A HISTORY OF HEISTS

A HISTORY OF HEISTS

Bank Robbery in America

Jerry Clark and Ed Palattella

ROWMAN & LITTLEFIELD
Lanham • Boulder • New York • London

Published by Rowman & Littlefield
A wholly owned subsidiary of The Rowman & Littlefield Publishing Group, Inc.
4501 Forbes Boulevard, Suite 200, Lanham, Maryland 20706
www.rowman.com

Unit A, Whitacre Mews, 26-34 Stannary Street, London SE11 4AB

British Library Cataloguing in Publication Information Available

Library of Congress Cataloging-in-Publication Data

Clark, Jerry (Gerald C.)
A history of heists : bank robbery in America / Jerry Clark and Ed Palattella.
pages cm
Includes bibliographical references and index.
ISBN 978-1-4422-3545-8 (cloth : alk. paper) — ISBN 978-1-4422-3546-5 (electronic)
1. Bank robberies—United States—History. I. Palattella, Ed. II. Title.
HV6658.C53 2015
364.15'520973—dc23
2014048711

♾️™ The paper used in this publication meets the minimum requirements of
American National Standard for Information Sciences Permanence of Paper for
Printed Library Materials, ANSI/NISO Z39.48-1992.

Printed in the United States of America

To our parents:
Jerry Sr. and Sandra Clark
Ed Sr. and Patricia Palattella

"We called him outlaw, and he was; but fate made him so."

—John Newman Edwards, newspaper editor,
on the death of Jesse James

"The successful bank robber is a king among thieves."

—George W. Walling, superintendent of the New York
City Police Department, 1874–1885

CONTENTS

ACKNOWLEDGMENTS

Bank robbery is as varied as a subject as any in American history, and the authors are grateful to many people for their research assistance. Two stand out: Bob Sparks, of the Nash Library at Gannon University in Erie, Pennsylvania; and John Fox, PhD, historian for the FBI, in Washington, D.C. The views expressed in this book, however, are the authors' alone, and do not necessarily reflect those of the FBI. Kathryn Knigge, at Rowman & Littlefield, was enthusiastic about this project from the start. We are grateful for her confidence. Our literary agent, John Talbot, provided guidance as well.

Jerry Clark: I consider myself extremely fortunate to have met and been associated with so many fine individuals in my twenty-seven years in law enforcement. I am deeply grateful to the many criminal justice officials, agents, and officers who taught me the professional skills and personal values I have used throughout my career and my life. Thanks also to my wife, Danielle, and children, Michael and Isabelle, for their patience and enduring support.

Ed Palattella: Crime coverage is a staple for the media in America, and I am fortunate to work for a news organization, the *Erie Times-News* and GoErie.com, that values context and insight in the reporting of crime and its effects on the community. Two top editors, Pat Howard and Doug Oathout, have been particularly supportive. Thanks to my wife, Chris, and children, Henry and Nina, for their patience, understanding, and encouragement.

INTRODUCTION

In the first week of October 1892, a historic bank robbery occurred in Coffeyville, Kansas. On October 5, most of the members of the Dalton Gang, the most feared group of bank robbers since Jesse and Frank James, were gunned down during a botched holdup of two banks at the same time. The Daltons had terrorized banks throughout Kansas and what today is Oklahoma, and the gang's decimation brought about national relief and national headlines.

Also in the first week of October 1892, a bank robbery shocked Erie, Pennsylvania, the hometown of the authors of this book. On October 3, four well-dressed young men walked into the lobby of the Keystone National Bank around half past twelve in the afternoon and tried to hold it up. One robber shot an assistant cashier in the cheek. The *Erie Daily Times* called the incident "a highly sensational attempt at bank robbing today that bristles with all the details wanting in the most lurid story that ever influenced the minds of impressionable youth."

For Erie residents, the attempted heist of their downtown bank was no less important than the Daltons' failed raid in Coffeyville, though the events in Kansas would be (and deservedly so) much more famous across the United States. Every bank robbery or attempted bank robbery affects the community where it takes place, but some heists are more notable for any number of reasons: the robbers involved, the historical context, whether the heist was an isolated incident or part of a wider trend. Banks are robbed every day in the United States, and bank robbery has been a fairly regular crime in America since shortly after the Revolution. But not all bank robberies are equally momentous.

In writing this history of bank robbery in the United States, the authors had to be selective. This book is not meant to be an encyclopedic volume, a work that details every bank robbery that has occurred in America since 1776. Instead, it examines bank robbery as a serious crime that has developed and changed as America has developed and changed. Bank robbery is not a crime unique to the United States, but it is a crime that, perhaps more than any other, has helped influence and define the nation, particularly how Americans have viewed crime over the centuries. The most famous bank robbers in the history of the United States—Jesse James, Butch Cassidy and the Sundance Kid, John Dillinger, Willie Sutton—are also distinct characters in our national drama. They are crooks who continue to captivate American imaginations into the twenty-first century, and who also reflected their times. As Jesse James helped define post–Civil War America, so Butch Cassidy and the Sundance Kid influenced the nation's views of the West, and John Dillinger and his gangster contemporaries became identified with the Great Depression. Many bank robbers went on to be portrayed in well-regarded movies, such as *Bonnie and Clyde* and *Dog Day Afternoon*, reinforcing bank robbery's hold on American thought.

Thieves are not the only characters in this book, though they are among the most colorful. Also introduced are the authorities who tried to stop the bank robbers, including governors, soldiers, U.S. marshals, presidents, and one official who, at the height of his control, was more powerful than any of them: J. Edgar Hoover, the director of the Federal Bureau of Investigation, an agency Hoover fashioned to be, more than anything else, the nemesis of bank robbers nationwide. As bank robbers became more skilled, so did the banks' methods of security, and so, too, the police and the federal agents. This book explores those relationships as well.

Like so many aspects of American society today, bank robbery has undergone a shift connected to the advance of the digital age and the Internet. The number of bank robberies has declined as the number of online financial frauds has increased. Why rob a bank, and risk getting captured or killed, when you can steal just as much money by duping someone while working anonymously on a computer? Yet bank robberies still occur, and they continue to draw attention and fascination. No single crime is more synonymous with crime in the United States than bank robbery, whether it ends in a bloody shootout in Coffeyville, Kansas, or with police finding four young thieves after chasing them through the streets of Erie, Pennsylvania. No matter where in America they have struck, bank robbers often have been unforgettable. Their heists—some strange, some sad, many of them violent—are intertwined with the larger story of the United States.

Jerry Clark
Ed Palattella
November 2014
Erie, Pennsylvania

I

BREAKING IN

Early Banks and Early Thieves

The first person charged with bank robbery in the United States set the standard for so many of the bandits who would follow: he became a celebrity.

The suspect was Patrick Lyon, who was arrested in 1798 in Philadelphia, then the capital of the young nation. He was a twenty-nine-year-old accomplished blacksmith and locksmith—and he was wrongly accused. The injustice churned public interest in the case, but so did the heist. Generations later, Jesse James, John Dillinger, George "Machine Gun" Kelly, Bonnie and Clyde, and Willie Sutton would become so well known as to become public enemies to some and folk heroes to others. Patrick Lyon and his ordeal preceded them all.

The offense in his case was, in a purely legal sense, a bank burglary. It was a case in which the thief broke into a financial institution, rather than a case of a bank robbery, in which a thief uses violence or the threat of violence to steal money or other valuables. The first armed bank robbery by a civilian in America happened decades later, on December 16, 1863, when a heavily indebted postmaster named Edward Green shot and killed a bank clerk in a robbery of $5,000 from Malden Bank, in Malden, Massachusetts, north of Boston.[1] Other early armed bank robberies took place during the Civil War; among the most notable of these wartime heists occurred on October 19, 1864, when a band of Confederate raiders robbed three banks in St. Albans, Vermont—the rebels' northernmost incursion.[2] The nation's first organized bank robbery—and first daylight bank robbery—occurred on February 13, 1866, when Jesse and Frank James and their gang of former Confederate guerillas held up the Clay County Savings Association in Liberty, Missouri. Before then bank burglaries and bank robberies were considered the same. Even the definitive contemporaneous account of Lyon's case states that he was accused of "robbing the Bank of Pennsylvania in 1798."[3] Whatever the crime was called, the case dominated the news of the day.[4]

The culprit made off with more than $162,821.21 in bank notes and gold the night of September 1, 1798—an astonishing amount of money that would equal about $3.2 million today.[5] The loot had been stored in the vault of the Bank of Pennsylvania, which had recently relocated to Carpenters' Hall on South Third Street, in Philadelphia. The hall, home to the Carpenters' Company, the oldest trade guild in America, hosted the First Continental Congress in 1774. The building that served as a home to the nation's early government was the scene of its first bank robbery.

Former tenants at Carpenters' Hall included the first two nationally chartered banks in America: the Bank of North America, which the Continental Congress established in 1781, and the First Bank of the United States, which, in 1791, four years after the signing of the Constitution and under the direction of Treasury Secretary Alexander Hamilton, became the nation's first federally chartered bank. The Bank of Pennsylvania moved to Carpenters' Hall in 1798, shortly before the robbery. The bank had been the victim of an attempted heist at its previous location in Philadelphia, and its owners hoped its new home would be safer. The bank brought with it the iron doors that had served it at its old spot. Pat Lyon had made those doors, and he had refitted them for the cash vault at Carpenters' Hall. He installed new locks he said could not be picked.

The thief used a key to get into the vault and steal the notes and gold.

The interest in the crime was intense. The Bank of Pennsylvania sent letters to banks in Wilmington, Delaware; New York; and Baltimore, warning those institutions of the enormous theft and asking them for help in "detecting the villains."[6] Advertisements with similar information circulated throughout the country, cautioning unsuspecting merchants and others against accepting the stolen cash. Officials offered rewards. The largest, $1,000, came in a proclamation from the governor of Pennsylvania, Thomas Mifflin.

Lyon had made the original key for the vault at Carpenters' Hall, and the bank officials immediately suspected him in the heist—though two days before the robbery he had fled to Delaware to escape a yellow fever outbreak in Philadelphia. He read in the newspapers that he was the prime suspect and returned to Philadelphia to prove his innocence. His lawyers would later proclaim, "He was 150 miles off when the robbery was committed!"[7] The exoneration would take some time. Upon arriving home, Lyon was locked up for three months in a twelve-foot-by-four-foot cell at the Walnut Street Jail, the world's first penitentiary.[8] He remained incarcerated despite the confession of Isaac Davis, a house carpenter elected to the Carpenters' Company in 1794. Davis told the authorities he had robbed the bank. Davis had visited Lyon's shop in late August 1798, as Lyon was working on the iron doors that he would soon attach to the new vault; Davis had studied the locks. When Davis later opened those locks and cleaned out the Bank of Pennsylvania, his accomplice was a bank porter, Thomas Cunningham. He had slept inside Carpenters' Hall the night of the robbery and had a key to the vault. The nation's first bank heist was an inside job.

As with many crimes, the crook was to blame for getting caught. Cunningham died of yellow fever two weeks after the robbery, eliminating the possibility that Davis's only co-conspirator would turn on him. Davis would have remained free from scrutiny—and Lyon likely a prisoner—had not Davis, according to one account, acted in a manner "that will live in the annals of stupidity, [for he] began depositing the missing money in the very bank he had robbed."[9] The authorities questioned him, and he confessed and agreed to return the money. Mifflin promised a pardon in exchange, but Davis disappeared and never went to prison. He repaid all but $2,000 and wrote a letter that cleared Lyon. Davis, now infamous, lost his standing in the Carpenters' Company. On January 21, 1799, the company's managing committee expelled him. According to the committee's minutes, "On motion resolved: that in consequence of Isaac Davis being concerned in an atrocious robbery on the Bank of Pennsylvania, the Company agree unanimously to erase his name off the list of members."[10]

Also in January 1799, a grand jury heard evidence in the bank robbery but refused to indict Lyon. He responded that year by writing a book, *The Narrative of Patrick Lyon Who Suffered Three Months Severe Imprisonment in Philadelphia Gaol on Merely a Vague Suspicion of Being Con-*

cerned in a Robbery of the Bank of Pennsylvania With his Remarks Thereon. Lyon's renown grew six years later, when he claimed his accusers had violated his civil rights. He sued the Bank of Pennsylvania's president and cashier, as well as a bank director and a high constable, for malicious prosecution and false imprisonment. A jury before the Pennsylvania Supreme Court in 1805 awarded him $12,000 in damages, which would amount to $243,000 today. Some of the best lawyers of the day represented Lyon, and the jury ruled in his favor in four hours. "The moment the verdict was delivered by the foreman of the jury, an universal clamor of exultation took place among the audience,"[11] according to one account.

The court later granted a new trial, but the case settled with a payment of $9,000 to Lyon, which bolstered the wealth he had already gained through his successful smithy and machining business. He would go on to build fire engines and become affluent enough to commission a self-portrait. The artist, John Neagle, completed two versions of *Pat Lyon at the Forge*—one in 1825–1826, which hangs at the Boston Museum of Fine Arts, and the other in 1829, which hangs at the Pennsylvania Academy of the Fine Arts, in Philadelphia. Both show Lyon at his bellows and anvil, in a triumphant pose, with the cupola of the Walnut Street Jail visible through a window in the background. The portrait represented "the last of many acts in Lyon's campaign of self-vindication,"[12] casting him as champion of justice for all. As Lyon wrote in his book, "It is an observation I have long made, that the great when they have power, will often make a wrong use of it, and that those who are inferior in rank, have very little chance of justice when opposed to them. . . . And what a horrid thing it is for an innocent man to suffer for another's guilt—the horror of such a thing, none but an innocent man can feel."[13]

Lyon's civil rights case against the bank officials and others turned out to be a landmark in Pennsylvania law. It showed how the state's constitution protected the rights of citizens from what could be the overreaching powers of government.[14]

The large amount of money Isaac Davis stole from the Bank of Pennsylvania reflected the institution's size and importance. Founded in 1793, it was the largest bank under state charter in the United States, and it had six offices throughout Pennsylvania, including at Carpenters' Hall. In colonial America, such large banks, which held deposits of bank notes as well as gold and silver, were nonexistent. Paper money was not uniform; currencies varied from colony to colony, and then state to state. The largely agrarian colonial communities used little of it; among their most valuable possessions were livestock, such as hogs. The need for banks grew as the post-Revolution states, particularly those in the North, turned to industry and prospered. To finance the new ventures, "money was needed, and to provide money there must be banks. So banks there were, everywhere."[15]

Aside from nationally chartered banks, such as the Bank of North America and the First and Second National Banks, state-chartered banks such as the Bank of Pennsylvania financed the nation's economy from the late 1700s to the mid-1800s. Twenty-eight state-chartered banks operated by 1800, 205 by 1815, and 329 by 1830.[16] The Union's drive to finance the military during the Civil War prompted Congress to pass the Legal Tender Act of 1862 and the National Banking Act of 1863, also known as the National Currency Act, which President Abraham Lincoln signed on February 25, 1863. The latter act increased the market for government bonds—which enabled the Union to raise money for the war effort—but, in conjunction with the Legal Tender Act, also established a uniform paper currency. The standardized bills "made possible the elimination of the motley array of state bank paper which had so long plagued the economy."[17] The number of nationally chartered banks surged after the passage of the National Banking Act of 1863 and the National Banking Act of 1864, which required banks to have reserves more closely in line with the amount of their deposits. The changes provided customers with a sense of protection, making banks more attractive for depositors.

The legislation all but eliminated what were known as wildcat banks—financial institutions, located mainly in the West, whose state currency was nearly worthless and that lacked gold and silver, known as *specie*, to redeem bank notes. Many wildcat banks printed money but were purposely situated in remote places so depositors could not redeem the notes for gold or silver, a practice that allowed the wildcat banks to hoard those assets. Wildcat banks, in a sense, robbed their customers; the banks took deposits and issued bank notes, but did everything possible to avoid fulfilling their financial promises.

As wildcat banks declined under the scrutiny of the new federal oversight, the number of more stable banks rose through the late 1800s. The boom arrived in rural communities following the Gold Standard Act, which President William McKinley signed on March 14, 1900. It placed the United States under only the gold standard and eliminated *bimetallism*, or the use of silver and gold to redeem paper money. The act also allowed the establishment of new nationally chartered banks "with capital stock of only $25,000 in communities of 3,000 inhabitants or less."[18] By 1911, the number of banks in the United States had increased to 25,000, up from fewer than 10,000 in the early 1890s.[19]

As the number of banks grew, so did the possibility of more bank robberies.

The prevalence of bank robbery and other crimes early in the history of the United States remains uncertain. Not until the Federal Bureau of Investigation introduced its Uniform Crime Reporting Program in 1930 would officials have reliable and comprehensive nationwide crime statistics to help lawmakers and police departments formulate responses to crime.[20] Tracking crime was also difficult without a public and well-administered justice system, which was absent in much of the United States during the nineteenth century. As happened in the case of Patrick Lyon, charged largely after an investigation by officials of the Bank of Pennsylvania, private interests—private citizens, private detectives, private prosecutors—functioned as the key players in the criminal justice system. Most municipal governments throughout the 1800s were too small and underfunded to create the public systems, such as police departments and district attorneys' offices, that would become standard in most cities by the 1900s.[21]

The heist at the Bank of Pennsylvania in 1798 is the first *known* bank robbery in the United States. The lack of reliable statistics requires the qualification, though the likelihood is high that, had another robbery preceded Isaac Davis's inside job, a newspaper would have reported it. Then, as now, bank robberies generated a large amount of media coverage. The heists can be daring and sometimes even lucrative. And an element of romance accompanies bank robberies in general. Especially as banks grew larger and, as in the Great Depression, developed a reputation for being unfair or unscrupulous, many would view bank robbery as a victimless crime, particularly in cases in which no one was hurt. How could a regular citizen in America, unemployed and alienated and partial, perhaps, to some kind of popular revolt, not cheer for a Jesse James, a John Dillinger, or a Pretty Boy Floyd? Perhaps no other crime in the United States owes as much of its allure to the media—first the newspapers and the popular magazines, and then the movies and television.

Though the heavy media coverage would seem to suggest bank robberies are rampant in the United States, bank robbery has historically been a rare crime. The number of bank robberies has spiked in some eras, but the incidences of bank robbery have remained low over time. Some of the most recent statistics show that, even in 2013, with 96,000 bank branches nationwide,[22] only about two of every one hundred robberies involve a bank, and bank robbery suspects are caught 60 percent of the time, among the highest clearance rates for all crimes.[23] The number of financial institutions robbed in the United States peaked at 9,388 in 1991. With the rise in online financial fraud, the number dropped to 5,086 in 2011, the lowest number since the FBI recorded 5,427 bank robberies in 1985.[24] The number of bank robberies rose to 5,684 in 2013, which was up from 5,484 in 2012, but still down considerably from the 7,465 recorded a decade earlier, in 2003.[25]

Bank robbery as a reliably profitable crime is another myth. Thieves can get away with blockbuster amounts of money, sometimes millions of dollars. But those takes are anomalies. Bank robbers in America have generally escaped with little cash—an average of less than $4,000 per heist, according to 2013 statistics.[26] Getting away with a bank robbery was much easier during certain periods, such as during the great crime wave that coincided with the Great Depression, but bank robbery has typically been a crime with low rewards.

So why rob a bank? The money is there, as is the potential for a big score. The risk of arrest might be high, but the risks inside the bank are usually minimal; tellers are taught, for safety reasons, to hand over the money. More than two-thirds of all bank robberies are over in three minutes or less.[27] And though the number of bank robberies has declined in recent years, the amount of money taken in bank robberies is still notable in the aggregate. In 2011, the most recent year for which complete statistics are available from the FBI, thieves made off with loot in 89 percent of the cases, and took a total of $38,343,501.96. Authorities fully or partially recovered the loot in 20 percent of the cases, for a total of $8,070,886.97.[28]

Desperation is another factor that drives robbers to try to beat the odds and not get caught. A bank robber cares little for statistics when he or she needs money to feed a drug habit or is a habitual criminal without legitimate work. In 2011, according to the FBI, of the 3,263 people identified in the bank robberies, authorities determined 1,229, or 38 percent, used narcotics, and 583, or 18 percent, had a prior conviction for bank robbery or related crimes. A correlation between poverty and bank robbery developed in the Great Depression and has persisted in other periods of economic uncertainty, such as the Great Recession, which started in 2008. Economic downturns lead to increased unemployment, which fuels hopelessness, destitution, and despair. Drug addiction, which often accompanies personal financial collapse, will motivate a robber to enter a bank in his hometown with no disguise, no plan, and no concern for the consequences. The motivations for bank robbery mirror constantly evolving societal changes.

In many cases, though, money may not be the driving force behind bank robbery. One researcher, committed to disabusing the glamorous perceptions of bank robbery conveyed in the movies and on television, found that "the act of committing a bank robbery often had very little, if any, relationship to the theft of money for personal profit. Rather . . . the bank can become an arena where psychological pressures are expressed as highly condensed action."[29] By robbing a bank, the thief might be channeling aggression or using the heist, and the violence it can entail, to subdue other drives, whether psychosexual or emotional.[30] Few bank robberies are planned; few originate with methodical and intelligent criminals. The typical bank robber acts with little deliberation, whether as the result of drug use or other personal dysfunction. "A case could be made," researchers wrote in another study of bank robbery, "for calling the majority of bank robbers 'losers,' born and raised. Their family backgrounds were overloaded with disorganized primary family relationships—lack of parental supervision, broken homes, poverty, alcoholism, promiscuity, general irresponsibleness."[31]

Other statistics suggest many bank robbers act on impulse. They tend to carry out heists by holding up the busiest banks that are closest to them, with most of the robberies occurring on Fridays between nine and eleven o'clock in the morning—right before the weekend.[32] In 2011, the heists the FBI recorded usually happened at the front counter of a bank (4,870 times) or at a bank branch (4,803 incidents) that was in the commercial district of a metropolitan area (2,066 robberies, compared to 928 in the suburbs, 1,734 in small towns, and 88 in rural areas).

Bank robbers are often men, and they can be prone to violence. The FBI determined 6,088 people were involved in the 5,086 heists in 2011; of them, 5,573 were known to be men and 429 women, with the gender of 86 unknown. Of the 6,088 people involved in bank robberies, the FBI identified 3,263 of them, or 54 percent. The most common way for a robber to hold up a financial institution in 2011 was by handing the teller or other bank employee a written note demanding money (used 2,958 times); the second-most common method was an oral demand (used 2,678 times). Robbers frequently accompanied these demands with weapons. In 2011, they included firearms (1,242, with 1,209 handguns among them); knives, clubs, hypodermic needles, and other weapons (31); and explosive devices, either used or threatened (154). Of the 5,086 bank robberies committed in 2011, according to the FBI, 201 involved "acts of violence," including the firing of a gun in seventy incidents, the use of explosive once, and 116 assaults. The violence caused eighty-eight injuries, led to the taking of thirty hostages, and ended in the deaths of thirteen people—one guard, two members of law enforcement, and ten bank robbers. If anyone is going to get killed during a bank robbery, the bandit is the most likely target.[33]

Even with such an ultimate risk, for many of these thieves, whether bright or dimwitted, desperate or debonair, the question is not so much "Why rob a bank?" as "Why not?" Where else would you go to get money quickly, other than a bank? "That's where the money is," according to the trademark phrase attributed to the iconic bank robber and author Willie Sutton (1901–1980; career earnings: about $2 million), who denied making the remark but agreed with its sentiment.[34] No matter what its provenance, that quip stands as the best explanation for why people rob banks, from Isaac Davis through the robbers of the twenty-first century. An additional insight indisputably comes from Sutton, who valued the thrill of a well-planned and well-executed heist. He wrote in his memoir, *Where the Money Was*,

> Why did I rob banks? Because I enjoyed it. I loved it. I was more alive when I was inside a bank, robbing it, than at any other time in my life. I enjoyed everything about it so much that one or two weeks later I'd be out looking for the next job. But to me the money was the chips, that's all. The winnings. I kept robbing banks when, by all logic, it was foolish. When it would cost me far more than I could possibly gain.[35]

A serial criminal carried out the nation's second known bank robbery. It was discovered on Monday, March 21, 1831, and was also the first bank robbery reported in New York City, the nation's financial capital. Sometime over that weekend, someone broke into the City Bank of New York (now Citibank), at 52 Wall Street, and stole $245,000 in bank notes and Spanish doubloons—an amount equal to $6.8 million today.[36] The crime, as was the heist at the Bank of Pennsylvania, was a burglary rather than a robbery; someone had slipped into the City Bank after hours.[37] The police had their man within a week: a suspect first identified as Edward Smith, also known as Edward Jones and James Honeyman, a thirty-five-year-old Englishman "short in stature, with sandy hair, and what may be termed a long head. The moral cast of his countenance is decidedly bad. The general expression of his face is intellectual, and marked by features of a strong character."[38]

Smith never admitted to the robbery, but the evidence was overwhelming. He was the person who, working with an accomplice, used two duplicate keys—one theory is that they were made from wax impressions—to open the doors to the City Bank the night of March 20.[39] Once inside, Smith and his accomplice opened the vault, whose inner door had no lock.[40] The morning of the robbery, a man by the name of Jones rented a room in a boarding house in the city, bringing with him three large trunks that attracted the attention of the landlord. Several days later, and after one of the trunks disappeared, the landlord contacted the police. Led by New York's Chief Constable Jacob Hays, the police picked the locks, opened the trunks, and found $185,783 in notes that matched those stolen from the City Bank six days earlier. The police arrested Smith, who was the tenant named Jones.

Smith ran a shoe store in the Bowery and, before moving to the rooming house, had lived with his wife and two young daughters at another residence in the city—a place that, when Smith stayed there, "became famous as the resort of dissipated profligates."[41] The authorities suspected Smith of other heists, including a store robbery in Brooklyn and two spectacular crimes: the "great robbery" of a mail coach in England years earlier, and the theft of cash from an English steamer en route to Providence, Rhode Island, the previous autumn.[42] Smith was never charged in those cases. His one-day trial in the City Bank robbery ended with a quick verdict on May 13, 1831. "The jury found the prisoner guilty without leaving their seats."[43]

Police later charged the accomplice, William J. Murray, whom Smith had met at a penal colony in Botany Bay, Australia, before they fled to England and, after committing robberies there, to the United States.[44] Murray was also convicted in the City Bank case, and he and Smith were sentenced to five years of hard labor at Sing Sing Prison in upstate New York. The influence of the robbery of the City Bank would have long-lasting effects. It made something of a hero out of Hays, the chief constable, though the public got upset when he was unable to find the last $42,000 from the robbery, which was never recovered. Smith and Murray vouched for Hays's honesty from prison in the first of what would be many symbiotic relationships between crooks and cops in bank robberies.[45] The heist at the City Bank is also credited as an impetus for the introduction of the bank safe in the United States in 1834—one of the first measures designed to foil bank robbers.[46]

The bank robbers who struck in the years after the City Bank heist were often more adept and more violent. Banks and police tried to stay ahead of them with new techniques, technology, and laws. The introduction of safes and other security innovations made bank robberies more difficult, but never impossible. Starting in the mid-1860s, no one proved that point more than Jesse James.

2

THE ORIGINAL OUTLAW

Jesse James, the Civil War, and Crimes Like No Other

Jesse and Frank James rode swift horses into Liberty, Missouri, on February 13, 1866. The brothers approached the Clay County Savings Association at about two o'clock in the afternoon. The Jameses had galloped into Liberty with as many as eleven other men, all of whom had fought as Confederate guerrillas—known as *bushwhackers*—in the Civil War. Clay County, in northwestern Missouri just east of the Kansas line, was the Jameses' home and base of operations. The brothers fought throughout the war with the secessionists in Missouri, a border state that sent troops to both the Union and Confederacy and whose deeply divided loyalties between the North and South triggered some of the bloodiest intrastate violence during the bloodiest period in American history.

This February afternoon in 1866 came ten months after Robert E. Lee and the Confederacy surrendered to Ulysses S. Grant and the Union at Appomattox Courthouse, Virginia, on April 9, 1865. Money was the secondary reason the thieves targeted the Clay County Savings Association for the first bank robbery of its kind in the United States—an organized peacetime heist carried out in daylight that was also the first holdup popularly connected to the James Gang.[1] A reason more important than money spurred the eighteen-year-old Jesse Woodson James; his twenty-three-year-old brother, Alexander Franklin James; and their cohorts to hold up this bank. That reason was politics.[2]

The Clay County Savings Association, to the Jameses, was a symbol of oppression. Prominent residents affiliated with Missouri's Radical Party, made up of stalwart abolitionists who sided with the Union, had founded and were running it. Though the Civil War officially ended at Appomattox Courthouse, James and his gang continued to fight for the South in Missouri. To make their force known on February 13, 1866, they robbed the Clay County Savings Association of $58,072.64 in bank notes, bonds, and gold and silver coins, which they stole from the bank's open vault. The robbery started with a ruse: A gang member walked in and asked the cashier to change a $10 bank note. Holding a revolver, the robber jumped over the front counter and threatened the cashier, Greenup Bird, and William Bird, his son, who worked as a clerk. Another man, also carrying a revolver, jumped over the counter. The two forced William Bird into the open vault and told him to stuff money into a cotton sack they gave him. The men had Greenup Bird collect paper currency, and then they shoved him into the unlocked vault and left. The bandits made off with the loot and joined the rest of their crew outside, where they had been keeping watch. The group fired their revolvers to clear the streets of Liberty and let out rebel yells as they fled the town on their horses. Jesse James sat atop the finest horse among the group—a bay mare named Kate. Stray gunfire killed one person, a bystander by the name of George Wymore. He was nineteen years old, a year older than the fiercest member of the group that murdered him.

Greenup Bird got out of the vault, opened the bank's window, and shouted a phrase that had been virtually unheard in America until then. Bird, in the middle of the afternoon, screamed that his bank had been robbed. He and his son had been prudent to hand over the money without a struggle. They otherwise would have risked the wrath of Jesse James, who later would espouse a ruthless philosophy on how to handle such situations. "A man who is a d———d enough fool to refuse to open a safe or vault when he is covered with a pistol ought to die," James wrote to a newspaper in 1872. "If he gives the alarm, or resists, or refuses to unlock, he gets killed."[3]

The heist at the Clay County Savings Association was a robbery of revenge, with the Union intended as the ultimate victim. The political motivations would be equally apparent in a crime that occurred nearly three years later—the armed robbery of the Daviess County Savings Association in Gallatin, Missouri, at twelve-thirty in the afternoon on December 7, 1869. It was the first heist unquestionably attributed to Frank and Jesse James, the only robbers who took part. The brothers rode off with a handful of worthless bank notes, though they were in high spirits nonetheless. Jesse James had killed the bank's cashier by firing his revolver once at the man's chest at point-blank range and again at his forehead. The cashier was John W. Sheets, who owned the bank. The Jameses stormed in and out of the Daviess County Savings Association thinking he was someone else—Samuel P. Cox, a former lieutenant in a state militia in Missouri and a former scout in the Union army. Almost five years earlier, on October 27, 1864, in Ray County, Missouri, Cox had killed William "Bloody Bill" Anderson, one of the most powerful of the Confederate guerrillas and a comrade-in-arms to Jesse and Frank James. They all fought under the black flag that Anderson and the other bushwhackers flew high during the Civil War.

Jesse James started the robbery in Gallatin with a familiar tactic. He asked the cashier to change a $100 bank note. Frank walked in, acting as if he and his brother were customers. Jesse took out his revolver and fired at the man he thought was Cox. Then Frank and Jesse grabbed whatever papers were on a desk and ran outside, where the townspeople of Gallatin opened fire with rifles. The noise spooked Kate, who threw Jesse. Frank hauled him on to his own horse, and the two escaped. But no longer would the brothers be able to hide their identities and keep low profiles. The murder of Sheets vaulted Jesse James into the newspapers, statewide and nationally, and infuriated Missouri Governor Joseph W. McClurg, who announced a reward for the capture of Frank and Jesse James of $500 each, more than double the usual bounty for fugitives in Missouri. It would be the first of many high prices that the public would put on the heads of the bandits, whose habits the locals already knew tended toward bloodshed and crime. The James boys, wrote the *Liberty Tribune* after the heist in Gallatin, "are regarded as desperate men."[4]

Just as the heists in Clay and Daviess counties were more than just bank robberies, Jesse James was more than a bank robber. He was a skilled criminal, but the politics behind his crimes would make him akin to a terrorist, a merciless proponent of a cause—in this case, the Lost Cause of the Confederacy—who had as many adherents as he had enemies. His influence cannot be overstated. Jesse James transformed bank robbery and the public's perception of the bank robber. He defined the outlaw in American culture.

When the country's first known armed bank robber, the financially and personally troubled postmaster Edward Green, shot and killed the bank clerk during the day in Malden, Massachusetts, in 1863, the crime was isolated and hastily conceived. Green, thirty-two years old, walked into the Malden Bank to get change and saw the only clerk present was the seventeen-year-old son of the bank's president. Green returned with a pistol; fatally shot the clerk, Frank Genovese; and escaped with $5,000. Green's lack of involvement in searching for the robber (as Malden's postmaster, he was supposed to be a civic leader) created suspicions, as did Green's payment, in the weeks after the slaying, of a $700 debt that was two years old. Green paid in bank notes from the Malden Bank, a clue that led to his arrest on February 7, 1864. He confessed and was hanged on April 13, 1866.[5]

Case closed.

That never happened to Jesse James.

James's pursuers included the militia, local posses, and the renowned private detective Allan Pinkerton and his Pinkerton's National Detective Agency, the first private detective agency in the United States. None of the pursuers caught or prosecuted James. His demise came when he was thirty-four years old and living under the assumed name of Thomas Howard in St. Joseph, Missouri, north of Clay County. One of his associates, Bob Ford, seeking a $10,000 reward that Governor Thomas T. Crittenden had promised ($5,000 for each of the James boys), shot Jesse James in the back of the head as James was dusting a picture at his house at about eight o'clock in the morning on April 3, 1882.

For sixteen years, James, his brother, and their different gang members robbed or attempted to rob as many as eleven banks in five states—Missouri, Iowa, West Virginia, Kentucky, and Minnesota. They also carried out as many as twelve train robberies; four stagecoach holdups; a robbery of a paymaster in Alabama; and a robbery of the box office at a state fair in Kansas City, Missouri, during which a little girl was shot in the calf. The Jameses' overall take is estimated to be as much as $350,000, or about $6.1 million today.[6] Bank robberies, train robberies, and similar crimes undoubtedly would have occurred had the James brothers never taken to the saddle. But Jesse James, who led the crew of lawbreakers, set the template—so much so that even today many bank robberies, especially those that are the successful work of skilled serial thieves, follow the pattern that James established.

Bank robberies became organized under the Jameses and their gang. They held up banks and trains, which also had safes, by deploying deception, shock, and other paramilitary techniques they mastered as Confederate guerrillas.[7] The Jameses' robberies often ended in unprecedented displays of violence—the result of the depth of Missouri's internecine hatred and the increase in the public availability of firearms after the Civil War, an era that demanded regular citizens carry firearms. In the words of historian T. J. Stiles, "The war had destroyed the social conventions and political institutions that had contained private disputes."[8]

Jesse James also proved himself proficient in public relations: He routinely wrote letters to newspapers to deny his participation in the bank robberies and other crimes, and his friendship with one of Missouri's most prominent newspaper editors, John Newman Edwards, provided James with an apologist and hagiographer without peer. The public's continued fascination with bank robbers exploded, to a large degree, because of the relationship between Jesse James and the media of his day.

Jesse James's other relationships contributed to the culture of bank robbery in the United States. Among his close friends and fellow thieves were the Younger brothers: Cole (born in 1844, three years before Jesse James), John (a year older than Jesse), Jim (three years younger), and Bob (six years younger). The Youngers lived in Lee's Summit, in Clay County, Missouri, about forty miles from the James homestead in the town of Kearney, then known as Centerville. They became Jesse and Frank James's partners in the James-Younger Gang. The Youngers' cousins were members of another infamous family of bank robbers: the Daltons, of the Dalton Gang, who lived in Cass County, Missouri, one county south of Clay, and whose crime spree would follow that of the Jameses. Jesse James boasts still other progeny, rooted in neither friendship nor bloodlines, but rather in imitation. These descendants were the men (and some women) whom he inspired to become bank robbers. They included Butch Cassidy and the Sundance Kid and their gang, called the Wild Bunch, as well as Clyde Barrow and Bonnie Parker and Pretty Boy Floyd. Jesse James did not invent bank robbery in the United States. But he did come to personify it.

The romantic legend of Jesse James persists. This is the legend that portrays him as the American version of Robin Hood, the English highwayman Dick Turpin, the Scottish rogue Rob Roy, and other "social bandits" or "noble robbers"—thieves who proclaimed injustice compelled them to steal to benefit the poor. James, in the words of historian Richard Maxwell Brown, was a "resister gunfighter"—"a notable lawbreaker paradoxically widely admired by law-abiding members of society."[9] In Brown's view, "In the post-1865 era, social bandits, in the James tradition of crime, looted banks and railroads, institutions whose rapacious economic exactions caused resentment among peaceable western farmers, ranchers, and townspeople."[10]

To many of his like-minded contemporaries, this description might have fit Jesse James. He was an inveterate rebel in an area of Missouri that despised the Union. In their first train robbery, near Adair, Iowa, on July 21, 1873, the Jameses and the Youngers wore masks that resembled the headgear of the surging Ku Klux Klan.[11] Jesse James's letters to the newspapers proved his boldness: In June 1870, about six months after James murdered the cashier John Sheets in Gallatin, the *Kansas City Times* published a letter James addressed to Governor McClurg. "It is true that during the war I was a Confederate soldier, and fought under the black flag," James wrote, "but since then I have lived as peaceable citizen."[12]

The five-foot-eleven-inch-tall Jesse James—whose angular face featured a slightly upturned nose and piercing blue eyes that constantly blinked[13]—was known to be sympathetic to some of his victims. During a train robbery near Blue Cut, Missouri, on September 7, 1881, he attended to a female passenger who had fainted. He soothed her face with a wet handkerchief, and returned the dollar he and his crew had stolen from her.[14] Frank James, known as Jesse's level-headed older brother (no bank-related killings are attributed to him), carried *The Pilgrim's Progress* with him on horseback and quoted Shakespeare.

The techniques of the Jameses and the Youngers were precise and pitiless, but laced with lightheartedness. Their preferred methods for robbing a train—methods they almost certainly learned from Confederate soldiers-turned-bushwhackers who attacked trains during the Civil War—were to place debris on the tracks or wave a red flag at the cab of the engine. The train would stop and two of the robbers—most likely Jesse and Frank James—would jump aboard and pilfer the passengers of their money, watches, and jewelry. They would look for the safe, which held money that belonged not to the railroads, but to express companies who paid the railroads to carry their valuable freight. Outside, one robber would hold as prisoners the conductor and the other train officials; two others would walk outside the train to monitor those who might try to crawl out the windows.

The Jameses liked to chat as they worked. During the James-Younger Gang's robbery of a train near Gads Hill, Missouri, at about four o'clock in the afternoon on January 31, 1874, they returned money to a passenger who said he was a minister, and they asked him to pray for them. Jesse and Frank took another passenger to a sleeping compartment and had him strip; the brothers suspected the man was one of Allan Pinkerton's detectives, and they claimed each of Pinkerton's men had a "secret mark on his body."[15] No telltale tattoo existed, and the Jameses released the man, unharmed. At the end of that same robbery, the Jameses returned a gold watch to the conductor, who said it had been a gift, and they shook hands with the engineer and let the rest of the train officials go.

The heist proved productive in terms of the robbers' take and what the holdup bought them in the priceless commodity of publicity. The Jameses and the gang made off with about $20,000 in valuables, including $1,080 in cash they pulled from the train's safe. The money had been under the care of the Adams Express Company, whose messenger aboard the train had opened the safe after one of the robbers thrust a shotgun into his chest. Before they departed the flustered messenger and the other passengers, the Jameses "left behind a prepared press release, with instructions that it be telegraphed to the *St. Louis Dispatch*" to claim the holdup at Gads Hill as their own.[16] The notice started, "The most daring robbery on record." It ended, "There is a hell of excitement in this part of the country."[17] The joke, to Jesse James, was on everyone else.

Jesse James and his men craved publicity. Like so many criminals since, public recognition of their robberies boosted their egos. In a robbery of the Ocobock Bank in Corydon, Iowa, on June 3, 1871, Jesse and Frank James, Cole Younger, and another robber used the presence of a famous man in town to their advantage. They robbed the town's bank of $6,000 while virtually all the townspeople were outside the Methodist church, enthralled by noted orator Henry Clay Dean. After the robbery, the gang stopped by the transfixed crowd and got upset when no one noticed them. They shouted that the town's bank had just been robbed, shook the money, and rode out of town. [18]

Jesse James, however, was no Robin Hood, and he was no saint, and the members of the James-Younger Gang were not the Merry Men. As a number of historians, particularly T. J. Stiles, have made clear, Jesse James was not known to disburse his loot among the poor, and he was never known to regret murdering John Sheets and other victims, who are believed to have numbered at least a dozen. Yet Jesse James succeeded in merging crime and political unrest in a way that would echo through American history into the next century, perhaps reaching a modern apogee when the newspaper heiress Patty Hearst held up a bank in San Francisco in April 1974 with members of the left-wing terrorist organization known as the Symbionese Liberation Army.

Jesse James picked his targets carefully: The banks and the railroads dominated the economy of the Reconstruction, in which, for former Confederates, the North sought to further ruin the South, which included the Jameses' beloved Missouri. The banks and railroads, for Jesse James, were totems of the evil Union. These institutions were also sources of illicit income to the Jameses and the Youngers, but in post–Civil War America a sentiment was already developing that robbery of banks (and trains) was an honorable crime, unless someone was killed. "No one was hurt, and no one loses anything save the express company," one newspaper declared after the James-Younger Gang robbed a train near Otterville, Missouri, on July 7, 1876. [19] In this line of thinking, Jesse James might have been a thief, but the banks (and trains, the equivalent of banks on rails[20]) were not much better.

His politics aside, James tapped the reservoir of antipathy toward banks that had built up throughout much of the United States thirty years earlier, when President Andrew Jackson, in one of his administration's most notable accomplishments, defeated the renewal of the charter of the Second Bank of the United States in 1832. Jacksonians decried banks as oppressive tools of authority that were designed to manipulate farmers, laborers, and other common folk—a populist philosophy so strong in the West that "when the Nebraska legislature passed its first criminal code in 1855, bankers were defined among the criminals and banking was made illegal."[21] Nebraska and other states eventually legalized banking, but the anti-banking sentiment lingered, leaving Jesse James to exploit it with his unique brand of post–Civil War rebellion.

Jesse and Frank James were born to two Kentuckians: Zerelda Cole, whose strong will and allegiance to the South influenced her sons throughout their lives, and Robert James, a Baptist minister whose widowed mother lived in Clay County, where Robert James and his young wife eventually settled. Robert James, who spoke out against abolitionists, later headed to California for the Gold Rush, and died there. Zerelda James remarried twice; her third and final husband, Reuben Samuel, a doctor and a farmer, kept slaves with her.

Jesse James experienced one of the signature moments of his youth on the farm on May 25, 1863, when he was fifteen years old. By then his brother had joined the ranks of the Confederate guerillas under the leadership of William C. Quantrill, a murderous criminal who, along with Bloody Bill Anderson, would lead the insurgency in Missouri. Members of a state militia under Union control invaded the Samuel farm, searching for Confederate bushwhackers. The soldiers flogged Jesse James, who had been plowing the fields. The soldiers then lynched James's stepfather, but halted after Reuben Samuel agreed to give up the hiding place of Quantrill's raiders, including his stepson Frank, who escaped with the others. The lynching shook Jesse James, the young would-be bank robber; the men who had attacked him and his stepfather were fellow Missourians, not troops from some Northern state. "That day in May, when the militia descended on the farm, has been described as the moment Jesse James set out on his quest for revenge," Stiles has written. "For Jesse and his family, the dream of returning to life in a peaceful, tight-knit society had now ended, never to recur; from this day forward, they would count every neighbor as either an ally or an enemy."[22]

The Jameses and their confederates the Youngers helped spread the terror among their enemies. On August 21, 1863, Frank James and Cole Younger—whose father had been killed by a militia member—befriended one another as they rode with Quantrill and about two hundred other bushwhackers across the border to raid the town of Lawrence, Kansas. Their supposed justification was to strike back at the Kansas "Jayhawkers" and "Red Legs" (so named for the color of their stockings), two groups of abolitionists who had attacked secessionists in Clay County and other areas of western Missouri during the Civil War. These cross-border raids were rooted in attacks that occurred nine years earlier, after Congress in 1854 passed the Kansas-Nebraska Act and repealed the Missouri Compromise, which had allowed Missouri to enter the Union as a slave state in 1821 and Maine a free state, with slavery banned in the territories west of Missouri. The Kansas-Nebraska Act empowered citizens of Kansas and Nebraska to vote on whether their territories should allow or prohibit slavery. The result was "bleeding Kansas," in which "border ruffians" from Missouri crossed into the Kansas Territory to fight for slavery against Jayhawkers and Red Legs, and proponents and opponents of slavery settled in Kansas, adding to the combat. During the Civil War, Missouri's border ruffians became the Confederate guerillas—Quantrill's raiders and Bloody Bill Anderson's irregular troops. Kansas remained a battleground, and Lawrence came under siege when Quantrill, Frank James, Cole Younger, and the rest of Quantrill's men stampeded in. They burned the town and murdered at least two hundred men and boys. "Kill!" Quantrill thundered. "Kill and you will make no mistake! Lawrence should be thoroughly cleansed, and the only way to cleanse it is to kill. Kill!"[23]

The enraged Union general who commanded a section of western Missouri issued General Order No. 11, which required every resident of several border counties (but not Clay) to leave within fifteen days. The Union soldiers cleared the landscape of people, livestock, crops, and buildings, increasing the enmity of the Jameses and the Youngers toward the Union and anyone who supported it.

By the summer of 1864, Jesse and Frank James had found another mentor: Bloody Bill Anderson, whose vicious tactics included scalping his Unionist victims. Jesse James was sixteen years old, a boy in age but an unforgiving terrorist in thought and bearing. He was never a standout marksman; a young James shot off the tip of his middle finger on his left hand while cleaning a pistol, earning him the nickname "Dingus," because he uttered the euphemism "O ding it! Ding it!" as the blood squirted from the wounded digit.[24] By the time he rode with Anderson, James had taken to carrying the twin six-shot revolvers—the six-shooters—that he and his fellow gang members would use as tools of crime and mayhem throughout their careers. The revolvers were weapons of war. They fired more rapidly than any other weapon (especially rifles), which made them ideal for bushwhacking and robbing banks.

As Frank James had the massacre at Lawrence, Jesse James had his own baptism in carnage. He and Frank and about eight other bushwhackers, with Anderson in the lead, pillaged the small railroad town of Centralia, Missouri, on April 27, 1864. They murdered twenty-two homebound and unarmed Union soldiers who had been on a train the guerillas commandeered as it was passing through. Anderson ordered the soldiers to strip before he and his minions started shooting. Jesse James was one of the killers, a cruel ringleader in what the lone surviving Union soldier called "a carnival of blood."[25] When another contingent of Union soldiers chased the rebels after the slaughter, James and the rest of the crew murdered them as well, and dismembered their bodies. Such sociopathic behavior was the norm for the bushwhackers.

Jesse James did not survive these exploits unharmed. He was shot in the chest in August 1864 while eluding the Union militia in Missouri; a farmer opened fire on James as he tried to steal the farmer's horse. James recovered quickly from that injury, unlike the bullet wound he suffered in a firefight with Union cavalrymen in Missouri on May 15, 1865—a month after Robert E. Lee's surrender. That wound left James bedridden for weeks, but it did not stop him from resuming his personal war. Nine months later, in February 1866, the Clay County Savings Association was robbed, and Jesse James's assault on banks had begun. His campaign of terror gained intensity with each heist. By 1868, Frank and Jesse James were regularly committing bank robberies, including the holdup in Gallatin, where Jesse James's lasting fury against the North blazed and he murdered the wrong man—and did not care.

If Jesse James can be forgiven for anything, it would be his feeling that he was invincible. He *was* invincible—until the very end, with his death coming at the hands of a traitor. He was among the best-known Americans of his time, the catalyst of countless manhunts and newspaper stories, but he never faced justice for his very public crimes. In response to the humiliating train robbery at Gads Hill, in January 1874, Missouri Governor Silas Woodson successfully asked the state legislature for $10,000 to hire "secret service men" to hunt down the Jameses, the Youngers, and other robbers. Woodson "pointed out that the recent acts of banditry were giving Missouri a bad reputation."[26]

The newly hired men never caught up to the Jameses, who could credit several factors for staying ahead of the law. As skilled guerrillas, they knew their environs better than their enemies knew them; they had spent their boyhoods roaming Clay County and exploring the lands around the Missouri River, which they turned into pockets of refuge as adult criminals. The Jameses' pursuers were disorganized, divided, and lacking in uniformity from state to state. The United States during the 1870s was still three decades away from creating the nascent national police force that would eventually become the Federal Bureau of Investigation. And even if the authorities managed to develop good leads on the Jameses, the Youngers, and the other gang members, the Jameses' Confederate bona fides appealed to many citizens and public officials who were more than willing to shelter Jesse James.

Stoking the sympathy for Jesse James, and helping to create his legend, was the newspaper editor John Newman Edwards. A former major in the Confederate army, Edwards was unsparing in his hatred of the Union, and he praised James and other bushwhackers as heroes, despite their bloody ways. He founded the anti-Union *Kansas City Times* in 1878, which published the letters to the editor in which Jesse James disavowed bank robbery and other crimes. Edwards later worked at the *St. Louis Dispatch* and other publications, and he would write Jesse James's obituary. In championing James as a rebel savior, Edwards also romanticized bank robbery—even armed bank robbery—as a kind of higher crime. Burglars and embezzlers continued to threaten banks far more than robbers when the Jameses and the Youngers rode across Missouri and applied the strategies and devices of war—most notably, the unquestioned need for planning, firearms, and violence—to bank robbery. Edwards considered their techniques enlightened.

Edwards's encomiums to Jesse James cultivated the nascent folklore that would portray the American bank robber as a special kind of criminal—a misunderstood but good-hearted soul whose thieving is society's fault, never his. Edwards manufactured the myth most notably in his most famous editorial, "The Chivalry of Crime." It appeared in the *Kansas City Times* on Sunday, September 29, 1872, three days after the Jameses and another masked man held up the box office at the Industrial Exposition, a state fair in Kansas City, Missouri. They struck at sundown, amid a crowd of ten thousand. The thieves took $978, and left behind a girl wounded in the leg. The gang had been after a much bigger haul, but about thirty minutes before their arrival, the fair's treasurer had removed from the booth about $12,000—equal to $212,000 today. In "The Chivalry of

Crime," Edwards likened the bandits to the Knights of the Round Table and the fearless fighters of Wagner's Ring Cycle, and he lauded them for what others would consider their frightening effrontery—robbing a ticket booth at a packed fair during daylight (and wounding a child). Above all, Edwards extolled the robbers' audacity. Edwards's editorial did not mention Jesse and Frank James, but he had been acclaiming their deeds since the fatal heist of the Daviess County Savings Association nearly three years earlier. In "The Chivalry of Crime," the Jameses, by implication, are the protagonists of Edwards's song of what he dreamed would be a resurgent border South. "There are men in [the counties of] Jackson, Cass, and Clay—a few there are left—who learned to dare when there was no such word as quarter in the dictionary of the Border," Edwards wrote.

> Men who have carried their lives in their hands so long that they do not know how to commit them over into the keeping of the laws and regulations that exist now, and these men sometimes rob. But it is always in the glare of day and in the teeth of the multitude. With them booty is but the second thought; the wild drama of adventure first. These men never go up upon the highway in lonesome places to plunder the pilgrim. That they leave to the ignoble pack of jackals. But they ride at midday into the county seat, while court is sitting, take the cash out of the vault and put the cashier in and ride out of town to the music of cracking pistols. These men are bad citizens but they are bad because they live out of their time. . . .
>
> Such as these are they who awed the multitude on Thursday. . . . What they did we condemn. But the way they did it we cannot help admiring. . . . It was as though three bandits had come to us from the storied Odenwald, with the halo of medieval chivalry upon their garments and shown us how the things were done that the poets sing of.[27]

Though Jesse James had plentiful secessionist allies, the many Unionists in Clay County and the rest of Missouri opposed him and his crimes, which undermined an already fragile state trying to recover from the Civil War. But sympathy for James and his gang surged in 1875 at the expense of Allan Pinkerton and his private detective agency, whose severe missteps made James and his family look like righteous victims of a callous and overreaching North.

Pinkerton had taken up the trail of the Jameses at the request of the Adams Express Company, whose safe the James-Younger Gang had emptied in the holdup of the train at Gads Hill on January 31, 1874.[28] The express company contacted Pinkerton after the robbery, hoping to stop the threat to its business. Pinkerton, who established his agency in 1850, appeared to be the man for the job. He was a giant figure in the nation's new private security industry, a Scottish-born emigrant (and committed abolitionist) whose cadre of investigators had guarded President-elect Abraham Lincoln and broken up the first gang of train robbers in the United States, Indiana's Reno brothers, in the late 1860s. Other businesses were doing work similar to Pinkerton's when he got the call to go after the James-Younger Gang: Wells Fargo started guarding stagecoaches in 1852, and Brink's Security, which would become the armored car company, began its operations in 1859.[29] Among them all, Allan Pinkerton was considered the best.

Jesse James defeated him. On March 10, 1874, Jesse, his brother, and another crew member shot to death Joseph W. Whicher, one of three detectives Pinkerton had sent to Clay County to try to infiltrate the James-Younger Gang. A week later, on March 17, 1874, two of the Younger brothers, Jim and John, got into a gunfight with the two other detectives, John Boyle and Louis J. Lull. Boyle survived, but Jim and John Younger fired fatal shots into Lull. Also killed were John Younger—shot by Lull before his death—and Edwin B. Daniels, a local deputy sheriff who had been assisting the detectives.

Allan Pinkerton tried to strike back, but that effort also ended in disaster. Working with Unionists in Clay County, as well as federal postal officials, Pinkerton planned a raid of the Jameses' family farm in Kearney, where Jesse and Frank were believed to be staying with their mother and their stepfather on the night of January 25, 1875. The James brothers had left by the time Pinkerton and a group of as many as nine men surrounded the darkened house. To light up the interior and to flush out the occupants, the detectives threw into the house an odd contraption: a burning iron ball filled with flammable liquid. Reuben Samuel used a shovel to toss the thing into the fireplace, and it exploded. Shrapnel tore through Zerelda James's right arm, which had to be amputated at the elbow, and shrapnel tore into the abdomen of eight-year-old Archie Sam-

uel, Zerelda's son and the half brother of Jesse and Frank James. Archie
died instantly. As one historian wrote about the attack, "Indignation was
nation-wide."[30] John Newman Edwards was among those who trumpeted
the defense of the Jameses and the demonization of Pinkerton.

On March 17, 1875, nearly three months after the explosion, the Missouri House of Representatives considered a resolution that would have
granted amnesty to Jesse and Frank James, the Younger brothers, and
other gang members "for any acts of lawlessness committed before or
during the Civil War and guaranteeing a fair trial on any charges for acts
since the war."[31] The resolution failed, showing the Unionists' hold on
the legislature. Despite that defeat, Jesse James seemed more powerful
than ever. He was still free. Allan Pinkerton, the nation's greatest detective, had given up trying to catch him.

Unchecked ambition finally undid Jesse James. His downfall—and the
deaths of some of his closest confidants—resulted from a hubris rooted in
unfettered rage, overconfidence, and a quest for what by the mid-1870s
had become an irrational pursuit: a Confederate Missouri. His end started
with a botched heist of a bank located 380 miles north of Clay County, in
Northfield, Minnesota. This attempted robbery would not be Jesse
James's last, but it would be the final crime for the James-Younger Gang.

Politics again drove Jesse James. He picked the First National Bank in
Northfield because it was connected to Adelbert Ames, a brigadier general in the Union army whose bravery at the Battle of Bull Run earned him
the Congressional Medal of Honor. During Reconstruction, Ames, a native of Maine, became the face of the Union in Mississippi. In 1868,
President Andrew Johnson appointed him provisional governor of that
state, where Ames worked to secure the rights of freed slaves. He later
served as a U.S. senator from Mississippi, and in 1873 was elected its
regular governor. For bushwhackers like Jesse James, Ames represented
yet another example of the North crushing the South.

Ames's father and brother ran a flour mill in Northfield, in southern
Minnesota, south of Minneapolis. Ames moved there in May 1876, after
he resigned the governorship in Mississippi amid political turmoil. Ames
worked at his family's mill, which owned a quarter of the First National
Bank; his father was the bank's vice president, and his brother was a

director.[32] As Bob Younger would say after the attack on the First National Bank, the gang knew Adelbert Ames, enemy of the Confederacy, had money there, and someone in the gang was upset with him.[33] Younger never identified who held the grudge, but that person almost certainly was Jesse James.

Eight bandits, each carrying two revolvers and wearing their trademark long linen dusters, rode into Northfield at about two o'clock in the afternoon on September 7, 1876. The eight arrived in three groups, each assigned a different task (a division of labor the robbers had learned as bushwhackers). Jesse and Frank James and another gang member, Charlie Pitts, were to enter the bank; Cole Younger and gang member Clell Miller made up the second group, and were to wait outside the bank to provide cover for the outlaws inside; Bob and Jim Younger and bandit Bill Chadwell (alias William Stiles), who was from Minnesota, were to wait at a bridge outside of town, and were to clear Northfield's streets if the robbery went awry.

It did, quickly.

The three robbers inside the bank met something that caught them by surprise—resistance. Despite having revolvers pointed at them, the three bank clerks on duty refused to hand over money, and refused to open the safe. Aiding the clerks was a chronometer time clock, the newest technological innovation to guard against bank robbery. The head clerk, J. L. Heywood, a twenty-three-year-old bookkeeper, told the robbers he could not open the safe, because it was on a time lock (though the safe was, in fact, unlocked).[34] Heywood and the other clerks struggled with the flustered bandits, who fled the bank empty-handed. Before they left, one of the robbers, most likely Jesse James, fatally shot Heywood in the head.

The resistance continued outside. Townspeople, suspicious of the strange men lingering around their streets, had armed themselves at the town's hardware stores and started to gather soon after the Jameses walked into the First National Bank. More residents, including Adelbert Ames, though he was unarmed, gathered when word of the heist spread. Those with rifles and shotguns fired at the bandits after they aborted the robbery and tried to join their cohorts and get out of Northfield. Clell Miller and Bill Chadwell were killed. Jim Younger was shot in the shoulder, and Bob Younger, in the arm. Jesse James and his brother were unhurt and escaped, but his plan and his gang had unraveled. He had gone too far in Northfield, which was in enemy territory. The James-Younger

Gang had reconnoitered the area around the town in the weeks before the robbery, but southern Minnesota still was a strange place to the boys from Clay County. Among the residents of Northfield, Jesse James and his fellow gang members had no sympathizers. The townspeople with the rifles and shotguns did not care about the South. They did not care about the Confederacy. They cared about their fellow citizens—and they wanted to kill the bandits.

Jesse and Frank James eluded a massive manhunt after the attempted Northfield robbery, though one of their shotgun-wielding pursuers wounded Frank in the right knee and Jesse in the right foot. The Jameses split up from the Youngers and Charlie Pitts, none of whom escaped. Pitts was killed and the three Youngers hurt in a firefight in Minnesota on September 21, 1876. The Youngers were arrested and faced execution in Minnesota for the attempted bank robbery and the death of the clerk Heywood. They pleaded guilty and were sentenced to life in prison, where Bob Younger died of tuberculosis in 1889. The two other Younger brothers were paroled in 1901. Jim killed himself in 1902. Cole died of a heart attack in 1916, after a short-lived career of forming a traveling road show with his old fellow guerilla and bank robber, Frank James.

After the Northfield fiasco Jesse and Frank James moved to Tennessee. They lived under assumed names with their families. Frank (B. J. Woodson) settled into a life of farming and timbering and playing the horses. Jesse (J. D. Howard or Thomas Howard) tried farming to support his wife, Zee (who was his first cousin; her full name was Zerelda, and she was named after his mother), and their two small children, Jesse Edwards James (the middle name was a tribute to the Jesse's favorite newspaper editor) and Mary James. But Jesse James found law-abiding professions unappealing, and he turned again to crime. He formed new gangs, including those with Charley Ford and his brother Bob.

Jesse James held up no more banks, but a series of other crimes—three train robberies, two stagecoach robberies, and the stickup of a paymaster near Muscle Shoals, Alabama—renewed his standing as one of the most wanted men in America, particularly in Missouri, where Governor Crittenden vowed to catch him. James launched his post-Northfield crime spree on October 8, 1879, with the robbery of a train near Glendale,

Missouri, outside Independence, in Jackson County, just south of Clay. The spree ended on September 7, 1881, when the crew robbed the train at Blue Cut, also near Independence. Politics did not primarily motivate Jesse James in these heists. Though still a rebel sworn to the South, he robbed now because he needed the money, and because he did not know how or want to do anything else. The thrill of the robbery swept away the boredom of a reputable life.

Jesse James was planning to rob a bank the day he died. He and his family had moved back to Missouri in April 1881, as Jesse fled the law once more, and by the spring of 1882 the Jameses had settled in their house in St. Joseph. Living with them were Jesse James's trusted fellow thieves, the Ford brothers: Charley, twenty-four years old, and Bob, twenty-one, who secretly had taken up Crittenden's offer to capture their leader—dead or alive. On Sunday morning April 2, 1882, James listened to Bob Ford read a newspaper story about the gang's crimes. James explained how he and the Fords in two days, on Tuesday, would rob the bank in Platte City, Missouri, in Platte County, just east of Clay. James planned to use a trick that had worked so well during the robbery of the bank in Corydon, Iowa, eleven years earlier. An orator would not have the attention of Platte City, but a murder trial would. James and his gang would rob the bank while everyone else was at the courthouse.

The morning was already hot as James spoke to Bob Ford. James took off his holsters and his two six-shooters, because of the heat. Jesse James was known to never take off his guns; Bob Ford had never seen him without them. James had his back turned as he dusted the picture. He was unarmed when Ford shot him in the back of the head.

Ford and his brother collected their rewards, but what many considered the dishonorable way in which they dispatched Jesse James branded them as cowards and fed the legend of the man they had conspired to kill. The Fords were convicted of murdering James, but Crittenden pardoned them. So strong was the public outrage over Jesse James's death that not only were the Fords tried and convicted, but Frank James, who surrendered after his brother's death, was also later acquitted of the bank robbery at Gallatin, in which John Sheets was killed. Frank would die on the family farm in Kearney in 1915, never found guilty of any of his crimes.

John Newman Edwards was among those who believed the James brothers were never guilty of anything. In his obituary of Jesse James, he wrote, "We called him outlaw, and he was; but fate made him so."[35] Two thousand mourners flooded Kearney the day of James's funeral, and his corpse was put on public display. In death, James was cast as the victim he made himself out to be while alive. "Murdered by a traitor and a coward whose name is not worthy to appear here," reads his tombstone. Shortly after his death, he was immortalized in song, in a folk ballad that railed against Bob Ford as "that dirty little coward" and lionized Jesse James as a brave family man. The first stanza of a well-known version goes like this:

> Jesse James was a lad that killed many a man.
> He robbed the Glendale train.
> He stole from the rich and he gave to the poor,
> He'd a hand and a heart and a brain. [36]

Jesse James died the apotheosis of the American bank robber. His most lasting legacy would play out not in the newspapers or in song, but rather on the streets and inside the banks of so many towns and cities across the nation. Soon after the death of Jesse James arrived another wave of bank robbers—people who, in many instances, would seem much like him.

3

ROBBERY ON THE RANGE

The Wild West, the Wild Bunch,
and the Rise of the Professional Bandit

The place called the Hole-in-the-Wall served as a fortress for bandits in the West. In Clay County and the other border lands of western Missouri, Confederate loyalties and anti-Union virulence—a combination that fueled rage—drove many residents to shelter Jesse James, the Younger brothers, and other bands of outlaws. Topography provided the asylum at the Hole-in-the-Wall, a natural wonder in the Big Horn Mountains in northcentral Wyoming. Its telltale configuration is not so much a hole as a mountain pass, an opening in a red sandstone escarpment—the "wall"— that, in the late 1800s, was virtually impenetrable to outsiders, especially those wearing badges. The denizens of the Hole-in-the-Wall were many: bank robbers, train robbers, cattle rustlers, and other assorted criminals. They hid in its warren of caves and tunnels that, along with the "hole," a prehistoric lake had most likely carved out of the earth.[1] But the Hole-in-the-Wall most notably served as headquarters and home to a group of bank robbers and other crooks already well known long before Paul Newman and Robert Redford immortalized them in an acclaimed movie a century later. They were Butch Cassidy, the Sundance Kid, and the Hole-in-the-Wall Gang, later known as the Wild Bunch.

Butch Cassidy was born Robert Leroy Parker to Mormon parents in Utah on April 13, 1866—two months after the holdup of the Clay County Saving Association in Liberty, Missouri. By the time Butch Cassidy, with and without the Wild Bunch, was robbing banks in the West from the 1880s to 1901, he and his cohorts had come to rival—but never eclipse—the James-Younger Gang as the preeminent thieves and fugitives in the criminal history of the United States. The ascent of Butch Cassidy and the Wild Bunch signaled a change in the culture of bank robbery. No longer were the heists the work of guerillas-turned-thieves. These bank robbers were born on the range, and they were cowboys before they were crooks. Butch Cassidy and the Sundance Kid robbed banks not to make political statements, but to make money. They honed many of the techniques Jesse James pioneered—the reliance on planning, surprise and swiftness, and even charm—but financial rather than societal forces mostly influenced how they chose to make a living. As the cattle economy collapsed, cowboys looked to bank robbery for a livelihood. The successes of Butch Cassidy and the Sundance Kid heralded the arrival of the professional thief—the crook who robbed banks for the adventure, but primarily for the loot.

Butch Cassidy and the Sundance Kid, one of the highest-grossing movies of 1969,[2] cemented the romanticized reputation of the eponymous bank robbers. Much of what the movie conveyed is accurate—in spirit. Butch Cassidy and his closest friend, Harry Longabaugh (later christened the Sundance Kid, after a town in Wyoming where he had been incarcerated), were known to be affable, intelligent, and lighthearted. Cassidy was more contemplative than the Sundance Kid, who was a better shot and whose use of a gun could border on intemperate. A beautiful and mysterious woman was part of their crew; she was Etta Place, who became the Sundance Kid's girlfriend. Butch Cassidy and the Sundance Kid, in the end, did leave the Wild Bunch and the United States for South America, where they settled in Bolivia. They died there in November 1908, after a shootout with soldiers in the mining town of San Vincente, 14,500 feet up in the Andes. The movie famously concludes with a scene in which the duo's demise is unsettled; they are last seen alive, surrounded by soldiers and trying to shoot their way out.

The reality is no less compelling.

The legacy of Butch Cassidy and the Sundance Kid is undeniable, not only because they were characters in a movie but also because they were real-life outlaws who helped reshape the public's perception of bank robbers. Butch Cassidy and the Sundance Kid, as well as Etta Place and other members of the Wild Bunch, were bandits you could like, not because you agreed with their bushwhacking politics, but because they seemed, from newspaper accounts and photographs and personal recollections, to be likeable rogues. They were bank robbers first, and criminals, but crooks whose good looks and mannered ways made them more forgivable than most. Butch Cassidy and the Sundance Kid also rode at the end of a time when the robbers were, for the most part, not known for indiscriminate violence. Butch Cassidy's general aversion to gunplay was not a product of Hollywood. Many of the professional thieves who succeeded the Wild Bunch did not care when they fired or whom they killed. The brutal trend eventually would terrify the nation and provoke the federal government to take up arms.

Along with the James-Younger Gang and the Wild Bunch, the Dalton Gang ranks as one of the most infamous groups of bandits in the United States of the 1800s. The members of the Dalton Gang rode neither with Jesse James nor the Wild Bunch, but the Daltons represented the transition between the two types of bank robbers: those who started as guerrillas and those who started as cowboys or frontiersmen. The main members of the Dalton Gang—brothers Emmett, Grat, and Bob—were born in the borderlands: Bob (1870) and Emmett (1871) in Cass County, Missouri, and Grat (1861) near Lawrence, Kansas.

Grat's name was short for Gratton,[3] after a statesman from Ireland, from which the Daltons' ancestors, the D'Altons, had emigrated; Emmett was named for an Irishman who had been hanged in the gallows in England.[4] The Daltons' mother, Adeline Younger Dalton, a native of Jackson County, Missouri, was a half sister of Colonel Henry Washington Younger, the father of the Younger brothers. Unlike their cousins, the Daltons left Missouri, the cradle of criminals or the "Mother of Bandits."[5] The Daltons settled in the southeastern Kansas town of Coffeyville, just north of the border with what was then known as the Indian Territory. Those lands, combined with the Oklahoma Territory, eventually made up Oklahoma.

Growing up in western Missouri and in Kansas exposed the Daltons to what remained of a culture of rebellion and guerilla warfare. Adeline Dalton's husband was James Lewis Dalton, a native of Kentucky and a horse trader and saloon keeper in Missouri who fought under General

Zachary Taylor during the Mexican War.[6] The Daltons, who had fifteen children (three who died young), made their home in 1890 in the Indian Territory, near Kingfisher, north of where Oklahoma City is today. Kingfisher was one of several towns that were populated virtually overnight when the federal government officially opened part of the Indian Territory to settlement at noon on April 22, 1889—the date of the Oklahoma Land Rush of 1889.

The Indian Territory was a land of ambitious settlers—the Sooners—and cowboys and cattle rustlers. The flood of people who crossed into the territory looking for employment and land impinged on the cowboys' work, as did hunters' decimation of the buffalo, another source of income.[7] With few skills other than the ability to herd cattle and handle a six-shooter, some cowboys stayed on the range but started stealing cattle and robbing banks. The Dalton Gang, though certainly modeled to a degree after the James-Younger Gang, also followed the Indian Territory's dark tradition of spawning gangs of criminals and of providing refuge to crooks and scoundrels. Those who fled to that new land after the Civil War found "a retreat safe from capture and punishment, made so by the difficulty of reaching them with legal process."[8] When the Daltons arrived, the Indian Territory had entered a period in which it "was one of the most lawless sections in the United States."[9]

The Indian Territory was a land where the law was struggling to take hold, a region, where, from 1884 to 1888, fifty federal deputy marshals were killed trying to keep the peace.[10] The Daltons intersected with that segment of Western society, too. Frank Dalton, the older brother of Emmett, Grat, and Bob, worked as a deputy U.S. marshal out of Fort Smith, Arkansas, on the state's western border with the Indian Territory. Fort Smith was the federal government's bastion of authority nearest the vast Indian Territory, created in 1834. The newly demarcated land resulted from the Indian Removal Act of 1830, which relocated five Native American tribes—the Cherokee, Choctaw, Chickasaw, Creek, and Seminole, known as the Five Civilized Tribes—from east of the Mississippi River to the Indian Territory. Native Americans enforced the laws against other Native Americans in the territory, but deputy U.S. marshals were in charge of enforcing the laws against non–Native Americans. The marshals patrolled the 74,000-square-mile Western District of Arkansas, which was based in Fort Smith and encompassed the Indian Territory and western Arkansas.[11]

Frank Dalton rode as a deputy marshal under the jurisdiction of U.S. District Judge Isaac Parker, of the Western District of Arkansas, who was known as the "hanging judge" for the method of punishment he frequently ordered. One member of Frank Dalton's posse was Grat Dalton. [12] Horse thieves and whiskey runners killed twenty-eight-year-old Frank Dalton in the line of duty in the Indian Territory, near the Arkansas border, on November 27, 1887. After his death, Grat and Bob Dalton rode as deputy U.S. marshals. Emmett, the youngest of the Dalton siblings, was known to ride as a guard for his brothers when they were lawmen. Bob Dalton later became chief of the Indian police in the Osage Nation in the Indian Territory, and Emmett joined his posse. They were accused, but never convicted, of killing a man who had tried to take up with Bob Dalton's girlfriend, who was also his cousin. Bob Dalton was accused of killing another man by mistake several months later. [13]

The Daltons, perhaps bored with searching for crooks on behalf of the federal government or caught up in the exploits of their cousins in Missouri or the criminals in the freewheeling Indian Territory, gravitated toward the other side of the law. Grat Dalton was accused of stealing horses in 1890, about the same time that Bob was accused of bringing whiskey into the Indian Territory, one of its most frequent crimes. [14] Their patrolling of the Indian Territory as lawmen aided the Daltons as criminals. They came to know many of the natural hiding places in the territory, including a limestone cave near where the Cimarron River meets the Arkansas River, at what is today Mannford, west of Tulsa. [15] The refuge was to become "Dalton Cave"—the Indian Territory's version of the Hole-in-the-Wall.

With their short careers in law enforcement over for the Daltons, the nascent Dalton Gang took shape in 1891 when Bob, the gang's twenty-year-old leader, and twenty-nine-year-old Grat headed to California, where they joined brothers Littleton and Bill. On February 6, 1891, Bob, Bill, and Grat were accused of trying to carry out their first heist: the attempted robbery of a Southern Pacific train near what was then the town of Alila, California (now Earlimart), in Tulare County, south of Fresno. The robbers wore masks as they stopped the train on horseback. One of them shot and killed the train's fireman, and the gang got away with no money. Detectives with the express companies found Bill and Grat and jailed them in Visalia, Tulare County. The comparisons to other famous train robbers were immediate. "The Daltons are said to be cousins of the notorious outlaws known as the Younger brothers," one newspaper reported upon the arrests of Grat and another brother, Bill Dalton. [16] Bill was acquitted of the attempted robbery. Grat was convicted and sentenced to twenty years, but escaped from prison and returned to Oklahoma, where Bob Dalton had fled after the holdup. [17] There the Dalton Gang regrouped.

The members of the reconstituted Dalton Gang were Bob, Grat, and Emmett (Bill did not join them this time, though he remained a lawbreaker), as well as a number of the Daltons' associates in crime, all fellow one-time ranch hands the Daltons had befriended while working as cowboys. They were Dick Broadwell, Charley Bryant, William McElhanie, George Newcomb, Charley Pierce, and, known to be among the fiercest of the pack, Bill Doolin, whom Emmett Dalton had met when they worked on the Bar X Bar Ranch near what today is Pawnee, Oklahoma. The Dalton Gang's crime spree lasted eighteen months and ended with a deadly bank robbery that recalled the James-Younger Gang's bloody fiasco in Northfield, Minnesota, sixteen years earlier.

As did the Jameses and the Youngers, the Daltons gained much of their notoriety by first robbing trains. Between May 1891 and July 1892, they held up four trains in what is now Oklahoma. The heists netted $14,000, $19,000, $11,000, and $17,000. These raids, unlike the botched attempted robbery of the train in California, succeeded each time. The advance scout on these missions was Bob Dalton's girlfriend, Eugenia Moore, who was attractive and drawn to a life of crime, not unlike the Sundance Kid's Etta Place.

The Daltons could have used Moore's advance work when they arrived at their hometown of Coffeyville, Kansas, at nine-thirty in the morning on October 5, 1892. Moore had died of cancer several weeks earlier, before the Daltons came up with an ill-fated plan in which they would target two banks in Coffeyville at the same time. [18] In this, the Daltons could be said to have been imitating the James-Younger Gang, or at least one of that gang's supposed feats in the Northfield fiasco. Popular belief at the time held that the Jameses and the Youngers split up shortly after they arrived in Minnesota and tried to rob two banks at the same time—the First National Bank in Northfield and another bank in Mankato, to the southwest. Contemporary newspaper reports and other accounts debunk that scenario, [19] though the Daltons truly were enamored of robbing two banks simultaneously and achieving what would be, among the realm of the thief, a peerless crime.

Emmett Dalton, who was twenty-one years old at the time of the Coffeyville raid, later said Bob Dalton, his then-twenty-three-year-old brother, came up with the idea of a "double-header" daylight bank robbery for two reasons: because Bob Dalton was in a desperate mood after the death of his beloved Eugenia Moore, and because Bob Dalton wanted to commit a crime that had never been done before and thus would outshine the deeds of his cousins.[20] The Daltons contemplated retirement in the Southern Hemisphere, not unlike Butch Cassidy and the Sundance Kid. "My brothers, Bob, Grat, and I, had decided to make one big haul and quit the outlaw game and go to South America," Emmett Dalton later told an interviewer. "We expected to get it here in this double bank robbery."[21]

The Daltons were mistaken in believing the Jameses and their cousins had executed a double bank robbery. But the Daltons still shared a sentiment that the James-Younger Gang tried to cultivate. The Daltons claimed that rewards posted for their capture had forced them to stay on the lam and break the law. Following the train robberies, authorities had offered rewards of $5,000 for each of the four Dalton brothers, Bill included, "dead or alive."[22] The Daltons' view, like Jesse James's view of himself, was that they were hunted innocents whom society forced into criminal behavior and who were, initially, blamed for crimes they did not commit. So the Daltons went on to commit more crimes anyway, following a philosophy characterized as "if they were blamed, they might as well have the gain."[23] The Daltons, like the Jameses and the Youngers, also projected an image of noble bank robbers, who refused to rob the passengers on trains and who routinely refrained from firing their revolvers and rifles during heists.[24]

Such supposed nobility did nothing to save the members of the Dalton Gang who rode into Coffeyville, a lumber, cattle, and railroad town of 3,100 people that a Kansan named James Coffey founded twenty-three years earlier. Coffeyville was busy, filled with so many cowboys and cafes, saloons, and gambling parlors that it was known in its early days as "Cow Town."[25] On October 5, 1892, many of the residents were familiar with the Daltons from when the brothers had grown up there. Bob, Emmett, and Grat Dalton arrived with fellow robbers Bill Powers and Dick "Texas Jack" Broadwell; a sixth man also made up the group, though his identity remains a mystery.[26] The members of the Dalton Gang carried Winchester rifles and six-shooters and wore fake beards and mustaches. They aimed to hold up the Condon Bank and the First National Bank, across the street from one another in the Plaza, at Ninth and Walnut streets, in the center of town. Grat Dalton, Powers, and Broadwell entered the Condon Bank, and Bob and Emmett Dalton walked into the First National Bank. As had happened to the Jameses and Youngers in Northfield, the Daltons were quickly caught in a deadly mess.

The Daltons had plotted the raid for months.[27] They were familiar with Coffeyville. Yet they did not know it well enough to realize that a hitching rail where they had intended to tie their horses was no longer there. By chance, street graders working in downtown Coffeyville had removed it.[28] The Daltons and the others had to use a fence one hundred yards away, which complicated their escape efforts. The source of the other problem was a merchant named Aleck McKenna, who quickly recognized one of the Daltons, despite their disguises. McKenna screamed that the Daltons were in town, and that they were robbing the banks. The townspeople gathered guns from the two local hardware stores—another detail that echoes what happened in Northfield—and assembled.

The Daltons had chosen a poor place for a bank robbery, and not just because they were trying to hold up two banks in their hometown. The locations of the two banks—in the center of Coffeyville—kept them under the constant watch of the town's residents, many of whom had deposited their life savings in the two institutions. The Daltons encountered the same problem in Coffeyville that the Jameses and Youngers had encountered in Northfield and that numerous other bank robbers would encounter in the years ahead. A bank's address was often one of its best defenses. "Although it is unlikely that any bank building offered much of a deterrent to robbery aside from the heavy vaults and safe it contained, it provided important physical security by its very location," according to one history of banking in the West.

> The typical bank stood close to the center of town, far enough away from the saloons to discourage alcohol-induced midnight pilgrimages by the bar patrons, but close enough that the next morning those same bleary-eyed (and broke) revelers could obtain more cash. The bank's interior wall bordered another business, and the vault was usually set into that wall or placed in the basement to prevent break-ins from the outside directly into the vault. Thus, any attempt at burglary or robbery

involved getting inside the building, which was in the middle of town, then inside the vault, which was in the most protected part of the building. [In addition,] a daylight raid carried entirely different risks. An escape with stolen money risked every gun in town being brought to bear on a set of rather obvious desperadoes.[29]

Inside the Condon Bank, the cashier, Charles Ball, frustrated Grat Dalton by telling him, falsely, that the safe was on a time lock and could not be opened for three minutes, until nine-forty-five in the morning—a ruse similar to the trick that stymied Jesse James in Northfield. Grat Dalton said he would wait, which allowed the Coffeyville residents more time to arm themselves and prepare for a gunfight. At the First National Bank, cashier Tom Ayres gave Bob and Emmett Dalton $21,000 from the vault, but not before delaying the handoff, which gave the armed towns-people even more time to congregate. When the members of the Dalton Gang ran out of the banks, blasting their six-shooters, the Coffeyville residents fired back.[30]

The bloodletting occurred in what is known today as Death Alley, which included the spot where the members of the Dalton Gang had tied their horses. A clean getaway was impossible. Residents blocked either end of the alley and shot away. Powers and Broadwell were killed, and so were Bob and Grat Dalton. Four townsmen were shot dead: Charles Connelly (the city marshal), Lucius Baldwin, Charles Brown, and George Cubine. Emmett Dalton was shot as many as twenty-three times, including through the groin, but survived. The total take in the robbery of the Condon Bank was $20—the only amount unaccounted for after the residents seized the other stolen cash.

The Coffeyville residents displayed their quarry with pride. They lined up the four dead robbers side by side on a hay wagon and photographed them. Powers and Grat Dalton were still wearing their fake mustaches; a rifle was left across the waists of Bob and Grat Dalton. The dead members of the Dalton Gang were trophies in what is often described as "the last big gunfight of the Wild West."[31] The raid lasted fifteen minutes and defined the Daltons and Coffeyville for a lifetime. The bank robbers had earned no glory there. "The city," reported the *Coffeyville Journal*, "sat down in sack cloth and ashes to mourn for the heroic men who had given their lives for the protection of property . . . and the maintenance of law in our midst."[32]

Emmett Dalton was sentenced to life at the Kansas State Penitentiary at Lansing, but Governor E. W. Hoch pardoned him after fourteen and a half years. He went on to work as a successful real estate agent in California, where he lived in Hollywood and had a role in a movie about the Dalton Gang.[33] As did Frank James, Emmett Dalton made a second career of exploiting his criminal past and preaching the message that crime, including bank robbery, does not pay. He told an interviewer in early May 1931—about three months after he published a book, *When the Daltons Rode*—that robbery had not made him and his brothers rich, and that they had hidden none of the stolen money as buried treasure. The missing-money myth corresponds with claims that Jesse James had stashed some of his gang's illicit earnings in caves. "We never buried any treasure," said Emmett Dalton, then sixty years old. "We needed all the money we collected for our own uses or to lend to our supposed friends."[34]

Emmett Dalton offered another downcast appraisal of his outlaw life a week later, on May 10, 1931, when he visited Coffeyville "to go over the old trails"[35] and to tend to the common grave of his two brothers and Dick Broadwell and Bill Powers. Dalton pointed at the gravesite as he delivered what he intended to be a timeless message:

> I challenge the world to produce the history of an outlaw who ever got anything out of it except that [motions to grave] . . . or else to be huddled in a prison cell.
>
> And that goes for the modern bandit of the skyscraper frontier of our big cities, too. The machine gun may help them get away with it a little better and the motor car may help them in making an escape better than to ride on horseback, as we did, but it all ends the same way. The biggest fool on earth is the one who thinks he can beat the law, that crime can be made to pay.
>
> It never paid and it never will and that was the one big lesson of the Coffeyville raid.[36]

The Dalton Gang's near-extermination in Coffeyville did nothing to deter Bill Doolin. The former cowboy and erstwhile member of the Dalton Gang formed his own group of misfits to rob banks and commit crimes in southern Kansas and the Indian Territory over four years, a

stretch that ended with a gunfight as bloody as the failed raid at Coffeyville.[37] Doolin called his gang the Oklahombres or the Wild Bunch, the
same name that Butch Cassidy adopted for his band of brigands.[38] One of
the main members of Doolin's Wild Bunch was Bill Dalton, who had
joined Doolin instead of riding with his brothers in Coffeyville.[39] The
number of deputy U.S. marshals who pursued Doolin grew over the years
until he and the rest of his Wild Bunch were among the most wanted
thieves in an expanse teeming with them. Some of these lawmen became
as well known as Doolin and Bill Dalton.

Doolin was born in 1858 near Clarksville, in Johnson County, Arkansas. He grew up one county east of Fort Smith and the Arkansas–Indian
Territory borderlands—a stretch known as "Hell's Fringe." Doolin at age
twenty-three left his family's farm and headed west, where he picked up
jobs on ranches in the Indian Territory, settled along the Cimarron River,
met Emmett Dalton, and joined the train-robbing Dalton Gang. Though
he and his gang members were akin to marauders, Doolin, not unlike
Jesse James, enjoyed popular support and had help staying on the lam.[40]
He adhered, after all, to a code that prohibited shooting federal marshals
in the back.

Doolin was the latest bank robber caught up in the mythology of the
social bandit. His renown grew after the Daltons' demise at Coffeyville,
where some thought him the mysterious and never-identified sixth bandit.
Whatever happened, Doolin was larger than life in the enormous Indian
Territory. He was a drifter-turned-cowboy-turned-gang-leader who was
also known to be quiet and loyal to his wife, Edith Ellsworth, a preacher's
daughter he married in 1893. Doolin had few rivals when he and his men
were in action. A reputed take that totaled $165,000 over the four years of
the Doolin Gang's exploits added to his stature among the public, other
thieves, and federal lawmen.[41]

The Doolin Gang often used Dalton Cave to rendezvous,[42] but the
gang's equivalent of the Jameses' homestead was their hideout in Ingalls,
about ten miles east of Stillwater, Oklahoma, in the Indian Territory. On
September 1, 1893, the enclave witnessed one of the West's deadliest gun
battles between outlaws and deputy U.S. marshals. Present were Doolin
and Bill Dalton and other members of the Doolin Gang, all erstwhile
working cowboys whose nicknames trumpeted their reputations: Dan
"Dynamite Dick" Clifton, George "Red Buck" Weightman, George "Bitter Creek" Newcomb, "Arkansas Tom" Jones (an alias for Roy Daugher-

ty), and Bill "Tulsa Jack" Blake. The federal government increased its fight against the Doolin Gang on July 1, 1893, when President Grover Cleveland appointed E. D. Nix the U.S. marshal for the Western District of Arkansas, under the jurisdiction of Judge Parker. Nix made the capture of the Doolin Gang a priority of his 150 deputy marshals, and he created an expert team of three of his best deputies to target the gang: Chris Madsen, Henry "Heck" Thomas, and Bill Tilghman, known as the "Three Guardsmen."

Nix knew the Doolin Gang was holed up at Ingalls, where Doolin, Bill Dalton, and the others would spend their loot at Ransom and Murray's Trilby Saloon. The deputies had little chance of surprising the robbers— not with many of the residents of Ingalls on the side of the Doolin Gang. A number of "citizens catered to their trade," Nix later wrote, "carried them news of the movements of the deputy marshals, furnished them with ammunition, cared for their horses, permitted them to eat at their tables and sleep in their beds."[43] Trying to convict any of the townspeople for harboring a fugitive, Nix reasoned, would be futile "by reason of the fact that the entire community was under duress and would not testify for fear of losing their lives and property."[44]

As a bank robber in the Indian Territory in the late summer of 1893, Doolin believed he was in an ideal position. He considered many of the law-abiding residents his allies. In addition, the efforts of deputy U.S. marshals to track the gang's movements would, he reasoned, become further complicated at noon on September 16, 1893, when the federal government would open for settlement 6.5 million acres of the Cherokee Strip, located in the northern Indian Territory along the Kansas border. The government had authorized other lands for settlement in the Indian Territory before, but the Cherokee Strip made up the biggest parcel, and the opening of those lands would create the largest land rush in American history. The marshals would have to spend so much time policing the newcomers, they would almost certainly have little left to make trouble for the likes of the Doolin Gang.[45]

The marshals found the Doolin Gang before the land rush, on September 1, 1893. Nix had dispatched to Ingalls four deputy marshals, with John Hixon in the lead, along with eight members of a posse. They wanted to sneak up on Ransom's saloon, but "as usual," Nix wrote to U.S. Attorney General Judson Harmon, "the outlaws had received notice of the proximity of the deputies and they sent a messenger to the deputies inviting them to come into town if they thought they, the deputies, could take them. The deputies accepted the invitation and after posting their forces, sent a messenger to the outlaws with a request to surrender and were answered with Winchester shots."[46] The Doolin Gang and the deputy marshals fired at one another, and bullets peppered Ransom's saloon. The gunfire, Nix wrote, made the saloon "too hot for the outlaws,"[47] and they fled out a side door. The deputy marshals blasted them with their rifles. The outlaws fired back, killing three deputies: Dick Speed, who died that day, and Tom Hueston and Lafe Shadley, who died of their wounds three days later.[48]

All the members of the Doolin Gang escaped, except Tom Jones, who was captured after Deputy Marshal Jim Masterson (the brother of Bat Masterson, the famous U.S. marshal of the West) tossed dynamite into the gang's hiding place in Ingalls. As Doolin, Bill Dalton, and the rest of the outlaws rode out of town, they stopped at the top of a ridge and fired parting shots at the deputy marshals and the posse members. A bullet killed an innocent bystander, Frank Briggs. "Eight or ten horses were killed and nine persons killed and wounded," Nix wrote.[49] The "Battle of Ingalls," as the gunfight was known, ended in a draw.

Though Doolin escaped, the Three Guardsmen never stopped looking for him. After the firefight at Ingalls, Doolin's Wild Bunch robbed a bank in East Texas, and attempted to rob a bank in Southwest City, Missouri, on May 20, 1895—a would-be heist that ended with the death of a state auditor, J. C. Seaborn, and left Doolin with a head wound. In January 1896, Doolin went to a health resort in Eureka Springs, Arkansas, to get relief from his rheumatism. Bill Tilghman, one of the Three Guardsmen, arrested him there and jailed him in Guthrie, Oklahoma, where Doolin masterminded a jailbreak in which thirty-seven inmates escaped.

Doolin appeared indestructible, though his affection for his family contributed to his downfall on August 25, 1896. He was visiting his wife and son in what is today Pawnee County, Oklahoma, northeast of Stillwater, when Deputy Marshal Heck Thomas, another of the Three Guardsmen, caught up with him on a road that was near his father-in-law's house. Thomas and his seven-member posse demanded Doolin surrender. Doolin refused, fired back, and was soon "cleverly riddled with buckshot."[50] He suffered more than twenty wounds. His death earned Heck Thomas a reward of $1,400, which he shared with his posse men.

The crime-induced chaos of the Indian Territory era appeared ready to pass away along with Doolin's death, which occurred eleven years before Oklahoma gained statehood. The day after Doolin's death, the *New York Times* declared on its front page that he was "the last of the noted outlaws of the South,"[51] and by then the Doolin Gang had disbanded, with many of its members also dead. Bill Dalton was the exception—for a time. Once out of prison he formed his own gang, another iteration of the Dalton Gang, in 1894, a year after the Battle of Ingalls. Bill Dalton and three other members of this Dalton Gang were badly injured in a failed bank robbery in Longview, Texas, on May 23, 1894. It was Northfield and Coffeyville redux: Townspeople opened fire on this version of the Dalton Gang as they tried to hold up the First National Bank. Two residents and one of the outlaws, Jim Wallace, were killed in the gunfight, in which some two hundred shots were fired. Bill Dalton and his other gang members got away with $2,000 in coins and bank notes, and Dalton escaped to a cabin in Oklahoma's Arbuckle Mountains. He remained one of the most wanted men in the Indian Territory. U.S. Marshal Nix intended to obliterate every last member of the Doolin Gang. His order: "Bring them in dead or alive."[52]

A posse found Dalton at his cabin on June 8, 1894, after a deputy U.S. marshal, Loss Hart, helped intercept a package of liquor that was on its way to a residence in the dry Indian Territory. Hart had no idea who was to get the package until Dalton's wife put in notice that it was hers. Having finally learned Bill Dalton's whereabouts, Hart and his men rode to the Dalton farm to arrest Bill Dalton for the killings at Ingalls. Dalton, armed, jumped from a second-floor window to escape. Hart fatally shot Dalton before he hit the ground.[53]

The Indian Territory, Missouri, and Western states bred bank robbers after the Civil War, but bandits thrived in other locales as well. As Wall Street powered the postwar economy, New York City's many banks were victimized. Among all that city's thieves in the late 1800s, George Leslie stood out—not just in New York City but across the nation. He was known as the "King of the Bank Robbers," though he typically burglarized banks rather than robbing them. As one of Leslie's chroniclers,

Herbert Asbury, noted (undoubtedly with some hyperbole) in *The Gangs of New York*:

> Practically every burglar and bank robber of note in the United States made New York his principal headquarters during the twenty years which followed the Civil War, but the only one to whom police were willing to award the palm of genius was George Leonidas Leslie, also known as George Howard and Western George. Leslie was the son of an Ohio brewer and a graduate of the University of Cincinnati, where he had specialized in architecture and won high honors. He could have probably amassed a fortune by the practice of his profession, but upon the death of his mother, soon after he had completed his work at college, he came to New York and fell in with bad company, and so became a criminal.
>
> Within a few years after the close of the Civil War Leslie had become the head of the most successful gang of bank robbers that ever infested the continent. [54]

One of the men who knew Leslie well was George W. Walling, superintendent of the New York City Police Department from 1874 until 1885, or seven years after Leslie died. In his book, *Recollections of a New York Chief of Police*, Walling characterized Leslie, who was born in 1842, as a master thief. Walling wrote that in the nine years Leslie's crew operated in New York, they stole hundreds of thousands of dollars from banks. "Throughout the United States," Walling wrote, "their plundering cannot have been less than $7,000,000, comprising 80 percent of all bank robberies perpetuated from 1860 to the date of Leslie's death."[55]

Leslie's innovative methods allowed him to achieve such staggering hauls. Elaborate planning preceded each of his heists, in which he directed a crew on how to break into the bank. Leslie often wasn't even at the scene of the crimes; his gang members followed his directions, succeeded, and gave him a portion of the proceeds. Once Leslie chose a bank, he would get the architect's plans for it or study the building himself and draft the floor plan based on his observations. He would have his men practice in rooms designed to resemble the actual chambers of a bank. He placed one of his cronies inside the bank as an employee, or he bribed a police officer to look the other way; these ruses provided him with even more inside information. Leslie was a calculating thief who approached bank robbery (or bank burglary) as a business. His gang members were his employees, and he was their chief executive. The group had a productive run. In Leslie's nineteen years of knocking over banks, "the police found ample indications of Leslie's skill and leadership in more than a hundred bank robberies."[56]

The police never caught him, though he was linked to robberies and burglaries of banks and jewelry stores in Philadelphia; Muncy, Pennsylvania; Milford, New Hampshire; Waterford, New York; and Dexter, Maine, where Leslie and his crew bound and gagged an elderly cashier, James W. Barron, who died during the heist on February 22, 1878. That murder, Walling wrote, so "completely unnerved" Leslie that he told his wife he would get out of the illicit trades, though he never did. Throughout his career, Leslie usually went from one heist to the next, at his own pace, with each case netting him and his crew more money. His skill, his intelligence, and his general distaste for violence made Leslie a model for the bank robber as a criminal of a higher class, a professional crook who thrived in the close quarters of moneyed big cities such as New York and Philadelphia. Walling wrote of Leslie and his ilk,

> The successful bank robber is a king among thieves, and so far as the skill and cunning which he exercises are concerned, he undoubtedly earns his reputation. As a rule, it is the most intelligent members of the criminal class who drift into this branch of wickedness. Experience has demonstrated that the expert bank robber is possessed of more than ordinary mechanical skill, and an amount of energy and patience that is phenomenal. Thousands of dollars are expended in purchasing tools, and in experimenting with new mechanical contrivances. They are enthusiastic in learning every detail of their occupation. Thus it is that every succeeding year adds to the knowledge of the criminal, and makes absolute protection against detection seem more possible.
>
> But the most notorious bank burglars, like famous men of action, are known by their achievements rather than by their reputation among their fellows. To the burglar the sacking of a bank is as the sacking of a town to a great warrior; if he accomplishes his object without suffering a maximum of loss he is for the time peerless and much sought after by the people—or their representative, the district attorney.[57]

Leslie's accomplishments outside of thievery added to his reputation. He developed a persona among his fellow crooks as a cultivated thief or a gentleman bank breaker. He cavorted with members of New York's high society, none of whom knew his real job. He grew up with money, and as an adult he collected art, frequented libraries, and went to the theater and museums. He was married to a woman named Mary Henrietta Coath, or Molly, whom he courted when she was fifteen years old, but enjoyed spending money on other women—too much money, his critics contended, explaining why Leslie ended his life broke. He had plenty of opportunities to make money without even entering a bank. "The success of Leslie's operations soon brought him nationwide renown," Asbury wrote, "and in the last years of his life he became a consulting bank robber, and was frequently called upon for advice by other gangs. For a stiff fee or a percentage of the gains, with a guarantee, he planned bank and store burglaries all over the United States."[58]

The reason Leslie gave for stealing was as straightforward as his heists were intricate. He told friends he longed for "easy money" in New York City.[59] But the way of life of the thief appealed to him as well. He grew up viewing Jesse James and Frank James as heroes, though he decided early on to forsake the gunplay that Jesse James employed so readily in war-fractured Missouri, a part of the country Leslie and his cohorts considered the American West. George Leslie's fascination with Jesse James earned him the nickname Western George.[60] Leslie lusted for the money and the fame, but not the violence. Jesse James was brash and flash; George Leslie would be cerebral.

When he was in his mid-thirties, Leslie planned the bank robbery that guaranteed his legacy. It took place in New York, and surpassed what had been Leslie's biggest heist up until that time in the city—the theft of $786,879 (about $13.6 million today) from the Ocean National Bank, at Greenwich and Fulton streets, on June 27, 1869. Leslie's boldest heist took him three years to plan, though he had no part in its execution. He was found dead five months before it happened.

The target was the Manhattan Savings Institution, in New York City, and Leslie's gang made off with $2,747,000 in bonds and cash on October 27, 1878—a figure that today would be a stunning $40.5 million. The stolen amount made the heist one of the largest bank robberies or bank burglaries in American history, though the actual take was much less. The amount of cash was a mere $11,000 and only $300,000 worth of the bonds was negotiable. The police recovered $257,000 worth of the bonds, but none of the cash.[61] Yet the initial amount reported stolen was enormous, and just as disturbing to the public was the fact that the thieves had hit the Manhattan Savings Institution, "the *Titanic* of American financial institutions."[62] The savings institution was more than a bank. "It was also a depository for the money, jewelry, securities, and other valuables of some of the most prominent, wealthy citizens of New York City."[63] The Manhattan Savings Institution, at Bleeker Street and Broadway, was a financial stronghold, composed of steel doors, vaults, and thick walls, Its security was unquestioned.

Leslie knew the bank in the years before the burglary. He had to. He realized this score was to be his biggest, and it would likely allow him to abandon his life of crime, as he had told his wife he would after the disaster at the bank in Dexter, Maine. After visiting the Manhattan Savings Institution repeatedly, Leslie created a replica of it inside a Brooklyn warehouse[64] owned by one of his main underworld benefactors. She was Fredericka "Marm" (or "Mother") Mandelbaum, known in New York as the "Queen of the Fences,"[65] and so close to Leslie that she was the person who nicknamed him Western George. Mandelbaum made her estimable living by selling the stolen goods that Leslie and others provided her, and Leslie often turned to her to front him money to plan his robberies and burglaries. While he and his gang rehearsed inside the warehouse, Leslie, on his own, went to work on a copy of the combination lock on the Manhattan Savings Institution's vault. He either bought the lock or bribed the vault maker to provide one.[66] "Leslie possessed great mechanical skill," Asbury wrote, "and was thoroughly familiar with every type of safe and bank vault manufactured in the United States, many of which he could open by manipulating the dial."[67]

Leslie broke into the Manhattan Savings Institution three times in March 1878 to prepare for the big heist. He got help from a crony, Pat Shevlin, whom he got hired as a bank guard by cozying up to the bank's president, Edward Schell.[68] Shevlin let him in the bank, where each time Leslie tried to crack the combination on the real vault. He succeeded the third time using the tool that most demonstrated his criminal genius. It was a thin piece of wire called "the little joker."[69] When one of Leslie's crew members burglarized a bank, he removed the dial from the vault or safe, and inserted the little joker into the recesses around the tumblers. The burglar later returned, and dents in the wire showed the approximate location of the tumblers when the vault or safe was unlocked. The indentations gave Leslie enough information to determine the combination when he returned to the bank to burglarize it himself.[70] The little joker foiled Linus Yale Jr.'s greatest invention, the combination lock, which he created in 1862. Leslie and an expert safecracker, Gilbert Yost, tried the little joker on the combination lock on the vault at the Manhattan Savings Institution. They came up with the combination: 80-9-25.[71]

Leslie never used it. His decomposed body was discovered on June 4, 1878, at the base of what was known as Tramp's Rock, about three miles from Yonkers, near the border of the Bronx and Westchester County. He died amid neither wealth nor glamour. He was shot once in the head and once in the chest, and a white-handled revolver was found nearby, as if to suggest he had killed himself.[72] Leslie was thirty-six years old.

Leslie's crew completed his work at the Manhattan Savings Institution on October 27, 1878, a Sunday morning. Led by Leslie's one-time contemporary in crime, Tom "Shang" Draper, five to eight men "had white handkerchiefs tied around their heads under their hats, and all wore half masks of black muslin covering their mouths."[73] They got into the adjacent apartment of the bank's janitor, Louis Werckle; bound him, his wife, and his seventy-three-year-old mother-in-law; and then entered the bank. They cracked the vault with the combination Leslie had obtained through his expert preparations. They pried open the vault's safe-deposit boxes, many of them filled with jewelry and other valuables of New York's wealthiest.

Crowds gathered around the Manhattan Savings Institution the day following the heist, but unlike in Northfield or Coffeyville, the bystanders were not there to fight. They were there to gape. By then, the thieves were long gone and the police, as the *New York Times* reported, had "no clue to the robbers."[74] "A Great Bank Robbery," the paper of record declared on its front page. It reported that the Manhattan Savings Institution "was the victim yesterday of one of the most daring and successful burglaries ever perpetrated."[75]

The police eventually solved the case. George Walling, the police superintendent, pledged a resolution. The clues poured in after Detective Thomas Byrnes, inventor of the "third-degree" harsh style of questioning, successfully interrogated Pat Shevlin, the insider whom Leslie had placed inside the Manhattan Savings Institution. Shevlin had reason to talk. His fellow gang members promised him a cut of $250,000 for his role, but he got only $1,200.[76] Shevlin confessed, and soon the authorities arrested and prosecuted most of Leslie's gang in the Manhattan Savings Institution case. The exception was Shang Draper, who was never charged for that heist, and Gilbert Yost, the safecracker, who ended up in an insane asylum.[77]

The police never solved the murder of George Leslie. His gang members were the prime suspects, and possible motives included a fight between Leslie and his confederates over the division of the proceeds from the heists; a concern that Leslie was spilling secrets about his gang's crimes, particularly the killing of the bank clerk in Maine; and a dispute over a woman, Babe Draper, the wife of Shang Draper.[78] Police believed Leslie was killed near Shang Draper's house and his body dumped at Tramp's Rock, where a police patrolman found it. Leslie's body was bloody, but his clothes were clean, leading the police to surmise that whoever killed him dressed him in fresh clothes. "A valuable diamond pin and pearl studs . . . remained in his shirt," the *New York Times* reported, though his wife later said the pin was much less valuable than the one he usually wore.[79] The newspaper reported upon Leslie's death,

> His parents were well to do and highly respectable people. He received a good education, and was destined for one of the learned professions. His mother died while he was quite a youth, and his father married again soon after her death. His stepmother treated him so unkindly that he ran away from home and fell in with unsavory companions, and he soon made his debut as a burglar. He was reputed to be one of the most skillful house-breakers in the country.[80]

Leslie got a funeral and a proper burial, which a crowd of curious onlookers attended.[81] The money for the arrangements came from Marm Mandelbaum, the benefactor he knew so well in life. He was interred in a $10 plot at Cypress Hills Cemetery, in Brooklyn, notable for being the first nonsectarian cemetery in that section of New York City.[82] Also buried there are the Dutch painter Piet Mondrian, Jackie Robinson, and Mae West.[83]

Butch Cassidy and the Sundance Kid were buried in unmarked graves in San Vincente, Bolivia. Their interment occurred on November 7, 1908, the same day soldiers killed them. The deadly showdown was over the pair's robbery of $90,000 in payroll that a mule train was carrying for a mining company on November 4. As one of their biographers, Thom

Hatch, has noted, the bandits died as *desconocidos*, or unknowns.[84] Butch Cassidy was forty-two years old. Harry Longabaugh, the Sundance Kid, was forty-one.

Myth has gradually ceded to fact in the case of the outlaws' demise. The cause and circumstances of their deaths are fairly certain today, due largely to the work of Anne Meadows, whose 1994 book *Digging up Butch and Sundance* details her travels to South America to trace the last days of the pair. More than six decades earlier, much of what the public knew about the bandits' demise came from an article in the April 1930 issue of *The Elks Magazine,* by journalist Arthur Chapman and based on the recollections of Percy Seibert, an American engineer who met Butch Cassidy and the Sundance Kid while working for a tin mine in Bolivia. Seibert did not witness the last stand of the *bandoleros Americanos,* but, according to Chapman, Seibert said they were found dead inside a house at a San Vincente hacienda after the Bolivian soldiers' siege of the complex, where much of the shooting took place in a courtyard. The Sundance Kid was mortally wounded, Chapman wrote, and Butch Cassidy, "though wounded, managed to pick up Longabaugh and stagger back to the house with his heavy burden."[85] The soldiers kept firing, all that day and night. At noon the next day, Chapman wrote, soldiers rushed into the house. "They found Longabaugh and Cassidy dead," according to Chapman. "Cassidy had fired a bullet into Longabaugh's head, and had used his last cartridge to kill himself."[86]

Growing up as Robert Leroy Parker, Butch Cassidy appeared destined to work on a ranch. He roamed the Circle Valley area of southcentral Utah, where his father and mother and five siblings settled as Mormons on 160 acres in 1879, when he was thirteen years old. The teen's aspirations started to shift when, while working at a neighboring ranch, he met a cattle rustler named Mike Cassidy.[87] He taught Bob Parker how to fire a six-shooter, and he regaled him with tales of life on the open range as well as the excitement of the West's cattle towns, with their saloons and women. Cassidy's escapades thrilled Parker, who was never a devout member of the Church of Jesus Christ of Latter-Day Saints. He left his family and set out on his own in June 1884, when he was eighteen years old.

Parker first made his way to Telluride, Colorado, where he sought work in gold and silver mines but was also accused of stealing horses. He then probably drifted to Wyoming and Montana, then both territories, before he returned to Telluride in 1887. There he met two men who would influence him just as much as Mike Cassidy had. They were fellow horse thieves Tom McCarty and Willard Erastus Christiansen, who went by the name Matt Warner. Both were into horse racing, but turned to bank robbery when their fortunes ran out. Bob Parker joined them. Many reasons could explain why he turned to crime. Maybe, still in thrall of Mike Cassidy, he yearned for adventure and riches, but wanted to work for neither. Perhaps he grew weary of laboring on ranches and in mines. Or maybe he and his cohorts struggled to find legitimate work, for theirs was a generation "not born of war but of depression in the cattle country and the changing social period."[88] A massive drought in 1883, the collapse of the beef market in 1885, and the Great Blizzard of 1886–1887 combined to force thousands of cowboys to search for work in an environment where "fortunes vanished overnight, small ranches were abandoned by their owners, and unemployment among cowhands was widespread."[89]

As with Jesse James's first bank robbery, the date of Bob Parker's first heist is uncertain. Some historians say he participated in the robbery of the First National Bank in Denver on March 30, 1889. The circumstances of the robbery are so unique that anyone involved would most likely admit being there, if only for bragging rights, but neither McCarty nor Warner ever did so, and they would have been there with Bob Parker. Two men walked into the bank, and one showed the bank president a vial that the robber said contained nitroglycerine. To avert the disaster of an explosion, the president gave the robbers $21,000, including a $1,000 bill.[90]

The first bank robbery that Bob Parker indisputably carried out, according to newspaper accounts, was the holdup of the San Miguel Valley Bank of Telluride on June 24, 1889. Four thieves—Parker, McCarty, Warner, and an unidentified man—used a technique that could have been borrowed from the Jameses or Daltons. One stayed outside near the horses, two stayed on the sidewalk, and the fourth went inside, where he presented a clerk with a check. The clerk leaned over to look at the check, the robber pulled his face down to a desk, and then the robber called for his partners outside. No one fired a shot inside the bank, and the gang left with $20,750, but not before letting those in Telluride know what had happened: "When they had ridden a couple of blocks they spurred their horses into a gallop, gave a yell, discharged their revolvers and dashed away."[91] The scene was like something out of a James-Younger Gang heist, albeit without the rebel scream.

The robbery of the San Miguel Valley Bank remade Robert Leroy Parker. He was now a criminal, a persona new enough to Parker that that he changed his name. Bob Parker became known first as George Cassidy and then, finally, Butch Cassidy. Parker's new surname was homage to his boyhood hero, Mike Cassidy. Many theories exist for why Parker adopted the first name "Butch." The most likely reason is that he took on the name after he worked at a butcher shop in Rock Springs, Wyoming, not long after the robbery in Telluride. Others claim McCarty gave Cassidy the name because of his problems firing a rifle. Either way, the name stuck, and it would ultimately instill more admiration than terror. Butch Cassidy, like Bob Parker, had plenty of friends. "My brother," Cassidy's sister wrote, "had a disarming way with people."[92]

Cassidy was also smart enough to realize when to avoid people. Shortly after the Telluride robbery, he is believed to have hidden out in a canyon-filled area of eastern Utah called Robbers Roost. It was a natural refuge not unlike the Hole-in-the-Wall, which Cassidy also came to know around this time. In 1890 he rustled cattle from a ranch he owned in Johnson County, Wyoming, about ten miles northwest of the Hole-in-the-Wall.

Cassidy sold the ranch and by 1891 was stealing livestock. He was charged with stealing horses in Fremont County, Wyoming, in 1892, convicted two years later, and sentenced to two years at the Wyoming State Penitentiary in Laramie. He was released on January 19, 1896, and quickly applied whatever lessons he had learned in prison to sharpen his techniques. On August 13, 1896, Cassidy and two associates robbed the Montpelier National Bank in Montpelier, Idaho, of $5,000–$16,500. Cassidy gave the money to an attorney to represent his friend Matt Warner, who was being tried in Utah on a charge of murder related to a gunfight. (Warner was found guilty of manslaughter.)

How Cassidy carried out the robbery in Idaho is as noteworthy as why he stole the money. He and his associates, Elzy Lay and Bob Meeks, never fired a shot. The robbers rode out of town quickly on their horses and outdistanced their pursuers. Cassidy and the others had fresh horses waiting at a mountain pass. "This bank robbery demonstrated the modus operandi of what was the signature holdup designed by Butch Cassidy—quick and well planned."[93] Cassidy employed the relay method again on

April 21, 1897, in Castle Gate, Utah, where he and Lay robbed the pay-master of the Pleasant Valley Coal Company of $7,000 in gold coins. Fresh horses allowed them to outrun a posse, whose members found calling for help difficult; Cassidy and Lay had cut telegraph lines to hasten their escape. Butch Cassidy, once again, had made a name for himself.

The Sundance Kid was born Harry Alonzo Longabaugh in the spring of 1867 to parents of German descent in Mont Clare, Pennsylvania, near Philadelphia. He worked on canals as a child with his father, whose brother ran a canal boat service, and then worked on a farm. Longabaugh read as much as he could. One of his favorite books was *Robbery Under Arms*, an Australian novel by Thomas Alexander Browne, whose pen name was Rolf Boldrewood. The book likely gave young Harry something to dream about: "The story centers on the lovable villains, who are adventures and thieves but nevertheless with high moral standards of honor and loyalty, and are trapped by circumstances of their own making."[94]

The boy's circumstances changed on August 30, 1882, when, at fourteen years old, he moved to a distant cousin's farm in southwestern Colorado. He found regular jobs as a cowboy throughout the West but, like many of his contemporaries, became unemployed around the time of the Great Blizzard of 1886–1887. With no hope of a steady income, he stole a horse near Sundance, in northeastern Wyoming, in February 1887. The twenty-seven-year-old Longabaugh was convicted and sentenced to eighteen months in the jail in Sundance, whose name he would take as his own. Even before then, Longabaugh had built a public reputation as a thief—and was willing to court publicity with the newspapers. On June 7, 1887, after the *Daily Yellowstone Journal* had characterized him as "one of the most dangerous outlaws in the West,"[95] Longabaugh wrote a letter to the editor that displayed his literate mind and fluency with language. "In your issue of the 7th inst.," he wrote, "I read a very sensational and partly untrue article, which places me before the public not even second to the notorious Jesse James."[96]

Soon the comparisons to James would be more than apt. After his release from prison, the Sundance Kid worked again as a cowboy, including a stint in Canada, but settled on banditry as his calling. He and an associate robbed the Great Northern train at Malta, Montana, on November 29, 1892, though they got away with only about $50. Five years later, on June 28, 1897, the Sundance Kid and five other men robbed the Butte County Bank in Belle Fourche, South Dakota, across the Wyoming border. They got away with only $97, and were nearly caught when the angry townspeople fired at them as they were riding away.

The Sundance Kid by now was wanted and believed to have fled to the Hole-in-the-Wall, where he met Butch Cassidy and the others who hid there to escape the law. Cassidy liked the newcomer. In the Sundance Kid, he had a coolheaded but sometimes edgy companion who had a reputation for being the fastest gun in the West. The Wild Bunch, so named by Cassidy, was born. The group's members varied over the years, but included, along with Cassidy and the Sundance Kid, William "News" Carver; Harvey Logan, known as "Kid Curry"; and Ben "the Tall Texan" Kilpatrick. In 1900, in one of the most iconic photographs of the era, the five, all wearing derbies and three-piece suits, posed for a formal sitting in Fort Worth, Texas. The Sundance Kid looks like he is about to break into laughter, and Cassidy wears a sly grin. These were not ordinary bank robbers. They were criminals with a sense of style.

Etta Place, the Sundance Kid's girlfriend, was another member of the Wild Bunch—one who, over the years, has become just as intriguing as Sundance and Butch Cassidy. Her origins and even her real name remain uncertain. Was she a schoolteacher, as portrayed in the movie? Was she a prostitute? Was she a cattle rustler? Whatever her true identity, Etta Place apparently was in love with the Sundance Kid. Another iconic photo shows the two of them posing for a photographer in New York City in 1901. The Sundance Kid, this time, looks severe. Etta Place, in a long dress with her hair up, looks elegant.

Appearances and demeanors aside, the members of the Wild Bunch were still bank robbers, still criminals, though a group whose leader, Cassidy, espoused a philosophy that stressed intimidation rather than deadly violence when robbing a bank or a train. The philosophy did not preclude the use of explosives. On July 14, 1898, the Wild Bunch robbed a Southern Pacific train near Humboldt, Nevada, of $26,000 in cash and jewelry stolen from the safe. The Sundance Kid used dynamite to blow open the safe, and the blast tore through the express car, where the safe was located; Cassidy was not believed to be present. The Wild Bunch members used dynamite in another train robbery on June 2, 1889, near Wilcox, Wyoming. Cassidy was not present at this heist either, but was believed to have helped plan it. The Sundance Kid and other gang members used dynamite to blow up a bridge, in an attempt to scare the train crew into opening the safe, and then finally blasted the safe directly. The take was $30,000–$50,000 in bank notes, jewelry, and other valuables.[97]

Butch Cassidy and the Sundance Kid were undeniably together on September 19, 1900, when they, along with William Carver, held up the First National Bank in Winnemucca, Nevada, and got away with $32,640 in gold coins and currency. They did not use dynamite, but the threat of violence. When the head cashier, George Nixon, told the trio that the safe was on a time lock and could not be opened, Cassidy held a knife to his neck. Nixon opened the safe. The three members of the Wild Bunch switched to fresh horses on the outskirts of town and escaped. They remained quarry. The Pinkerton detectives had declared the members of the Wild Bunch wanted dead or alive, with a bounty of $10,000 each.

Even the Hole-in-the-Wall could no longer provide security. Butch Cassidy and the Sundance Kid were fugitives on a national scale, so they sought refuge out of the country. After a stay in Forth Worth, they headed to South America. The photo they sat for in Forth Worth had hurt their efforts to hide in the United States. It was widely circulated, making the members of the Wild Bunch even more widely wanted. After a stop in New York City (and another photograph, this one of Place and the Sundance Kid), Cassidy, Place, and the Sundance Kid took a steamship to South America. The international flight marked the trio's recognition that their era—the era of the bank robber in the Wild West—was coming to a close. The Pinkertons were more organized, the posses were more vigilant, and photography was just one of the many tools their pursuers could use to try to catch them. Their time in the United States—or at least their time to survive in the United States—had passed. According to biographer Thom Hatch, "The two outlaws were not stupid or stubborn men. They were perceptive enough to know that the days of the Wild Bunch and the Wild West were gone forever. They could not run from modern technology and coordinated law enforcement efforts—the system—and hope to escape."[98]

Cassidy, the Sundance Kid, and Place (now thought to be Mrs. Harry Longabaugh) worked as ranchers for a time in South America, but could never stop being criminals. On December 19, 1905, they held up the Banco de la Nacion in Villa Mercedes in San Luis, Argentina. The take was the equivalent of $90,000 in American currency. A switch to fresh horses outside of town speeded their getaway. Soon after the robbery, Place disappeared from contemporary accounts of the exploits of Cassidy and the Sundance Kid. Her fate remains unknown.

For so many years, uncertainty could also describe what happened on the final day of Butch Cassidy and the Sundance Kid, at that hacienda in San Vincente, Bolivia, where the soldiers had tracked them following the payroll robbery. Did the two escape, as some have theorized? Did they return to the United States? Or did they both die in the firefight with the Bolivian soldiers? And, if so, how did they die? Did Butch Cassidy really kill a badly wounded Sundance Kid before killing himself?

The available evidence suggests that Butch Cassidy and the Sundance Kid were killed by the soldiers and buried in unmarked graves, according to the findings of Hatch and biographer Anne Meadows. The doubters persist, and their refusal to accept such an unromantic conclusion is understandable—particularly in light of the enduring account of Butch Cassidy killing the Sundance Kid out of a sense of mercy and then ending his own life. Robert Leroy Parker and Harry Alonzo Longabaugh were towering figures in their own time—figures who have transcended their own times. Nothing helps create celebrity, posthumous or otherwise, like an immensely popular movie.

However they died, Butch Cassidy and the Sundance Kid were the last of a kind. Soon bank robbers throughout the United States would drive cars, rather than ride horses, and their crimes would become more mechanized in so many other ways, including the weapons they used. One robber who straddled the two eras was Henry "Bearcat" Starr, known as "the last of the horseback outlaws,"[99] but also the first bank robber to use a car during a heist. Starr had a link to Jesse James as well.

Starr was born on December 2, 1873, in the Indian Territory, in Fort Gibson, in eastcentral Oklahoma, two counties west of the Arkansas line. His parents were of partial Cherokee descent—hence Starr's high cheekbones and his other nickname, "The Cherokee Bad Boy." His aunt and uncle, by marriage, were Sam and Belle Starr. The latter, years earlier, had been the girlfriend of Cole Younger, Jesse James's confidant, and she went on to become the "Outlaw Queen," a friend, often intimately so, with bank robbers and thieves throughout the Indian Territory. She was not a blood relation to Henry Starr, who was known to distance himself from her,[100] but she was nonetheless a member of the Starr clan, who had a long history of outlawry.

Henry Starr started out as a cowboy and then became a horse rustler. He formed a gang and began robbing stores and trains in 1892. On December 13, 1892, he shot and killed a deputy U.S. marshal, Floyd Wilson, who had been searching for Starr near Nowata, in the northwestern Indian Territory. Like so many other criminals, Starr stood trial at Fort Smith, Arkansas, in the courtroom of Judge Parker. He twice sentenced Starr to hang after two convictions, the first of which was overturned on appeal,[101] though Starr ultimately got a fifteen-year sentence for manslaughter. He won a pardon from President Theodore Roosevelt, partly for his role in defusing a shootout in prison, and he was freed on January 16, 1903. Starr named his son Theodore Roosevelt Starr.

Starr did not use his second chance to reform himself; he robbed banks in Oklahoma, Texas, and Arkansas until his death in 1921. Many of the heists occurred in between prison stints, from which Starr was invariably paroled. And when he was not robbing banks, he wrote an autobiography, *Thrilling Events: Life of Henry Starr*, and played a bank robber in a silent movie, *Debtor to the Law*.[102]

The book deal put Starr in the same league with Emmett Dalton; Starr, as did Dalton, spoke out against bank robbery and the pitfalls of crime. Starr resembled Frank James as well, in that he, too, tried to make a living starring in a Wild West show.[103] Yet Starr's biggest act was his final bank robbery, when he used a Nash automobile to try to escape. The heist occurred on February 18, 1921, at the Peoples National Bank in Harrison, in northwestern Arkansas, two counties east of the Oklahoma line. He and some members of his gang got away with $6,000, but also met a surprise: The former president of the bank, W. J. Myers, set a "bandit trap" by placing a loaded thirty-eight caliber Winchester rifle inside the bank's vault. When the robbers confronted him, Myers reached for the gun and fired at Starr, hitting him in the spine, as he was leaving town in the car.[104]

Neither the Nash automobile nor Starr recovered. Starr and his accomplices abandoned and burned the car after fleeing the bank. Starr died in jail of his bullet wound four days later, on February 22, 1921. He was forty-seven years old and mindful of his reputation. "I've robbed more banks than any man in America," Starr told the doctor on his deathbed. [105]

Bank robbers struck in the West and Midwest well after the death of Henry Starr; their numbers exploded as the United States battled an unprecedented spike in crime. These were different characters, with different weapons, with backgrounds much different from those of Starr, Butch Cassidy and the Sundance Kid, Bill Doolin, and the Daltons. After the death of Henry Starr, bank robbers were no longer erstwhile cowboys. They were professional robbers, like George Leslie, but many also were professional killers. They battled what the federal government designed to be the most professional police agency in the land.

4

THE G-MEN GET GUNS

Bank Robbery and the Birth of the Modern FBI

J. Edgar Hoover was ready to declare war once again. The forty-year-old director of what was then known as the Department of Justice's Bureau of Investigation had spent much of the Great Depression telling the public he was taking on America's most notorious criminals—crooks who had further alarmed a nation already struggling under economic collapse. Hoover's bulldog-like mien personified what he considered the persistence of his agents, known, primarily because of his public relations prowess, as "G-men."

The kidnapping of the twenty-month-old son of renowned aviator Charles A. Lindbergh, in March 1932, prompted Hoover to declare war on kidnappers. The capture of George "Machine Gun" Kelly in September 1933 showed that Hoover and his men were going after gangsters. And the crime sprees and prison breaks of bank robber John Dillinger, whom bureau agents killed in Chicago in July 1934, sent Hoover into a battle against the arch felons. The worst of these was Dillinger. Hoover is said to have labeled him America's first Public Enemy Number One[1] on June 22, 1934—Dillinger's thirty-first birthday.

On April 5, 1935, Hoover declared another war—on bank robbers. "We are making the same kind of a drive on them as we did on the kidnappers," he said. "We have been getting set for some months and are now going forward with increasing momentum."[2]

One of the news agencies Hoover addressed used military metaphors to summarize his initiative. The Associated Press called it "a special offensive by the Federal Government."[3] In 1932, Hoover had created the Bureau of Investigation's first crime laboratory and, regarded by even his critics as an organizational genius, he demanded his agents work methodically and adhere to protocols he designed to stress uniformity and precision of investigation. These were some of the weapons—science and investigative rigor—that Hoover said his agents would use to fight the bank robbers. Their allies would be a crime-weary public and grateful bank employees.

"The first thing we tell them is not to touch anything; to leave the setting of the crime free from disturbance for the analysis of our agents," Hoover told the reporters. "Now that we have fast automobiles at our offices and an adequate supply of firearms, we are equipped to go after the robbers if we are informed about a robbery soon enough."[4]

As for the size of the enemy's army: Hoover, who had also instilled an emphasis on statistical analysis at the Bureau, had a figure. He told the reporters the number of "known bank robbers" he was up against was five thousand.[5]

Three months later, on July 1, 1935, Hoover renamed his own army of agents. The force had grown to the point that a new moniker was necessary. His agency could no longer be known as the Bureau of Investigation, or, as it was briefly, the Division of Investigation. Those were faceless names for an organization that, by this time, had become even more prominent in the public imagination than the Department of Justice, of which it was a part. Hoover renamed the Bureau of Investigation the Federal Bureau of Investigation. From then on, whenever a bank robber worked a heist, he or she would have to contend with the FBI.

Just several years earlier, J. Edgar Hoover's Bureau of Investigation seemed bound for legal obscurity. It was a middling agency, beset by scandal, lack of clear purpose, and Congress's reluctance to impede states' rights and the Constitution by creating the equivalent of a national police force. Hoover's government career appeared to be on course for a premature end. He had been loyal to the Department of Justice, joining it as a law clerk in 1917, when he was twenty-two years old and a former clerk at the Library of Congress. He impressed presidents and attorneys general with his work ethic and sharp mind. He reached the position of director of the Bureau of Investigation on May 10, 1924, when he was twenty-nine years old. But that agency had a limited role in fighting crime; few federal laws gave the bureau jurisdiction. The size of the role soon grew—the result of the Great Depression and the great national crime wave that came with it. The FBI and Hoover, more than anything, owed their existence and the expansion of their powers to criminals—especially bank robbers.

The FBI originated in a piece of bureaucratic gamesmanship bordering on deceit. Congress never intended it to exist. In 1871, the year after it created the Department of Justice, Congress appropriated $50,000 to the department for the detection and prosecution of federal crimes. The Department of Justice typically used the money to hire private detectives, such as those with the Pinkerton Detective Agency, until Congress prohibited such expenditures in 1892. The Department of Justice and its head, the attorney general, were left to piece together a detective force by borrowing agents from other federal departments, particularly the Treasury Department, whose Secret Service had been created after the Civil War to investigate counterfeit currency.

President Theodore Roosevelt, elected in 1901, pushed for the Department of Justice to have its own detective force. Roosevelt wanted a corps of professionals to investigate the kind of government corruption he had vowed to eradicate as the Progressive nominee for president. Roosevelt had an ally in Attorney General Charles J. Bonaparte (a grandnephew of Napoleon I), whom Roosevelt appointed in 1905. Bonaparte continued to cobble together "special agents"—so called because they investigated "special crimes"[6] or were outsiders called in for "special" cases[7]—from the Secret Service and other government agencies; he also had a small cadre of Department of Justice employees—"special representatives of this Department," as he described them.[8] But Bonaparte pressed Congress to establish a detective agency for the Department of Justice.

"The attention of the Congress should be, I think, called to the anomaly that the Department of Justice has no executive force, and, more particularly, no permanent detective force under its immediate control," Bonaparte wrote in his annual report to Congress for 1907. He did not fault the work of the borrowed special agents, but, he also wrote, "it seems obvious that the Department on which not only the President, but the courts of the United States must call first to secure the enforcement of the laws, ought to have the means of such enforcement subject to its own call; a Department of Justice with no force of permanent police in any form under its control is assuredly not fully equipped for its work."[9]

Congress turned down Bonaparte, and took further action. In May 1908, it barred the Department of Justice from using Secret Service agents—a backlash traced to Congress's anger at a number of indictments the Secret Service helped secure against members of Congress in 1905 on charges of fraudulent land deals. Congress also remained wary of expanding federal powers, with one lawmaker warning of "a great blow to freedom and to free institutions if there should arise in this country any such central secret-service bureau as there is in Russia."[10]

Roosevelt authorized Bonaparte to act boldly. Despite Congress's clear disinclination to staff the Department of Justice with special agents of its own, on July 26, 1908, Bonaparte formed an investigative unit of thirty-four special agents within the Department of Justice and placed it under the control of the Department of Justice's chief examiner, Stanley W. Finch. What would become the FBI was born. Bonaparte in his annual report for 1908 seemed brazen in explaining how the new unit came about. He wrote that, because of Congress's ban on the use of Secret Service agents, "it became necessary for the department to organize a small force of special agents of its own. Although such action was involuntary on the part of this department, the consequences of the innovation have been, on the whole, moderately satisfactory."[11]

The special agents investigated a limited number of federal crimes, among them bankruptcy fraud; nonviolent violations of the national banking laws; mail fraud; crimes committed on federal government land and reservations; and peonage, or involuntary servitude of laborers in debt.[12] Bank robbery was not yet a federal crime, though the Department of Justice was responsible for investigating and prosecuting fraud, embezzlement, and other crimes, such as defalcation, or misappropriation of funds, involving the national banks. These types of crimes particularly concerned Bonaparte. In his annual report to Congress for 1908, he asked lawmakers to allow the Department of Justice to hire "a small number of trained accountants" to investigate banking violations, rather than forcing the Department of Justice to continue to rely on "national-bank examiners," who worked for the Treasury Department's Office of the Comptroller of the Currency. Reflecting on how crimes against banks deeply affect the public confidence, Bonaparte wrote,

> The number and gravity of offenses against the national banking laws by officers or employees of national banks constitute matters of reasonable solicitude and regret. The moral culpability involved in such offenses seems often to be imperfectly appreciated and, although they usually excite great indignation and provoke loud complaints from the sufferers when they are first discovered, so much time is frequently lost in the preparation for trial and actual trial of these long and complicated cases that the crime itself has faded from public memory when the criminal is at last convicted, and there is need of vigilance lest he finally escape with wholly insufficient punishment. The department has felt bound in duty energetically to assist the several United States attorneys in bringing this class of offenders to justice, and to do all in its power to assure them adequate penalties. [13]

Bonaparte's successor as attorney general, George W. Wickersham, took over as head of the Department of Justice for President William Howard Taft in 1909. Wickersham inherited Bonaparte's investigators, and gave the group a name: the Bureau of Investigation. The bureau remained small, but its potential was great. Its special agents were in a position to fight crime on behalf of their fellow Americans, to be the avengers of ordinary citizens against criminals and their terrors, which were soon to grow more severe. As an authority on the FBI, Richard Gid Powers, has observed, the Bureau of Investigation "could have a significant impact on the country because its actions could reduce complex problems to understandable dramas of crime and punishment. The bureau's cases were important not so much for any effect they had on the crime rates, but as a way of reinforcing the public's perception of the president as the ultimate public defender." [14]

Congress gradually gave the Bureau of Investigation power to investigate some interstate crimes, though the bureau's overall jurisdiction remained restricted. Congress in 1910 passed the White Slave Traffic Act, or the Mann Act (after Congressman James Robert Mann of Illinois), which outlawed the transportation of women across state lines for prostitution and what lawmakers considered other immoral purposes. And in

1919, Congress responded to the rise in automobile ownership and automotive theft by passing the Motor Vehicle Theft Act, or the Dyer Act (after Congressman Leonidas C. Dyer of Missouri). It prohibited interstate transportation of stolen automobiles. Congress and the courts justified the Mann and Dyer Acts under the commerce clause of the Constitution, which allows the federal government to regulate interstate trade. The passage of the acts showed Congress's willingness to let the government investigate some serious crimes that traditionally fell under control of the local police. The Mann and Dyer Acts, according to Athan G. Theoharis, a scholar of the FBI, "captured a growing conviction that local and state police could not by themselves address certain crimes and, thus, that there was a need for a supplementary federal role."[15] Years later, as part of President Franklin D. Roosevelt's New Deal, Congress would embrace this philosophy to make bank robbery a federal crime.

The Bureau of Investigation first had to recover enough public confidence for Congress to even consider expanding its powers. After World War I, Congress rebuked the bureau for rounding up those whom agents had labeled subversives, including alien residents as well as U.S. citizens who had attended meetings of the Communist Party of America and the Communist Labor Party of America. These "Palmer raids," which occurred nationwide in late 1919 and early 1920 and were named after Attorney General A. Mitchell Palmer, resulted in few deportations and further damaged the credibility of the Bureau of Investigation.[16] The raids also involved J. Edgar Hoover, who helped plan them as chief of the Bureau of Investigation's new Radical Division, later called the General Intelligence Division. Palmer named him to that post in 1919, when Hoover's tenure at the Department of Justice was only two years old and he was already a twenty-four-year-old special assistant to the attorney general.

The bureau's abuses continued during the corrupt administration of President Warren G. Harding, whose nadir was the Teapot Dome scandal. Senator Thomas J. Walsh of Montana led a 1923 Senate investigation that showed Albert B. Fall, the secretary of the Department of the Interior, had accepted $409,000 in bribes from two oil tycoons in exchange for granting them no-bid exclusive leases to lucrative U.S. Navy oil reserves in Teapot Dome, Wyoming (so named for its unique shape), as well as Elk Hills and Buena Vista, California. Harding's attorney general, Harry M.

Daugherty, had refused to have the Department of Justice investigate the deals.

Montana's junior senator, Burton K. Wheeler, led an investigation of Daugherty, who was Harding's former campaign manager and a friend of Fall's. The probes revealed how agents with the Bureau of Investigation attempted to intimidate and blackmail Wheeler and Walsh. Agents spied on the senators and their families, wiretapped their telephones, broke into their homes and offices, and opened their mail. Hoover was second-in-command of the Bureau of Investigation at the time; Daugherty had promoted him to assistant director of the bureau in 1921. By 1923, with the bureau's antics a national disgrace, the Department of Justice had become known as the Department of Easy Virtue—a refuge for cronies and scoundrels. [17]

In 1923, after Harding died in office, reform came with the new president, Calvin Coolidge, Harding's vice president. In 1924, Coolidge demanded and received Daugherty's resignation, and named as his attorney general Harlan Fiske Stone, dean of the Columbia University Law School. Stone, later a Supreme Court justice, appointed the twenty-nine-year-old Hoover director of the Bureau of Investigation, first as its acting chief and then its permanent director. Under Stone's firm directives, Hoover overhauled the bureau. He fired rogue agents and established many of the protocols and organizational structures—including a national crime laboratory and a national fingerprint file under the bureau's Division of Information and Identification—that the FBI continues to use to this day.

The Bureau of Investigation nonetheless continued to lack the standing of many other federal agencies. Its jurisdiction still encompassed few crimes—among them were mail fraud, bank fraud, and violations under the Mann and Dyer Acts—and its agents still could not carry firearms or make arrests on their own; they had to call U.S. marshals or local or state police officers to take suspects into custody.

The bureau even had a secondary role in what was considered the crime of the century—the Lindbergh kidnapping, in March 1932. In June 1932, Congress passed the Federal Kidnapping Act, known as the Lindbergh Law, which made kidnapping a federal crime—with federal jurisdiction triggered only if authorities had proved the victim of the kidnapping had been transported across state lines. The law was not retroactive; the state police in New Jersey, where the kidnapping occurred at the

Lindbergh residence, retained control of the case, though the Bureau of Investigation later coordinated the probe. President Herbert Hoover, Coolidge's successor, reluctantly signed the Lindbergh Law; however, his concerns about states' rights virtually ensured that he and his attorney general, William DeWitt Mitchell, would decline to seek more powers for the Bureau of Investigation for the rest of Hoover's time in the White House.

Two years before the Lindbergh kidnapping, in a speech in which he decried racketeering, public corruption, and "gangster crime," Hoover had told the nation that the states must hold the ultimate authority in fighting crime. "Every single State has ample laws that cover such criminality," Hoover said. "What is needed is the enforcement of these laws, and not more laws. Any suggestion of increasing the Federal criminal laws in general is a reflection on the sovereignty of State government."[18] In addition, the local and state police agencies did not make an arrest in the Lindbergh case until 1934. The long investigation eliminated the publicity that a quick end to the case would have immediately brought J. Edgar Hoover, who repeatedly arranged to have the Bureau of Investigation (and himself) be part of the media coverage of the case.

In the early 1930s, Hoover was not yet the seemingly indispensable director he would become later, when he would go on to lead the FBI for nearly a half century, working, until his death in 1972, for eight U.S. presidents and sixteen attorneys general. In fact, Hoover appeared to be on his way out as director of the Bureau of Investigation in 1933, when President Franklin D. Roosevelt succeeded President Herbert Hoover. Roosevelt appointed a new attorney general, Senator Walsh of Montana, whom the Bureau of Investigation had targeted during the Teapot Dome scandal. Many in the new administration expected Walsh would fire Hoover. But the seventy-three-year-old Walsh died of a heart attack in North Carolina on March 2, 1933, while on a train that was traveling from Florida to Washington for Roosevelt's inauguration on March 4, 1933.

Roosevelt appointed a new attorney general, Homer S. Cummings of Connecticut, a former prosecutor and a former chairman of the Democratic National Committee. He retained Hoover. Aided by New Deal legislation, and with Hoover carrying out his orders, Cummings would go on to make fighting crime, including bank robbery, a priority of the Roosevelt administration. In terms of the enlargement of federal authority, the anti-crime initiative would be just as important as Roosevelt's creation of federal programs to ease and end the hardships that had started when the stock market crash of October 1929 plunged the United States into the Great Depression.

Cummings's initial job was to give Roosevelt a legal opinion on whether the president could shut down the nation's beleaguered banking system—an action that, once approved, coincidentally would lead to legislation that helped define the scope of the later statutes that made bank robbery a federal crime. With the nation in the throes of the Great Depression and desperate Americans pulling their money out of banks, on March 6, 1933, two days after he took office, Roosevelt sought to end the runs on banks and strengthen the national banking system by declaring a four-day bank holiday. The legislation that followed reflected the popular belief that speculation had caused the financial crisis. To trust the banks again, Americans needed to know their deposits were safe. The bank holiday ended the immediate concerns about the banks imploding, and the National Banking Act of 1933, also known as the Glass-Steagall Banking Reform Act, provided long-term assurances. The act, which Roosevelt signed on June 16, 1933, created the insurance fund that, after the Banking Act of 1935, would become the Federal Deposit Insurance Corporation. The fund initially covered deposits of no more than $2,500 per individual when the insurance became effective on January 1, 1934. The banks in the new system numbered 13,201.[19]

Roosevelt and Cummings soon employed the activist federal government of the New Deal to subdue another national threat—crime. The still-unsolved Lindbergh kidnapping continued to horrify the nation, but it was part of a wave of notorious crimes that swept the country in 1933 and 1934—perhaps the greatest crime wave in American history. The end of Prohibition, with the ratification of the Twenty-First Amendment, on December 5, 1933, left bootleggers, rum runners, and their confederates looking for new lines of work. Prohibition had cultivated a sense of lawlessness in the United States, with bootleggers and other gangsters acting with impunity. During the Great Depression, that culture of lawlessness fused with individual financial desperation and a popular anger at banks. The ire was understandable: Many banks had foreclosed on their customers' homes or, when the banks went under—as nine thousand of them (a full third) did between 1929 and 1933—swallowed their depositors' savings.[20] The gangsters and bank robbers and kidnappers reflected how the Great Depression had warped the American ethos of self-reliance, so that crime, for many, had become an understandable and even acceptable way to survive.

Technology aided the robbers. The telephone and telegraph let them communicate with one another easily in the planning of their heists. The rise of the automobile (as Henry Starr showed) and the airplane allowed bank robbers to flee and cross state lines quickly, which put them out of the jurisdiction of the police in the locale where the heist occurred.[21] Many of the robbers were heavily armed, and some were using the new Thompson submachine gun. "Federal men," Roosevelt said, "are constantly facing machine-gun fire in the pursuit of gangsters."[22] By 1933, according to one estimate, robbers were said to be holding up banks "at the rate of almost two a day."[23]

"We are no longer a nation whose problems are local and isolated," Cummings said in a speech about the need for the federal government to fight crime. "The growing density of our population and the development of high-speed methods of transportation have resulted not only in a large increase in our crime rate, but, also, have given to many offenses an interstate character."[24] Bank robbers in the Midwest and South were particularly adept at jumping from state to state—Ohio, Indiana, Illinois, Minnesota, Missouri, Arkansas, Texas—and capitalizing on the jurisdictional deficiencies of local and state law enforcement. For years, the stretch between Minnesota and Texas—the same area that Jesse James once terrorized—had been known as the nation's "crime corridor."[25]

Since the time of James, states had tried to establish their own forces to combat the criminals, with the Missouri militia being one of James's most notable enemies. Yet these forces still were restricted to enforcing laws within their own states, much as the U.S. marshals who patrolled the Indian Territory for the Daltons, Bill Doolin, and Henry Starr did not have national jurisdiction. The marshals' sphere of law enforcement was limited to the Indian Territory, which, before Oklahoma's statehood, was federal land.

The inkling of a national or seminational police force originated in the West in the spring of 1898, when Butch Cassidy, the Sundance Kid, and the Wild Bunch were riding high and frustrating the governors of Colorado, Utah, and Wyoming, just as the James-Younger Gang had infuriated

Missouri's heads of state. The governors in the tri-state area met in Salt Lake City in the spring of 1898 "to discuss eradicating the outlaw gangs—the Wild Bunch in particular. . . . The governors thought that perhaps they could be successful by dispatching peace officers who could cross boundaries and be authorized to make arrests in all three states."[26] The breakout of the Spanish-American War, in April 1898, derailed the governors' plans, which would become realized with the FBI under Roosevelt.

The New Deal's banking reforms and other economic legislation evinced Roosevelt's belief that federal intervention was a solution to the country's financial woes. Along with J. Edgar Hoover, Roosevelt and Cummings came to believe that federal intervention was a way to quell the crime wave. Cummings considered the possibility of creating an American version of Scotland Yard and, with Roosevelt's backing, lobbied Congress to give the Bureau of Investigation expanded crime-fighting powers.

Roosevelt prepared for the proposed changes on June 10, 1933, when he signed an executive order that created the Department of Justice's Division of Investigation, which combined the Bureau of Investigation, the Bureau of Identification, and the Bureau of Prohibition. Roosevelt's and Cummings's demands for more powers for the Division of Investigation gained greater urgency on June 17, 1933—the date of the Kansas City Massacre, a case that, along with the Lindbergh kidnapping and the exploits of John Dillinger, more than anything, provided the impetus for the creation of the modern FBI. Cummings raged in public over the death of Special Agent Raymond J. Caffrey, who was killed in the Kansas City gunfight along with three other lawmen and Frank "Jelly" Nash, an escaped bank robber (whose nickname was slang for nitroglycerine). As 1934 started, Cummings and Roosevelt focused on federal involvement in the control of bank robbery and other crimes.

Roosevelt unveiled the new effort in his annual message to Congress on January 4, 1934. He said Americans "have been shocked by many notorious examples of injuries done our citizens by persons or groups who have been living off their neighbors by the use of methods either unethical or criminal." He cited white-collar criminals, such as tax cheats and "reckless speculators." "In the other category," Roosevelt said, "crimes of organized banditry, coldblooded shooting, lynching, and kidnapping have threatened our security. These violations of ethics and these violations of law call on the strong arm of Government for their immediate suppression; they call also on the country for an aroused public opinion."[27]

Cummings stirred up that public opinion. On February 19, 1934, he introduced a package of twelve anticrime bills to Congress, including the Federal Bank Robbery Act, which would make bank robbery a federal crime. Cummings based the constitutionality of the proposals on the commerce clause. Other bills would make the interstate flight of felons a federal crime if they were trying to avoid prosecution; strengthen the federal kidnapping law; and require the registration of machine guns, sawed-off shotguns, and rifles—the types of weapons gangsters favored. "We are now engaged in a war that threatens the safety of our country—a war with the organized forces of crime," Cummings told the Daughters of the American Revolution on April 19, 1934, in a speech that included his exhortation that the nation's crime problems were no longer "local and isolated." Cummings gave a history lesson. "At the time of the adoption of the Constitution of the United States," he said, "there was little need that the Federal Government should concern itself with the problem of crime. Due to the isolation of the different settlements, the operations of criminals were, of necessity, local in their nature." Cummings was careful to put limits on the federal government's quest for new powers; the government, he said, "has no desire to extend its jurisdiction beyond cases in which, due to the nature of the crime itself, it is impossible for the states adequately to protect themselves."[28]

Cummings nonetheless placed some of the blame for the surge in crime on incompetent and corrupt local authorities and police officers, many of whom, he said, "are given positions on a basis of political prefer-ment." "Clearly the institutions and agencies upon which we have relied for the enforcement of the law have not adequately performed their proper functions," Cummings said. "In many localities there exists an unholy alliance between venal politicians and organized bands of racketeers." Exacerbating these unfortunate realities, he said, was a "lack of coopera-tion" that can exist among various law enforcement agencies. The criminal, especially the criminal on the run, benefited from the interagency distrust. "Another serious phase of the problem," Cummings went on, "has to do with the relative uncertainty which exists with respect to the dividing line between the jurisdictions of the Federal and State Governments. Here lies an area of relative safety—a twilight zone—in which the predatory criminal takes hopeful refuge."[29]

Cummings's push for his Twelve Point Program grew even more relevant on April 23, 1934, when John Dillinger and his gang took advantage of that "twilight zone" of jurisdictional confusion. They escaped the Bureau of Investigation and local police in a botched raid on a lodge where Dillinger and his crew had been hiding out in the summer resort town of Little Bohemia, in northern Wisconsin. The most violent member of Dillinger's gang, George "Baby Face" Nelson, fatally shot a special agent, W. Carter Baum, and wounded another agent and a local constable. The next day, as the *New York Times* reported on the escape on its front page, another story had Roosevelt asking Congress to approve the anticrime bills, with the president "aroused by the latest escapade of the bandit John Dillinger."[30] Few in Congress objected, unlike during the presidency of Herbert Hoover, when the White House and many in Congress raised concerns over the erosion of states' rights. Roosevelt and Cummings faced little opposition to the anticrime bills; Americans worried the bank robbers and other crooks were winning.

The bills in Cummings's Twelve Point Program speeded through Congress. On May 3, 1934, the House Judiciary Committee referred the Federal Bank Robbery Act to the full House of Representatives. The act made any robbery of a national bank or a member bank of the Federal Reserve System to be a federal crime. The act set forth the penalties for a convicted bank robber, penalties that still are on the books: up to twenty years in prison and a $5,000 fine for most cases; up to twenty-five years in prison and a $10,000 fine "if an assault be committed or the life of any person put in jeopardy, by use of a dangerous weapon in the commission of an offense"; and "if murder or kidnaping [*sic*] be committed in connection therewith the penalty shall be imprisonment from ten years to life, or death if the jury shall so direct in the verdict."[31]

Cummings submitted a statement to the Judiciary Committee in support of the legislation. Replete with references to the great crime wave of the Great Depression, his statement represents the sine qua non commentary on the establishment of bank robbery as a federal crime in the United States:

> This bill is directed at one of the most serious forms of crime committed by organized gangsters who operate habitually from one State to

another—the robbery of banks. From all sections of this country Federal relief has been requested. It is asserted that these criminals are sufficiently powerful and well equipped to defy local police, and to flee beyond the borders of the State before adequate forces can be organized to resist and capture these bandits. There would seem to be no logical reason why the Federal Government should not protect the institutions in which it is interested from robbery by force or violence equally as well from defalcation, embezzlement, and willful misapplication of funds. This bill provides punishment for those who rob, burglarize, or steal from such institutions, or attempt to do so. A heavier penalty is imposed, if in an attempt to commit any such offense and person is assaulted, or his life is put in jeopardy by the use of a dangerous weapon. A maximum penalty is imposed on anyone who commits a homicide or kidnaping [*sic*] in the course of such unlawful act.

The bill specifically provides that jurisdiction shall not be reserved exclusively to United States courts. There is no intention that the Federal Government shall supersede the State authorities in this class of case. It will intervene only to cooperate with local forces when it is evident the latter cannot cope with the criminals. [32]

Congress acted quickly. Without taking a record vote, the House on May 5, 1934, passed six of the twelve anticrime bills, including the Federal Bank Robbery Act; the Senate approved the bills ten days later. The Federal Bank Robbery Act defined a bank as including "any member bank of the Federal Reserve System, and any bank, banking association, trust company, savings bank, or other banking institution organized or operating under the laws of the United States." The act defined a bank robbery as committed by "whoever, by force and violence, or by putting in fear, feloniously takes, or feloniously attempts to take, from the person or presence of another any property or money or any other thing of value belonging to, or in the care, custody, control, management, or possession of, any bank."[33] Three years later, Congress amended the Federal Bank Robbery Act to include larceny, or the unlawful taking of property without force, and burglary.[34]

On May 18, 1934, Roosevelt signed the Federal Bank Robbery Act and the five accompanying anticrime bills. They outlawed the following on the federal level: the killing or assault of federal officers, such as special agents in what was then the Division of Investigation; extortion by means of telephone, telegraph, radio, oral message, or otherwise; the transportation of kidnapping victims across state lines, with the presumption that such a transfer occurs if the kidnapping victim is not returned within seven days; the fleeing from state to state to avoid prosecution for certain felonies, such as murder, kidnapping, and robbery; and inciting a riot at a federal prison.[35]

Congress was not yet done. Lawmakers soon passed and Roosevelt signed other legislation that gave the Division of Investigation more powers and tools. On June 6, 1934, Roosevelt signed an act that allowed federal authorities to offer awards of up to $25,000 to capture anyone accused of violating federal laws. On June 18, 1934, he signed an act that allowed supervisors and special agents in the Division of Investigation to carry firearms and make arrests. And on June 26, 1934, Roosevelt signed an act that allowed the federal government to tax the making and sale of machine guns and other firearms, and to regulate the interstate transfer of those weapons.[36]

Bank robbers had a new foe. A total of 391 gun-carrying special agents of the Division of Investigation, backed by 451 support staff members and an annual budget of $2,589,500, were ready to pursue the robbers, put out award money for their capture, and arrest the robbers anywhere, even if they did not cross state lines.[37] "It had become evident by the beginning of my Administration that the Federal legal and administrative machinery for the detection, prosecution and punishment of crime required complete overhauling,"[38] President Roosevelt said in signing the first six anticrime bills on May 18, 1934.

By the summer of 1934, that legislative overhaul was complete. Thousands of banks for decades had been members of the Federal Reserve; yet bank robbery during all those years had not been a federal crime, though embezzling from or otherwise defrauding a national bank always had been. Under the anticrime legislation, a bank's inclusion in the Federal Reserve did not make robbing it a federal crime; the commerce clause of the Constitution made that legal transformation. Roosevelt used the same New Deal activism to prompt a new perspective of the economy, and of bank robbery and other crimes. "The Congress," Roosevelt also said in signing the bills on May 18, 1934, "decided that it would have to take advantage of its constitutional power to enact crime legislation based on the interstate commerce clause, the tax clause and the implied right of the Federal Government to protect its various agencies and instrumentalities."[39]

The intersection of New Deal legislation and bank robbery became even more apparent on August 23, 1935. Congress passed a law that expanded the Federal Bank Robbery Act to include all banks insured by the new Federal Deposit Insurance Corporation, not just those in the Federal Reserve. "The Justice Department is expected to reach out soon to protect the small-town bank, long victimized by America's 5,000 known bank robbers," the Associated Press reported in advance of the passage of that legislation. "'Country bankers' have feared, since Federal agents were put on the job last year, that the bank robber, frightened away from 'big game,' would concentrate on small-town banks." The new law, the Associated Press said, affected another $18 billion in deposits and gave "'G man' protection" to 14,280 banks, national and state, with deposits now totaling $41 billion.[40]

J. Edgar Hoover relished the newly renamed FBI's role as protector of the nation's banks and their depositors. On November 18, 1935, like a field general detailing the results of a battle, Hoover reported that the bureau's special agents, since the passage of the Federal Bank Robbery Act in May 1934, had obtained convictions of eighty bank robbers, with three life sentences, and other sentences totaling 1,807 years. "When we started investigating national bank robberies there were fifteen or sixteen robberies a month," Hoover said. "This month there have been three. Bank officials tell me, too, that the dollar loss in the robberies has decreased 84 percent since we took over. That means the robbers are getting less loot in their raids."[41]

Hoover's G-men had slowed the enemies—the bank robbers—by the end of 1935. But the G-men had not eradicated them. No one would.

5

MARQUEE MAYHEM

John Dillinger, Bonnie and Clyde,
and the Glamorization of the Gangster

FBI agents gunned down John Dillinger in an alley shortly after he and two women left Chicago's newly air-conditioned Biograph Theater around a half past ten at night on July 22, 1934. The setting was appropriate. The thirty-one-year-old Dillinger, the nation's first-ever Public Enemy Number One, the man whose gang had robbed fifteen banks in fourteen months and made off with $300,000, had escaped the 101-degree heat for an hour and thirty-three minutes by going to see the newest hit movie, *Manhattan Melodrama*, about crime and its consequences. In the film, William Holden plays Jim Wade, an upright district attorney who prosecutes his childhood friend, Blackie Gallagher, a gangster played by Clark Gable; Blackie's girlfriend, Eleanor, is played by Myrna Loy. Gallagher gets the electric chair in the end.

John Dillinger, known as "Handsome Johnny," whose dimpled chin added to his movie-star good looks, died at the height of a cultural crescendo for criminals that originated in Hollywood, where the studios capitalized on the popularity of bank robbers and gangsters during the Great Depression. Dillinger and other bank robbers of this period—a period when bank robbery all but justified the FBI's existence—mirrored the image of the bank robber and gangster projected on the movie screen. These bank robbers—Dillinger; Machine Gun Kelly; Pretty Boy Floyd; Alvin "Creepy" Karpis, who operated with "Ma" Barker and her boys;

and Bonnie Parker and Clyde Barrow—were merciless, but, for much of the public, so were the banks they robbed.

Manhattan Melodrama was one of many films the movie studios produced in the early 1930s about gangsters who had fixed themselves to the public consciousness during Prohibition-era exploits of bootleggers and kingpins such as Al Capone. Gangster films had been around for years, but in the early 1930s, movies like *The Public Enemy* (1931), starring James Cagney; *Little Caesar* (1931), starring Edward G. Robinson; and *Scarface* (1932), starring Paul Muni, glamorized the underworld with violent scenes that predated the enforcement of the Motion Picture Production Code. Led by Will H. Hays, its first president, the nascent Motion Picture Producers and Distributors of America (MPPDA) drew up the code in 1930 but left it toothless until 1934. Starting in that year, public criticism about sex and violence in the movies led to an outright ban of films with content related to gangsters.[1]

Renewed enforcement of the Production Code, also known as the Hays Code, prompted the MPPDA's president himself to fulminate against the production of any movie about Dillinger. Hays expressed his displeasure in March 1934, after Paramount Studios announced it intended to make a film about the famous outlaw and fugitive who was then still very much alive and holding up banks; the movie would be called *A Man without a City*.[2] "No picture on the life or exploits of John Dillinger will be produced, distributed or exhibited by any member," Hays wrote. "This decision is based on the belief that the production, distribution or exhibition of such a picture could be detrimental to the best public interest. Advise all studio heads accordingly."[3]

Paramount never made the Dillinger film. Nonetheless, Handsome Johnny turned into a headliner, a sly villain who earned the condemnation of two of the country's most influential moralists: Will H. Hays and J. Edgar Hoover, who saw him as the public enemy of America's banks and minds. Dillinger was a prince of thieves in the middle of a dangerous decade that was thick with them. Many of the bank robbers who preceded and followed him gained similar notoriety for the same reasons Dillinger did. They were usually good, often ruthlessly so, at robbing banks. And some did have movies made about them.

In the 1920s and early 1930s, before John Dillinger's criminal career peaked for fourteen months in 1933–1934, John Harvey Bailey ruled as the preeminent bank robber in the United States. Bailey, who went by Harvey, by the end of his career had become known as the dean of American bank robbers, or the "king of the heist men."[4] By some accounts, he was behind the Kansas City Massacre, which triggered Homer Cummings to lobby Congress to pass the laws that gave the FBI the legal authority and the firepower to hunt down and kill Dillinger.[5]

Bailey was born on August 23, 1887, and was a product of the Midwest and, later, Oklahoma. He grew up on a farm in northcentral Missouri and worked as a fireman on the railroads before he was drafted into the army in World War I. He followed his army buddies to Chicago after the war, where he got caught up in bootlegging and was connected to the operations of Al Capone.[6] As Bailey said later, he soon "graduated to banks. There was more money in robbing banks. I robbed about two banks a year during the twelve years I was in that business."[7] Working alone and with gangs, such as the Holden-Keating Gang, and as far north as Minnesota and as far south as Texas, Bailey robbed as many as twenty banks between 1920 and 1932. He participated in some of the most stunning heists of the Jazz Age, making "his career of outlawry . . . the most spectacular the southwest has known since the days of Jesse James."[8]

Bailey's business attire and suave countenance on the job were reminiscent of George Leslie's coolness. Bailey was known for his impeccable English (largely devoid of slang), his calm demeanor, and manners "so gentlemanly he termed the female hostages he loaded into his getaway cars 'hostesses.'"[9] Bailey was known to carefully plan his robberies and getaway routes, and he discouraged gunfire. His first signature heist occurred on December 18, 1922, when he and four others held up a Federal Reserve Bank delivery truck outside the Denver Mint and made off with $200,000. No one was charged in the case, though police had enough evidence to show Bailey masterminded the scheme.[10]

The stolen money helped fund a law-abiding life for Bailey, for a time. He returned to Chicago with his wife and two children and operated a chain of service stations and car washes until "he lost almost everything in the 1929 stock market crash."[11] Around this time, Bailey teamed with Machine Gun Kelly and other bank robbers, such as Frank "Jelly" Nash and Alvin "Creepy" Karpis, Ma Barker, and her sons Freddie and Arthur "Dock" Barker, members of the Karpis-Barker Gang. Bailey long had been a friend to Pretty Boy Floyd, whom he considered an honorable thief. Bailey liked to tell a story of how, in 1924, he and Floyd broke into a grocery store in Sallisaw, Oklahoma, near where Floyd grew up. It was west of Fort Smith, Arkansas, in the Cookson Hills area of Oklahoma, a spot that served as yet another hideout for criminals in what had been the Indian Territory. Bailey said he and Floyd gave the stolen food to Cherokees, who were starving during a drought, and that their generosity saved the lives of the Native Americans. [12]

Bailey's largest heist was also the largest armed bank robbery on record at the time. It occurred on September 30, 1930, when Bailey and a group of others stole $2.5 million in cash and securities from the Lincoln National Bank and Trust, in Lincoln, Nebraska. The daylight holdup was bold: "gunmen looted the bank while a machine gunner stood guard on the corner." [13] Bailey was never arrested in the case, though he got caught in another heist. Agents with the FBI arrested him on July 7, 1932, while he was playing golf (and wearing knickers) on the Old Mission Golf Course, near Kansas City, Missouri. The federal agents were looking for Bailey's two golfing buddies (and fellow bank robbers), Francis "Jimmy" Keating and Tommy Holden, who were on the lam from the federal penitentiary at Leavenworth, Kansas. They had been there on twenty-five-year sentences for stealing $135,000 from a U.S. Postal Service truck after holding it up in suburban Chicago in 1926. And with the help of fellow inmate Machine Gun Kelly, they had escaped in 1930.

The federal agents returned Holden and Keating to Leavenworth, and quickly made a case against Bailey. They found in one of his pockets a $500 Liberty bond that had been stolen during a holdup of the Citizens National Bank in Fort Scott, Kansas, three weeks earlier. Bailey netted $4,000 from the total take of $47,000 in that heist, whose crew was made up of some of Bailey's closest confederates: Holden, Keating, Freddie Barker, Alvin Karpis, and another robber, Verne Miller. That raid had been spectacular. The robbers kidnapped three women from the bank and placed two of them on the running boards of their getaway car, a new seven-passenger Hupmobile sedan. [14] Bailey, using a method common among his gangland cronies in Chicago, correctly figured the police would not fire at the car with the female hostages standing on the running boards. Bystanders were said to have let the getaway car go by because they mistook the women and the men inside and outside the Hupmobile as "silly young lovers." [15]

Bailey soon settled in Kansas City, only to be caught on the golf course. He was convicted in the bank robbery in Fort Scott and sentenced to ten to fifty years at the state prison in Lansing, Kansas, which he entered in August 1932. The imprisonment marked the first time Bailey had been nabbed during his criminal career. He wanted out. His escape would start the chain of events that would result in the Kansas City Massacre.

Bailey broke out of the prison with eleven other inmates on Memorial Day 1933. Frank Nash was not one of them, but he played a key role. He was on the lam from Leavenworth, where he had been serving a sentence for train robbery, and helped smuggle into the state prison at Lansing guns that Bailey and the others used to escape. Bailey and his crew fled to their version of the Hole-in-the-Wall, in Cookson Hills, Oklahoma.

The Kansas City Massacre occurred the morning of June 17, 1933. Many historians contend that Bailey had no part in it, while others—most significantly, L. R. Kirchner, who has thoroughly studied and written about the event—put Bailey in the middle of the firefight. Whatever the level of his direct involvement, Bailey knew all the criminals connected to the shooting. The episode revolved around the fugitive Nash. The day before the massacre, federal agents had found him in Hot Springs, Arkansas, where he had been on vacation. The agents drove Nash to Little Rock, Arkansas, and got on a train with him headed to Kansas City, Missouri. Once the train entered the station at a quarter after seven in the morning on June 17, the agents planned to drive Nash thirty miles to Leavenworth.

The drive never happened. A bloodbath derailed it.

The train arrived on schedule, and Nash got off, but then he never got as far as the front passenger seat of the armor-plated car to be driven by FBI Special Agent Raymond Caffrey, who was escorting Nash with a contingent of six other lawmen. Machine-gun fire erupted just before Caffrey could get in. The spray of bullets killed him, as well as Nash; two Kansas City police officers, Frank Hermanson and Bill Grooms; and Otto Reed, the police chief in McAlester, Oklahoma. Reed had assisted in the search for Nash in Arkansas because he was an expert on Nash and could identify him.[16] Caffrey was the third FBI agent to be killed in the line of duty, out of a total of thirty-six slain through 2014.

If the gunmen's intent was to free Nash, they failed. They murdered him and ignited the national furor that enraged President Roosevelt, Cummings, and J. Edgar Hoover. Whoever was responsible for the Kansas City Massacre, Hoover thundered, "must be exterminated, and they must be exterminated by us."[17] As the Roosevelt administration launched its war on crime, investigators were left to unravel who had carried out the Kansas City Massacre. The prime suspect was Bailey's buddy Verne Miller, but agents also considered Pretty Boy Floyd, Bonnie Parker and Clyde Barrow, and Bailey, though Bailey wrote to the investigators to say he was innocent because he had robbed a bank in Arkansas the same day of the Kansas City Massacre.[18]

Hoover believed the killers to be Miller, Floyd, and Floyd's partner, Adam Richetti, another bank robber. Richetti was the only one of the three to be convicted and executed for the Kansas City Massacre. Miller would be found dead in a drainage ditch in Detroit more than a year later, in November 1934, and Floyd would die in a shootout with federal agents, in East Liverpool, in northeastern Ohio, in October 1934. The authorities never charged Bailey in Nash's death.

Bailey was convicted, wrongly, in another crime that added to Hoover's furor over the crime wave of the 1930s. Machine Gun Kelly and his wife, Kathryn, kidnapped a millionaire oilman from Oklahoma City, Charles Urschel, on July 23, 1933, and demanded a ransom of $200,000. The FBI took over the case because the Lindbergh Law had expanded its jurisdiction. The kidnappers got their ransom on July 31, and the agents interviewed the newly released Urschel. When he was held captive, he had so closely listened to the planes overhead that the agents were able to establish the planes' flight patterns. That and other information led the agents to pinpoint that Urschel's kidnappers had been on a farm in Paradise, Texas. Machine Gun Kelly's father-in-law, Robert Shannon, owned the place.

Agents raided the farm on August 12, 1933. Kelly and his wife were not there, but Bailey was, asleep. He had robbed a bank in Kingfisher, Oklahoma (the erstwhile home of the Daltons), on August 11, and then found refuge at the Shannon farm. During the bank robbery, Bailey had borrowed Kelly's signature weapon, his submachine gun, which he returned to Shannon at the farm. Waiting for Bailey at the farm was cash Kelly had left him to pay off a debt. The cash was from the $200,000 ransom, whose notes the federal agents had cataloged by serial number. The investigators found $640 of the cash on Bailey, and he was finished, though he had no part in the kidnapping. The main culprit, Kelly, was done as well. Agents and local police tracked him to a farm near Memphis, Tennessee, on September 26, 1933. Surrounded, Kelly supposedly pleaded with the agents and the police by shouting, "Don't shoot, G-men, don't shoot," thus coining the G-man moniker that Hoover proudly used to describe his newly empowered agents.

Whether Kelly said those words remains in dispute—press accounts of his capture had him saying only "Okay, boys, I've been waiting for you all night"[19]—but the results of the Urschel case were undeniable. Hoover's men had solved it, even if the agents wrongly charged Bailey. While awaiting trial, he escaped from an "escape-proof" prison in Dallas, but the escape was only for a day, and Bailey was convicted of kidnapping and sentenced to life in prison in October 1933. The pursuit of Bailey had been a national priority. "Right or wrong, we have orders to put you away," Hoover's first assistant, Harold "Pop" Nathan, told Bailey in the Urschel case.[20]

Bailey served part of his sentence at the federal prison at Alcatraz, in San Francisco Bay, where, he said, he protected fellow inmate Al Capone from those who wanted to stab him.[21] Bailey was paroled in the mid-1960s and went on to live in Joplin, in the southwestern corner of Missouri, where he married and retired as a cabinetmaker. He must have felt at home in Joplin, which was fifty miles northwest of Cookson Hills, and long had been a gathering spot for criminals, with Hot Springs, Arkansas, and St. Paul, Minnesota. "Liquor flowed freely in this bootlegging headquarters," according to one writer's account of Joplin, "and customers from the traditionally dry states of Oklahoma, Arkansas and Kansas flocked to the gaudy little metropolis."[22] For a time, Joplin was also home to Bonnie and Clyde.

Bailey cooperated with a 1973 biography, *Robbing Banks Was My Business . . . The Story of J. Harvey Bailey*, and remained a minor celebrity until his death, at age ninety-one, in 1979. In some of his many interviews with newspaper reporters, the retired dean of American bank robbers regretted his past at the same time he reveled in it. "Crime does not pay. You do! I did!" he said in one account.[23] He spoke in 1973 about how a bank robbery then would be far different from a holdup in his heyday, in the 1920s and 1930s. "It can't be done today in towns of 65 or 75 thousand people when we robbed them," Bailey said in his dotage. "Today there's helicopters, airplanes, and two-way radios. You just can't do it without getting caught."[24]

Harvey Bailey offered an example of how to make a living as a bank robber in the Jazz Age. John Dillinger showed how robbing banks during the Great Depression could be just as profitable. If Dillinger adopted his style of living from the likes of Bailey and his cronies, he learned the mechanics of how to rob a bank from the disciples of an equally impressive criminal, Herman K. Lamm, a former Prussian military officer. Lamm left the German army before World War I—he was caught cheating at cards, according to some accounts—and immigrated to Utah, the land of Butch Cassidy.[25] Lamm turned to bank robbery in his adopted country, was caught, and served time in 1917 in the Utah State Prison, where he came up with a near foolproof system for holdups.

The workings of "The Baron," as he was known, recalled the exploits of Jesse James in how Lamm applied military precision to bank robberies. His most notable tool was a stopwatch, which he used to time heists to make sure his confederates got in and out of banks before the police arrived. Lamm's methods also recalled the thoroughness of George Leslie. Lamm cased his targets and relied on the floor plans of the real banks to rehearse heists in vacant warehouses. Unlike Leslie, who traveled by foot or by horse, Lamm built his meticulous getaways around the automobile and a full understanding of an area's back roads, or "cat roads." He called his getaway maps "gits,"[26] and he made sure that he had enough fuel to outrun the police. Lamm liked to keep a gas can in the back of the getaway car.[27]

Lamm's gang perfected his methods in the 1920s, when the men robbed banks throughout the West. One of Lamm's influences was Butch Cassidy, though he was most likely never a member of the Hole-in-the-Wall Gang, despite speculation otherwise.[28] Lamm and his crew developed a reputation as the most efficient bank robbers of their time. His end came on December 16, 1930, when the forty-year-old was killed after police and more than two hundred area residents caught up with him and his gang following the robbery of $15,567 from the Citizens State Bank in the westcentral Indiana town of Clinton. Lamm's makeshift getaway car stalled near a field in Sidell, Illinois, across the Indiana line, and he was surrounded. Two of his gang members, Walter Dietrich and James "Oklahoma Jack" Clark, survived and were convicted and sentenced to life at the Indiana State Penitentiary at Michigan City, on Lake Erie.

Dietrich taught Lamm's techniques to another inmate, John Dillinger. In return, Dillinger let Dietrich join his gang, which had been plotting bank robberies from behind bars.[29]

You immediately knew if John Dillinger had robbed your bank, even if you were unable to see his unforgettable face. Handsome Johnny was also known as "Jackrabbit." He routinely vaulted the counters—some as high as seven feet—of the banks he and his gang hit. The display of athleticism was the flourish for Dillinger, whose heists followed the precise planning he had learned indirectly from the Baron. Get familiar with the inside of the bank, go back and rob the bank, get out of the bank as fast as you can, and make sure you have enough fuel to drive a long distance: Those were the four basic steps John Dillinger applied, with vaulting the counter thrown in as a bonus.

Dillinger's professionalism and his dramatic flair made him both successful and popularly appealing, and so did his understanding of the zeitgeist. The public, he and his fellow gang members knew, would never see them as evil as long as they victimized the banks, which had left so many people with so little during the Great Depression. Said "Handsome Harry" Pierpont, one of Dillinger's closest confidantes, after his (Pierpont's) arrest, "My conscience doesn't hurt me. I stole from the bankers. They stole from the people. All we did was help raise the insurance rates."[30] This thinking, which in some respects persists to this day (because banks are federally insured, no one really loses any money in a bank robbery, or so the rationalization goes), fails to take into account the terror, injuries, and death the tellers, bank managers, and customers can suffer during bank robberies. Dillinger was careful to craft his crimes as those against an institution or the ineffective government rather than against the fellow citizen struggling to survive. He portrayed himself as a champion of the little guy and the nemesis of society's behemoths.

Dillinger knew the little guy. He grew up as one. John Herbert Dillinger was born on June 22, 1903, in the Oak Hill neighborhood of Indianapolis, where his father, John Wilson Dillinger, a former farmhand, ran a small grocery store next to their house. The younger Dillinger's mother, Mollie, died of a stroke when he was three years old, creating a lasting emptiness from which her lawbreaking son, despite his hard and sardonic persona, could never recover. "I only wish I had a mother to worry over me, but she died when I was three," Dillinger once said. "I guess this is why I was such a bad boy. No mother to look after me."[31]

Dillinger worked at his father's grocery store and showed a keen mechanical aptitude while in school, but he also got into mischief.[32] In 1920, perhaps concerned about his son's future, his father moved the family to Mooresville, a Quaker farming community of 1,800 people northwest of Indianapolis. It was the hometown of the senior Dillinger's second wife, with whom the son did not get along. Dillinger dropped out of high school in Mooresville, worked hard and well at a machine shop, played baseball, and bought and fixed a motorcycle and cars, but he remained troubled. His relationship with his father, never good, was now strained, partly due to the younger Dillinger's inveterate womanizing and failed attempt to marry his stepcousin.

John Dillinger, twenty years old, grew embittered with his family and the norms of society, and he drew closer to a life of crime. Around this time Jesse James intrigued Dillinger and his closest friend, Delbert Hobson. "Excessive in everything, Dillinger began to read volume after volume of Wild West stories," wrote John Toland in his 1963 biography, *The Dillinger Days*. "His favorite hero was Jesse James and he would bore Hobson with involved accounts of the famous gunman's Robin Hood qualities; he seemed obsessed not only by Jesse's courage and daring but also by his kindness to women and children."[33] Writing forty-one years later, another biographer, Dary Matera, concluded of Dillinger,

> Quick to realize that he was a cowboy about as much as he was a farmer, John Jr. took the James persona and melded it with the city gangster he saw portrayed during the popular Saturday matinees he caught at the Idle Time theater. Soon, he was wearing his hat tilted to the side, and walked with a mobster swagger. Friends noticed that he began to talk tough and take on the air of a hoodlum.[34]

At first, Dillinger was a small-time crook. In July 1923, armed with a pistol, he stole a car from the parking lot of his family's church in Mooresville and drove to Indianapolis, by some accounts to go on a date with a girlfriend who was pregnant with his child.[35] Two police officers stopped Dillinger—he said his given name was "Charley"—but he got away, even as the officers fired at him as he fled. The next morning Dillinger further escaped by enlisting in the navy. He got through basic training but went AWOL for a day in October 1923, while his battleship, the *Utah*, was docked in Boston. Dillinger eventually deserted the navy and returned to Mooresville and, still only twenty years old, married his sixteen-year-old neighbor. He worked as an upholsterer, played shortstop on a semiprofessional baseball team, and fell under the influence of one of the umpires in the league, Ed Singleton, ten years older than Dillinger and a heavy drinker and ex-convict.

Ed Singleton was John Dillinger's Mike Cassidy. The crime that Singleton and Dillinger committed ruined any respect Dillinger had for justice and set him in the direction of being a bank robber. Singleton and Dillinger robbed a Mooresville grocer, B. F. Morgan, the night of September 6, 1924, as Morgan was walking down a street, carrying the day's receipts. Dillinger had a revolver, which went off when Morgan grabbed it. No one was injured, and Dillinger and Singleton were quickly arrested. Dillinger confessed to the county prosecutor under the assurance that he would get a light sentence—an assurance that he believed to be so credible that he saw no reason to hire a lawyer to represent him for his guilty plea and sentence. The more experienced Singleton hired a lawyer, was convicted at trial, and got a sentence of two to fourteen years at the Indiana State Reformatory at Pendleton. Dillinger got ten to twenty years. He was furious. If Singleton got a lighter sentence than he did, Dillinger had said before Dillinger's trial, "I'll be the meanest bastard you ever saw when I get out."[36]

Dillinger, even more miserable because he suffered from gonorrhea, started his sentence at Pendleton, which was more of a reform school than a prison, a place designed for juveniles rather than hard-core inmates. Dillinger tried to escape and constantly misbehaved. His wife divorced him in April 1929, which further added to his antisocial behavior. Dillinger came up for parole in July 1929, was denied, and—at his request—was sent to the home of many of Indiana's most dangerous inmates, the Indiana State Penitentiary at Michigan City. While there, Dillinger fell into a group that included a fellow twenty-six-year-old, Harry Pierpont, the head of a gang that had held up banks throughout Indiana. Three years later, Walter Dietrich, the acolyte of Baron Lamm, joined the gang of prisoners. They made a list of banks to rob once Dillinger got out. If Dillinger had asked to go to Michigan City with the intention of learning to how to be a professional criminal, as some have suggested, he got the education of a lifetime behind bars.[37]

After nine years in prison, Dillinger, then thirty years old, got out on parole on May 22, 1933. He had promised Pierpont and his other buddies that he would not forget them. A month later, a rash of holdups occurred in Indiana, Ohio, and Kentucky, but the first heist indisputably connected to Dillinger happened on July 17, 1933—a month after the Kansas City Massacre. Dillinger and an accomplice robbed the Commercial Bank in Daleville, Indiana, near Muncie, northeast of Indianapolis. They got away with $3,500 and four diamond rings, which one of the robbers—presumed to be Dillinger—helped collect after he jumped the counter when the twenty-two-year-old teller, Margaret Good, refused his command, delivered while pointing a gun at her: "This is a stick-up, get me the money, honey."[38] The men, who locked the bank employees and customers in the vault and escaped in a Chevrolet coupe, knew where they were going, as they had made themselves familiar with the layout of Daleville.[39] Dillinger had struck, and struck well, using the Baron's step-by-step techniques.

Handsome Johnny was on his way, as economic and societal chaos roiled the nation. The list of target banks he had received from his fellow inmates gave him a head start, as did the links those same inmates had with the criminal underworld in Indiana and elsewhere. Dillinger's ability to escape from the law repeatedly was grounded in his personal magnetism, which allowed him to introduce himself to his new underworld contacts and then quickly earn their trust and admiration.

No one could question Dillinger's commitment to keeping his word after what happened at the Indiana State Penitentiary at Michigan City on September 26, 1933. Three weeks earlier, on September 6, Dillinger had recorded his biggest haul to date: nearly $25,000 stolen in a holdup of the Massachusetts Avenue State Bank in Indianapolis. The police caught up with him later, in Dayton, Ohio, on September 22, where he had been visiting a girlfriend, twenty-three-year-old Mary Longnaker. Several days before his arrest, however, he had managed to get revolvers smuggled into the state prison at Michigan City, by having a middleman place them in a crate full of thread. On September 26, Dillinger's friends—ten in all, including Harry Pierpont and Walter Dietrich—got the guns, overwhelmed the guards, kidnapped a sheriff who was visiting the prison, and escaped.

Dillinger by then had been transferred to a prison in Lima, Ohio. He wasn't there long. Five of the Michigan City escapees showed up at the Allen County Jail the night of October 12, 1933, and asked to speak to Sheriff Jess Sarber's most famous inmate. Sarber requested their credentials; Pierpont fatally shot Sarber. The gang got the keys to the cells, let out Dillinger, and locked up Sarber's wife and a deputy sheriff. Dillinger finally had a bank-robbing gang, which included Pierpont, Homer Van Meter, Charles Makley, Russell Clark, John "Red" Hamilton, and Edward Shouse. For the most part, it was made up of the gang he had helped form in prison, and whose members he had helped break out. Later in October 1933, Dillinger and some accomplices raided police stations in Auburn and Peru, Indiana, and on October 23, 1933, Dillinger, Pierpont, Makley, Clark, Hamilton, and another accomplice pulled off Dillinger's biggest heist—the robbery of $75,000 from the Central National Bank in Greencastle, Indiana. The newspapers by now were referring to the escapees as the Dillinger Gang.[40]

The most famous photograph of John Dillinger, the photo that captures the hold he had on the United States, was snapped January 30, 1934. It was taken at the Crown Point Jail, in northwestern Indiana. The authorities had flown Dillinger to Crown Point from Tucson, Arizona, where he and his gang had sought to disappear after the January 15 bank robbery of the First National Bank of East Chicago, Indiana, north of Crown Point. Dillinger, the populist thief, was said to have told a patron in the bank, "We don't want your money. We just want the bank's."[41] Dillinger and John Hamilton got away with $20,000, but not easily. Outside the bank, Dillinger got into a firefight with a local police officer, William O'Malley. He shot Dillinger four times in the chest, to no avail: Dillinger was wearing a bulletproof vest. Dillinger shot O'Malley eight times and killed him—"the first and only killing ever laid at his feet."[42] Dillinger was no longer solely a bank robber. He was also a murderer of a police officer.

The Tucson police caught Dillinger and his twenty-six-year-old girlfriend, Mary Evelyn "Billie" Frechette, without firing a bullet on January 25. The investigators found the pair after heading to a house where two of Dillinger's gang members, Makley and Clark, had been staying after a fire had broken out in their hotel room. To the surprise of the firefighters, who tipped off police, Makley and Clark had been storing "trunks filled with guns and money and bulletproof vests."[43]

Dillinger was a star when he was flown from Tucson to Chicago and then driven to Crown Point. Air travel was a rarity, reserved for the wealthy and important and, in Dillinger's case, the notorious. While awaiting extradition to Indiana, Dillinger bantered with reporters and guests in the jail for Pima County, Arizona. "I guess my only bad habit is robbing banks," was one of his remarks. "I smoke very little and I don't drink much."[44] The quip encapsulated Dillinger's bravado, his dark sense of humor, and his winking acknowledgment that, though a bank robber and an accused murderer, his personality could blunt his misdeeds.

The famous photograph displayed Dillinger's magnetism in a way that produced grudging respect for him and anger at his captors. Goaded by photographers, the two officials responsible for making sure Dillinger would be brought to justice in Indiana posed alongside him at the Crown Point Jail. To his far right is the sheriff of Lake County, Indiana, Lillian Holley. Standing next to her, and immediately to the right of Dillinger, is the prosecutor, Robert G. Estill. Dillinger is grinning at the camera, and Estill and Holley are looking at one another. Estill is smiling and has his left arm around Dillinger's shoulder, as if embracing an old friend, and Dillinger is smiling and leaning on Estill's shoulder. The photo eventually ended the political careers of Estill, who was voted out of office, and Holley, who resigned. The photo enraged Homer Cummings, who said he would have removed Estill and Holley from office immediately if he could. "Such disgraceful conduct, such negligence, violated all canons of common sense and made law enforcement doubly hard," the U.S. attorney general said.[45] Dillinger's charisma, on full display in the photo, was another of his weapons.

So were his wits. Dillinger, in his boldest escape, broke out of the Crown Point Jail on March 3, 1934. He used a fake gun that he had carved from a piece of wood and dyed with black shoe polish. He and another inmate, Herbert Youngblood, in on murder charge, held up the prison staff, including the warden, and headed to Chicago. They drove

Sheriff Holley's car, which they had stolen from the prison. A United Press story soon referred to Dillinger as "Houdini of the outlaws."[46]

Dillinger kept disappearing, at least from the police. He got to work with a new gang, made up of some of his old crew, as well as the twenty-four-year-old Baby Face Nelson, an up-and-coming gangster who joined Dillinger on March 4, 1934, in St. Paul, Minnesota, a city known for its blatant harboring of criminals. Two days later, the gang robbed $46,000 from the Security National Bank, in Sioux Falls, South Dakota. FBI agents, still without expanded police powers, were able to issue a warrant for Dillinger's arrest under the Dyer Act, because he had driven a stolen car across state lines. A week later, the gang got into a shootout while stealing $52,000 from the First National Bank in the northcentral Iowa town of Mason City, with the Minnesota line to the north and the Wisconsin line to the northeast. The gang, who had cased the bank, estimated it held nearly $250,000 in cash. This was to have been the heist of Dillinger's lifetime, based on what he told one of his gang members, Jim Jenkins. With his share of the loot, or about $40,000, Dillinger "would at last be able to do what he and Jenkins had spent so many hours talking about in prison: escape to Mexico or South America to 'live like a king.'"[47] Or, perhaps, like Butch Cassidy.

Instead, the robbery left Dillinger with far less than what he had hoped for, as well as a bullet wound to the shoulder. The shootout showed that not everyone bowed to Dillinger and his gang, even when they were toting machine guns. A bank guard, Tom Walters, fired tear gas at the robbers, which sent them scrambling. Nelson fired away with his machine gun. Police and a crowd of townspeople, many of them armed, surrounded the bank building. From his third-floor office, an elderly judge, John C. Shipley, fired at Dillinger and hit him in the shoulder. Dillinger and his crew fled in a waiting Buick and, using the trick that Harvey Bailey had found so effective, took women from the bank as hostages and forced them to ride on the car's running boards and fenders. A family driving by thought the overcrowded Buick was part of a wedding celebration until the family's car got closer and was hit by bullets.[48] Nelson shot at anything that moved. Dillinger, Nelson, and the rest of the gang finally drove back to St. Paul, where Dillinger got care for his shoulder and plotted where to hide next. He would not go to South America, but to northern Wisconsin and the lodge at Little Bohemia.

John Dillinger and his gang's escape from Little Bohemia, as well as Baby Face Nelson's killing of Special Agent W. Carter Baum during the failed raid on the Sunday night of April, 23, 1934, ranked among the biggest blunders in J. Edgar Hoover's career. He nearly lost his job over it, and the fiasco threatened the jobs of many others in the FBI, particularly one of Hoover's most trusted special agents, Melvin Purvis, who was in charge of the bureau's Chicago office. Following the Kansas City Massacre, Hoover had installed Purvis as the head of a special squad dedicated to catching the bank robbers and gangsters terrorizing the Midwest. The prize was Dillinger, whom the FBI code-named JODIL.

Purvis believed Dillinger was all but finished when he got a tip that Dillinger and his gang were hiding near Mercer, Wisconsin, in the lodge at Little Bohemia, which had been attracting criminals since Prohibition, when it was a playground for bootleggers. [49] An underworld contact had suggested Dillinger go there. [50] Hoover was so sure of an imminent arrest that he notified reporters to get ready to report it. They were all at Little Bohemia, the latest incarnation of Dillinger's gang: Dillinger; Nelson and his wife; Homer Van Meter; Tommy Carroll; and John "Red" Hamilton. Purvis and his agents were there as well. They had flown into Rhinelander, Wisconsin, driven to Little Bohemia, and surrounded the lodge.

Then a dog barked.

Purvis mistakenly thought the noise had alerted the bank robbers, so his agents started firing when three men stepped out of the lodge and into a car. One was killed, and two were injured—and none was Dillinger or his gang members. The victims were workers who had stopped by Little Bohemia for a drink. The gunfire alerted Dillinger and the others, and they rushed out the lodge's back windows and escaped. The trigger-happy Nelson, twenty-five years old, killed Baum in a shootout on a back road leading away from Little Bohemia.

Dillinger's getaway, while tragic, had the makings of a farce. A photo in the *New York Times* on April 25, 1934, showed a group of townspeople pointing to the window from which Dillinger's gang had jumped. An embarrassed Hoover and an alarmed press portrayed Dillinger as a wild-eyed bogeyman who threatened the safety of every man, woman, and child in the middle of the United States. The *New York Times* reported, also on April 25, that five thousand men were hunting Dillinger, and that "in the thirty-six hours since Dillinger and his crew shot it out with pursuers at Mercer, Wis., on Sunday night, fear of his depredations has spread through the Middle West until tonight in a score of towns extraordinary precautions were taken against his coming." So far, the *New York Times* also reported, the federal government had failed in its "efforts to make Dillinger eat his words, that there was no jail in the country strong enough to hold him."[51]

Baby Face Nelson only added to the ferocity of Dillinger's gang. He had not been friends with Dillinger before the two started collaborating after that meeting in St. Paul on March 5, 1934, two days after Dillinger escaped from the Crown Point Jail. Nelson, needing more men to help him rob banks, had agreed to aid Dillinger after he broke out of prison. Nelson already had picked a number of banks to rob once Dillinger was free, including the institutions they eventually hit in Sioux Falls, South Dakota, and Mason City, Iowa. Helping to broker the deal between the Nelson and Dillinger gangs was Alvin Karpis, head of his own bank-robbing crew and a friend of Harvey Bailey's. Nelson would have liked Bailey as a partner, but by then Bailey was in prison. John Dillinger would have to do.[52]

The interplay between bank robbers and gangsters was another hallmark of the great crime wave during the Great Depression. While organized crime and syndicates existed, individual gangs were more likely to join forces sporadically in de facto confederations. And though many of the gangs and bank robbers knew one another, such as Floyd and Bailey, "they were actually loosely assembled bands, raiding parties that occasionally shared personnel. To give one example . . . Baby Face Nelson worked at different times with the Barkers, Pretty Boy Floyd, and John Dillinger."[53] Nelson, armed with a submachine gun, proved an adept but volatile and unpredictable bank robber who killed three federal agents during his career, a brutal record that remains unbroken.

Nelson, whose given name was Lester Joseph Gillis, was five feet, four inches tall, and his oversize ego matched his penchant for reckless violence. Born to Belgian immigrants in Chicago on December 6, 1908, he grew up in a law-abiding family, but turned to bank robbery and other crimes to support his own wife and two children during the Great Depression. Nelson had been an auto mechanic before then, and he liked to steal cars as much as he enjoyed working on them. He fell into regular criminal activity in 1928, when he started working at a gas station notorious as a gathering place for hoodlums. Nelson and his friends at the station organized into a gang of petty thieves, with Nelson advancing to house burglaries, bank robberies, and other bolder crimes to make more money. He most likely got his nickname on October 6, 1930, when he mugged Mary Walker Thompson, the wife of Chicago Mayor William "Big Bill" Thompson—an armed holdup that illustrated the tight hold that thieves and organized crime had on the city where Al Capone had once reigned. Nelson stole a diamond ring, a diamond bracelet, and a brooch, all valued at $18,000, from Mary Thompson, who described the assailant in a newspaper account. "He had a baby face," she said. [54]

Nelson went on to rob taverns, and was convicted and sentenced to two terms of a year to life. He went on the lam in February 1932, however, when he held up a cab that was supposed to drive him to prison. Nelson fled to San Francisco and then Reno, Nevada, where he met fellow bank robber Alvin Karpis in late 1932. Karpis, perhaps wary of Nelson's temper and liberal use of a submachine gun, passed on bringing Nelson into his bank-robbing gang. But Karpis made the introductions that created enough familiarity between the Dillinger and Nelson gangs that they eventually agreed to join forces.

Karpis, in this instance and many others, was a broker for criminal activity during the Great Depression. He was born Albin Francis Karpowicz to Lithuanian immigrants in Montreal, on August 10, 1907, and eventually moved to Kansas, where petty crimes landed him in the state penitentiary at Lansing. There, Karpis met Fred Barker, one of the four Barker brothers, from a poor farming a family originally rooted in southwestern Missouri, in an area not far from Joplin. The clan was headed by the boys' overprotective mother, Arizona Donnie Barker, known as Kate "Ma" Barker.

Karpis, whose cold demeanor earned him the nickname "Creepy," was considered the brains of the Karpis-Barker Gang. Ma Barker spent most of her time defending her sons and Karpis, whom she considered one of her own, to police and parole agents, and was not known to be a criminal genius. "The old woman couldn't plan breakfast," Harvey Bailey once said of Ma Barker, whom J. Edgar Hoover would make out to be a queen of the underworld. [55] Ma Barker nonetheless embraced her role as a criminal matriarch whose boys turned out to be not unlike those other outlaw brothers from Missouri—the Jameses, the Youngers, and the Daltons. One of Ma Barker's childhood heroes was said to have been Jesse James, who was assassinated when she was ten years old but whom she had once seen in Carthage, Missouri. As head of the Barker clan, she was like Zerelda James.

After her son Herman was accused of stealing a car in Joplin, in 1915, Ma Barker moved her brood to Tulsa, where they continued to cause problems. After Freddie Barker and Karpis left prison in Kansas, they reunited in Tulsa and took up burglary. They fled from the police to the southcentral Missouri town of Thayer, on the Arkansas border, where they lived with Ma Barker. Karpis and Freddie Barker fled again in December 1931, after Karpis fatally shot a sheriff, C. R. Kelly, as he was investigating the pair for a store robbery in West Plains, Missouri, near Thayer. Ma Barker decided that she and the boys should head to St. Paul, where they would fall in with other criminals and get started on a career of bank robberies and kidnappings—the only way Karpis believed he could make a living.

In St. Paul, Freddie Barker and Karpis frequented the Green Lantern tavern, the unofficial headquarters for big-time criminals in the Midwest. They met Harvey Bailey there, as well as Tommy Holden and Francis Keating, and Frank Nash and Machine Gun Kelly, then known as George Barnes. With inspiration and support from these and other hoodlums, the Karpis-Barker Gang was on its way, another group of desperadoes who would thrive along with John Dillinger, who was still Public Enemy Number One. But following his death, the designation would fall to these other bank robbers, in order: Pretty Boy Floyd, Baby Face Nelson, and Alvin Karpis.

The second-most dangerous man on the federal government's list was nicknamed Pretty Boy because of his tailored suits and other sharp clothes and pomaded hair. Hoover classified him as a public enemy because of his supposed role in the Kansas City Massacre. But among his fellow Oklahomans, particularly those who knew him from his days growing up near Sallisaw, Charles Arthur Floyd was known as "Choc" or "Charley," a friend to many and a hero to even more. Of all the formidable bank robbers of the Great Depression, Floyd, while violent, stands out as a thief with one of the largest Robin Hood personas, whether deserved or not. His funeral attracted twenty to forty thousand people, "more than 10 times the population of Sallisaw in the 1930s."[56]

Like Baby Face Nelson, Floyd was not physically imposing: He was five feet, eight inches tall, with a stocky build, slicked-back hair, and a full face. He knew how to dress well and wield a gun, and he knew how to rob a bank, but his strongest attribute was his public support, despite his violent ways.

Floyd was born in Georgia on February 3, 1904, and soon moved with his family to the Cookson Hills area of the Oklahoma Territory, where they had relatives. Charley Floyd came from a solid family, grounded in the Baptist faith, and as a young man he tried to make a living harvesting wheat in Kansas. As the economy in Kansas and Oklahoma fell apart, largely due to a collapse in the market for oil, gas, and other natural resources—a collapse the Dust Bowl later exacerbated—Floyd found robbing banks a better way to get money. One of his major influences, in terms of how to carry out a heist (during the day, quickly, with a ready getaway plan), was Jesse James.[57] He also considered Emmett Dalton something of a role model. Charley Floyd was not much of a reader, but his relatives said he enjoyed *When the Daltons Rode*, Emmett Dalton's biography of his days as a bank robber.[58]

Like Baby Face Nelson, Pretty Boy Floyd despised his nickname, which, like Nelson, he got from a woman. She is said to have bestowed it upon him at a card game in Kansas City, in late 1929, when he was twenty-four years old. Floyd was well dressed and well coiffed, as usual. "Hello, pretty boy," said the woman, a twenty-year-old by the name of Beulah Baird. "Where did you come from?"[59] The newspapers soon picked up the name as they reported on Floyd's robberies in the same frenzied tones reserved for the likes of Dillinger. Floyd, like James and Dillinger, worked hard to perpetuate an image of the bank robber as a man of the people. No matter what Floyd was called, he did not want to be known as a criminal. He tried hardest to shape his image in early 1932, when the governor of Oklahoma, William "Alfalfa Bill" Murray, announced a $1,000 reward for his capture.[60] Floyd requested that the governor withdraw the reward, and wrote him in a letter, "I have robbed no one but the monied men."[61]

Floyd forfeited any reprieve from the governor on April 8, 1932, when he fatally shot Erv A. Kelley, a former sheriff connected to the State Crime Bureau in Oklahoma. Kelley's job was to catch Floyd, and he and a posse had staked out Floyd's hideout in Bixby, near Tulsa, when the firefight broke out shortly before two thirty in the morning. The murder fueled the police's desire to nab Floyd, but it did little to dull the popular admiration for him, particularly in the Cookson Hills. When Floyd arrived in Sallisaw on November 2, 1932, to rob a bank, cheers greeted him and his submachine gun. Banks in eastern Oklahoma had become so unpopular that even regular citizens had been robbing them; Floyd, the professional, was treated like royalty. "Give 'em hell," a farmer shouted as Floyd prepared to rob the bank of $2,530.[62]

By late 1932, Floyd had joined bank robber Adam Richetti, though Floyd soon seemed to tire of life as a thief. He yearned to retire to a life of baking pies, "his favorite way to relax."[63] Floyd instead headed to Missouri, where he and Richetti soon would be linked to the Kansas City Massacre.

Bonnie Parker and Clyde Barrow operated well outside the orbit of Pretty Boy Floyd, Baby Face Nelson, and John Dillinger and his associates, which was how Dillinger liked the situation. He considered the murderous couple from Texas to be sloppy punks as they shot up the lower Midwest and Southwest in 1933 and 1934. "They're giving bank robbery a bad name," Dillinger is reported to have said.[64] Bonnie and Clyde held up gas stations and grocery stores but did not rob many banks. When they did, the banks were in small towns and Bonnie and Clyde's take was often small: a few hundred dollars here, a thousand dollars there—nothing like the five- or even six-figure hauls of a Dillinger or a Bailey, or a Nelson or a Floyd.

Their violence further set Bonnie and Clyde apart from the bank robber in the mold of Dillinger and his ilk, though Barrow appears to have seen Dillinger as a criminal template, at one time mimicking his tailored clothing and polite diction.[65] Certainly Dillinger and the others were killers, and Nelson was prone to spray a bank with his submachine gun whenever he could. But these killings, though inexcusable, typically came in the course of a bank robbery. For Bonnie and Clyde and their ring of thieves, called the Barrow Gang, murder was a way of life and even the aim of life. This was particularly true for Clyde, who is believed to have committed most, if not all, of the killings attributed to the gang: at least thirteen slayings across Missouri, Arkansas, Oklahoma, and Texas, with seven lawmen among the dead.[66] Bonnie and Clyde were sociopaths who happened to rob banks. Their bloody methods led to their eventual shunning among law-abiding citizens and lawbreakers alike. "They were, in short," John Toland wrote in *The Dillinger Days*, "not only outlaws but outcasts."

Hollywood immortalized them as such in 1967's *Bonnie and Clyde*, which, like *Butch Cassidy and the Sundance Kid*, was a critical and financial hit.[67] Warren Beatty and Faye Dunaway portrayed the couple as poor, bored, and by turns menacing and comic. The film turned Bonnie and Clyde into sympathetic thieves who became countercultural symbols, much like Paul Newman's Butch Cassidy and Robert Redford's Sundance Kid. The Bonnie and Clyde on the screen were complex and anti-authoritarian, lost innocents trying to survive in an oppressive world in which banks were the enemies of Dust Bowl farmers. A tagline of a promotional poster for *Bonnie and Clyde* read, "They're young . . . they're in love . . . and they kill people." Beatty uttered lines that became among the best known from the 1967 movie: "This here's Miss Bonnie Parker. I'm Clyde Barrow. We rob banks." The film, directed by Arthur Penn, was filled with scenes unprecedented in their violence. In that regard, it unquestionably resembled the lives of the real Clyde Barrow and Bonnie Parker.

The pair did not operate totally alone. They were the main members of the Barrow Gang, which carried out its first holdup in March 1932. The gang's initial members were Bonnie and Clyde and ex-convicts Ralph Fults and Floyd Hamilton. In late 1932, after Fults and Hamilton left, the gang added sixteen-year-old William D. "W. D." Jones, whose family was friendly with the Barrows. In March 1933, the gang grew by two more: Buck Barrow (Clyde's older brother) and Blanche Barrow (Buck's wife). No matter what the variations of the Barrow Gang, Clyde was the leader.

Clyde Barrow was born on March 24, 1909, in Telico, Texas, a dot of a town southeast of Dallas.[68] His father was a junk man. Bonnie Parker was born on October 1, 1910, in another small town, Rowena, Texas, southwest of Dallas and west of Waco. Her father was a mason. Neither Bonnie nor Clyde was physically intimidating. She was four feet, eleven inches tall and weighed 90 pounds, and walked with a limp due to injuries from an automobile accident in June 1933. Clyde was five feet, seven inches tall and weighed 135 pounds. Each seemed bound for lives of anonymous poverty when they first met at a party in Dallas on January 5, 1930. Except for Clyde's prison stints, they would be with one another until they died.

Bonnie was nineteen years old, married, and out of work as a waitress. Clyde was twenty years old, and already wanted for crimes such as car theft and burglary. She aspired to be a poet or to make it big on Broadway; he aspired to be a saxophone player or the owner of an auto parts store, and to be his own man—"the one in charge"[69]—though he, like Bonnie, struggled with the other rural poor.

A deep feeling of injustice drove Clyde Barrow, who had been raped while in prison (he killed the rapist, a fellow inmate named Ed Crowder, by beating him with a lead pipe) and had problems with the police while out. In January 1932, so desperate was Clyde to leave a prison farm where he had to pick cotton that he had his left big toe and part of a second toe cut off with an ax. He was soon paroled and got a job near Dallas. After losing his job in mid-March 1932, after the police stopped by his workplace, Clyde declared that he was done working for a living. With his ne'er-do-well older brother as an influence, he decided to become a full-time thief. His full-time partner and lover was his own Bonnie Parker, who never divorced her husband, a murderer named Roy Thornton, then in prison.[70] Soon the other members of the gang joined Bonnie and Clyde in their two-year crime spree.

Bonnie and Clyde did not much like to rob banks. They preferred to hold up grocery stores, gas stations, liquor stores, or small jewelry shops; the heists often yielded little money, but they also did not attract a flood of police. Or they held up armories, where they stole submachine guns and other firearms that kept them outfitted like a militia. Robbing banks was so much riskier—the tellers, the guards, the location in the center of a large town or city—that Bonnie and Clyde, for much of their time together, "didn't consider robbing a bank to be a good option."[71] In the years the Barrow Gang operated, including Bonnie and Clyde's spree, the gang is estimated to have robbed fewer than fifteen banks, including some the gang robbed more than once.[72] Bonnie typically did not participate in the bank robberies and took on lesser roles when she did.[73]

Bonnie and Clyde were not professionals, which was apparent during a bank robbery they worked together. On November 30, 1932, they and two associates along for this one heist, Frank Hardy and Hollis Hale, held up the Farmers and Miners Bank of Orongo, Missouri, just northeast of Joplin. Bonnie went in the day before to survey the interior, but her observations did not seem to help Clyde the next day. Though he walked into the bank with a submachine gun, the teller fired a pistol at him. The pistol jammed. Clyde opened fire, but the teller had ducked behind the counter and was not hit. Clyde and the others—Bonnie was not with him—ran outside, where townspeople fired upon them. The crew drove away in their getaway car with a take of $110.

Bonnie and Clyde's dark genius was rooted not so much in their crimes and how they carried them out, but in their understanding of the relationship between fame and crime, including bank robbery. They yearned to be celebrities—he a sax player, and she a starlet—and given that they chose crime as a way of life, they understood that being notorious was just as powerful as being notable. They constantly took snapshots of one another, and had others take snapshots of them. In one, Bonnie is smoking a cigar, holding a pistol, and leaning on the front headlight of a getaway car. In another, she is jokingly pointing a shotgun at him. And in another, they are kneeling in a clearing in the woods, where Clyde is cleaning a submachine gun. Whether the pair posed for these photos with the public in mind is uncertain, but this much is clear: Bonnie and Clyde saw themselves as glamorous. If Bonnie Parker would never appear in the movies she liked to see, she could still be a star with Clyde.

These photos turned Bonnie and Clyde into a national phenomenon. The photos were on a roll of undeveloped film the police found on April 13, 1933, after raiding a house in Joplin where Bonnie, Clyde, and the rest of the Barrow Gang had holed up. Two lawmen died in the firefight that preceded the gang's flight. When newspapers published the photos, Bonnie and Clyde were the best-known criminals in the United States, complete with their own playfully defiant gangster style. Their identity was tied to bank robbery and other crimes, and they were proud of the connection, and their ability to fashion myths of out of their lives. They were stars in their own movie.

They also knew how that movie had to end. At the house in Joplin, police discovered an unfinished poem by Bonnie, "The Story of Suicide Sal." It tells the story of how Sal's boyfriend, a gangster, brings her into a life of crime. Sal relates her tale to the narrator, who appears to be writing from prison, according to the first stanza:

> We, each of us, have a good "alibi"
> For being down here in the "joint;" [*sic*]
> But few of them are really justified,
> If you get right down to the point. [74]

The newspapers published "The Story of Suicide Sal," and they also published a poem Bonnie wrote in the spring of 1934, as the police continued to close in on Clyde and her. "The End of the Line," popularly known as "The Story of Bonnie and Clyde," is Bonnie's ode to the outlaw and the outlaw's unavoidable fate. The sixteen-stanza poem opens:

> You've read the story of Jesse James—
> Of how he lived and died;
> If you're still in the need
> Of something to read
> Here's the story of Bonnie and Clyde.

The poem ends with these two stanzas:

> They don't think they're too smart or desperate,
> They know the law always wins;
> They've been shot at before,
> But they do not ignore
> That death is the wages of sin.
>
> Some day they'll go down together;
> And they'll bury them side by side,
> To few it'll be grief—
> To the law a relief—
> But it's death for Bonnie and Clyde. [75]

Bonnie Parker and Clyde Barrow were alone in their stolen Ford when a posse gunned them down on May 23, 1934, on the outskirts of Gibsland, in northern Louisiana, east of Shreveport. The Barrow Gang's membership had dwindled nearly a year earlier, in July, when a posse caught up with the gang in Dexfield, Iowa, days after Buck Barrow had been wounded in a shootout with police in Platte City, Missouri. Buck died five days after he was caught in Dexfield with Blanche. Bonnie, Clyde, and seventeen-year-old W. D. Jones escaped, though Jones soon dropped out of the gang to be with his mother in Houston. Bonnie and Clyde continued to outrun the authorities. The FBI got jurisdiction in May 1933, after the pair drove a stolen car across state lines. The public by now wanted them caught. The image of free-spirited desperadoes had vanished after Clyde and his newest gang member, twenty-two-year-old Henry Methvin, killed two motorcycle police patrolmen—E. B. Wheeler, twenty-six, and H. D. Murphy, a twenty-two-year-old rookie—near Grapevine, Texas, outside of Dallas, on April 1, 1934 (Easter Sunday). Murphy's death particularly incensed the public; he was to have been married in twelve days. From the date of Murphy's murder onward, Bonnie Parker and Clyde Barrow "would be more reviled than celebrated."[76]

Their end came in an ambush. Texas Governor Miriam "Ma" Ferguson had commissioned a decorated retired Texas Ranger, Frank Hamer, to find Bonnie and Clyde. Hamer created a posse with interstate authority, and he got a tip on the outlaws' whereabouts from Methvin's family. Hamer and the other five lawmen, who were from Texas and Louisiana, opened fire on Bonnie and Clyde's car shortly after nine in the morning on May 23, 1934. Bonnie was shot with fifty rounds, Clyde with forty. Inside the car, police found "three rifles, two sawed-off shotguns, nine pistols, three thousand rounds of ammunition, stolen license plates from several states, and Clyde's saxophone."[77] She was twenty-three years old. He was twenty-five.

The visitations at two Dallas funeral homes for Bonnie Parker and Clyde Barrow attracted ten thousand to twenty thousand people. Shortly after their deaths, popular newsreels at theaters showed footage of them, their faces still bloody, from the coroner's laboratory.[78] Bonnie and Clyde had finally hit the big screen.

Few people in American history earn such enmity from the government than that person whom the chief executive himself cites when signing laws that significantly enlarge the government's powers. Jesse James achieved such dubious status when the governor of Missouri declared his capture a priority. That was only in one state. John Dillinger caused President Roosevelt to roar with anger in May 1934, when he cited Dillinger as a reason for Congress to pass the New Deal crime legislation. J. Edgar Hoover's aggressive special agents and the new laws eventually trapped and dismantled Dillinger and his gang, with the world-famous outlaw meeting his demise not far from the bright lights of the Biograph Theater.

In mid-April 1934, a little more than a week before the botched raid in Little Bohemia, FBI agents had arrested Dillinger's longtime moll, Billie Frechette, in a Chicago tavern. The next month she was convicted of harboring Dillinger and sentenced to two years in federal prison. Also in May 1934, Dillinger and Homer Van Meter robbed the First National Bank in Fostoria, Ohio, of $10,000, and they were suspected of getting into a gunfight in East Chicago, in which two police officers were killed.

In a development that showed Handsome Johnny valued survival more than vanity, he and Van Meter in May 1934 had two underworld-connected doctors in Chicago perform plastic surgery on them at the home of Chicago crime figure Jimmy Probasco. For $5,000 each, Dillinger and his buddy had their faces altered and their fingerprints obliterated; one of the doctors cut off the skin on their fingertips and treated what remained with a mixture that included hydrochloric acid.[79] As for Dillinger's photogenic face, the doctors removed moles between his eyes, "cut the cheek along the ear and the edge of the jaw and transplanted some of the flesh to the dimple on the chin. Finally they tightened up the cheeks with kangaroo tendons."[80]

The bizarre procedure was enough to disguise Dillinger, but not to make him unrecognizable. His visage, blown up on so many wanted posters, had been seared into the memory of the public. Dillinger dyed his hair and wore a mustache and glasses, though he still went out to the movies and other public venues in Chicago, where he was now living. He and his gang, including Baby Face Nelson, committed their final bank robbery on June 30, 1934, when they stole nearly $30,000 from the Merchants National Bank in South Bend, Indiana—a heist in which a policeman was killed and at which, according to some writers, Pretty Boy Floyd was present.[81] Dillinger soon was short on money and short on gang members, and under the watch of Hoover's man in Chicago, Melvin Purvis. Dillinger could not hide, especially when he was Public Enemy Number One, whose capture would win a reward of $10,000.

Purvis, who had received the tip that had led him to Little Bohemia, also worked the tip he and his fellow agents used to track Dillinger to the Biograph Theater. On July 21, 1934, an Indiana policeman told Purvis that a brothel madam who went by the name Anna Sage was willing to turn over Dillinger's whereabouts in exchange for the reward money and the federal government's help in eliminating her threatened deportation to Romania. Sage, whose real name was Ana Cumpanas, said Dillinger had been dating one of her boarders, a waitress named Polly Hamilton. Sage said she, Dillinger, and Hamilton had plans to see *Manhattan Melodrama* at one of two Chicago theaters, including the Biograph, the night of July 22, 1934. Purvis and his men staked out the theaters. Purvis knew Dillinger had gone into the Biograph when he saw Sage outside, "wearing an orange skirt that looked blood red in the lights of the marquee."[82] Sage was forever known as "the woman in red," the woman who betrayed John Dillinger.[83]

Dillinger was surrounded when he, Sage, and Hamilton left the Biograph at about a half past ten that night. Purvis and a group of agents, including Sam Cowley, who was under Purvis but headed the squad that was targeting Dillinger, were waiting outside, undercover. Dillinger, suspicious, ran down the alley next to the theater. Purvis yelled at him, and he refused to surrender. Dillinger pulled out his .38-caliber Colt automatic pistol—and was shot dead by gunfire from three special agents: Herman Hollis, Clarence Hurt, and Charles Winstead. Dillinger was hit in the left side, right eye, and back.

Purvis telephoned a grateful Hoover in Washington, D.C. Radio stations blared the reports, and the curious took to the streets. Thousands were "crowding around the entrance to the Biograph. A car parked nearby with Indiana license plates was being dismantled by those who mistakenly thought it was Dillinger's. Others were dipping handkerchiefs and pieces of paper into the tiny red pools in the alley. Some women were even soaking the hems of their skirts with blood."[84]

Some fifteen thousand people gawked at Dillinger's body at the Cook County Morgue, in Chicago, and his burial, in Indianapolis, attracted another five thousand. Dillinger's death catapulted Special Agent Melvin

Purvis into the realm of a national hero. He wrote a book, *American Agent*, and later appeared on cereal boxes and hosted a radio show—though Hoover grew so jealous of his protégé that he all but forced Purvis out of the FBI and undercut Purvis's efforts to find work elsewhere.[85] Hoover linked himself to Dillinger's fatal capture. From then on, and until he died, Hoover made sure a glass display case in the FBI's headquarters contained John Dillinger's death mask.[86]

More deaths of public enemies soon closed out "The Year of the Gangster," as 1934 was known. Hoover's men, still investigating the Kansas City Massacre, shot and killed the thirty-year-old Pretty Boy Floyd on the farm near East Liverpool, Ohio, on October 22, 1934. Floyd admitted nothing before he died. On November 27, 1934, FBI agents killed Baby Face Nelson near Barrington, Illinois, in a gun battle in which Nelson killed two special agents, Sam Cowley and Herman Hollis, who had both staked out Dillinger outside the Biograph. Agents killed Ma Barker and her son Fred on January 16, 1935, in Ocklawaha, Florida. On May 1, 1936, the FBI, with Hoover present, arrested Alvin Karpis—the last Public Enemy Number One, wanted for kidnapping, bank robbery, and other crimes—in New Orleans. He was convicted and sent to Alcatraz, where he spent twenty-six years, the longest tenure for an inmate at the Rock, until he was paroled in 1969.[87]

By 1935, when Hoover launched the FBI's battle against bank robbers, the agency had already achieved huge public-relations coups with the deaths of Dillinger and the others. The FBI went on to triumph on the movie screen as well. Gangster movies, so popular before the imposition of the Hays Code, gave way to equally popular movies that celebrated the FBI. Though strict imposition of the Hays Code went into effect in 1934, virtually prohibiting the making of gangster movies, the Motion Picture Producers and Distributors of America approved an exemption. It allowed on-screen violence to occur in antigangster movies—films whose heroes were FBI agents. What followed, through September 1935, was a cycle of G-men movies about J. Edgar Hoover's FBI. They included *Public Hero Number One* (May 1935), starring Lionel Barrymore; *Whipsaw* (December 1935), starring Myrna Loy and Spencer Tracy; and *Show Them No Mercy* (also in December 1935), starring Cesar Romero.[88]

These movies were still violent, and still focused on gangsters: "They now made the FBI agents the nominal heroes, but gave the same fat parts to the gangsters. As a sop, they had the gangster killed or punished at the end."[89] Just as bank robbery helped create the modern FBI in real life, so bank robbers, gangsters, kidnappers, and other crooks provided the foils that made the FBI agents stars of the G-men movies.

The most influential of these films, the movie that most shaped the public image of the FBI, was *G-Men*, released in April 1935. It was made by Warner Brothers, which had produced so many of the gangster movies (*The Public Enemy*, *Little Caesar*, *Scarface*), and its star was James Cagney, also the lead in *The Public Enemy*. In *G-Men*, Cagney plays James "Brick" Davis, a lawyer who trains as a G-man after his friend, already an agent, is killed while trying to arrest a gangster. Davis pursues gangsters as the G-men's agency—a cinematic stand-in for Hoover's FBI—demands more police powers to fight the crime wave. The G-men win in the end, to the adulation of an adoring nation. *G-Men* and other movies in the genre "redefined the FBI agent as the latest incarnation of a century-old stereotype in popular entertainment: the action detective hero who customarily works outside the cumbersome institutions of the government and the law," according to author Richard Gid Powers.[90] The same movie industry that, before the enforcement of the Hays Code, had mythologized gangsters now used violence to mythologize the FBI.

Hollywood refocused its myth making on bank robbers and gangsters three decades later with *Bonnie and Clyde*. Screenwriters Robert Benton and David Newman started working on a treatment for what would become *Bonnie and Clyde* shortly after John Toland's *The Dillinger Days* was published in 1963. Toland interpolated the narrative about Dillinger with an account of the two young lovers/killers. This subplot fascinated Benton and Newman, particularly Toland's line about the pair being outcasts as well as outlaws.[91] Toland also portrayed Bonnie and Clyde as something of sexual rogues: He wrote that the pair enlisted W. D. Jones in their gang "not only to assist in the robberies but to help satisfy Bonnie's sexual aberrations. Clyde, who had homosexual tendencies, didn't object to her peculiar tastes. In fact, he enjoyed sharing her pleasures."[92] The final version of *Bonnie and Clyde* eliminated, over the objections of Benton and Newman, a sexual ménage a trois with Clyde, Bonnie, and their getaway driver, C. W. Moss, whose character resembled W. D. Jones and Henry Methvin, the last member of the Barrow Gang. The final script, again against the wishes of Benton and Newman, also portrayed Clyde as heterosexual rather than bisexual. His supposed impotence remained a theme, which added to the movie's sexual tension.[93]

Under the direction of Arthur Penn, *Bonnie and Clyde* recast the popular image of bank robbers and gangsters in a film that was sexually charged, darkly comic, and unusually bloody. Perhaps its most famous scene—the ambush of Bonnie and Clyde and their deaths in a barrage of bullets—would have been banned under the Production Code of Will Hays. The code still existed when *Bonnie and Clyde* appeared in theaters in 1967, but it was all but finished. Acolytes of the French New Wave had been challenging the strictures of the code for years, just as the counterculture was challenging mainstream American society in the 1960s. The Production Code gradually relaxed (*Bonnie and Clyde*'s release alone showed how much it had changed) and finally collapsed into obsolescence. Its replacement, effective on November 1, 1968, was the more permissive Motion Picture Association of America ratings system, which continues today. Bonnie and Clyde and the other gangsters and bank robbers had defeated the moral code of authority—at least in the movies.

Patrick Lyon, a blacksmith from Philadelphia, was the first person accused of bank robbery in the United States—the theft of gold and bank notes from the Bank of Pennsylvania at Carpenters' Hall, in Philadelphia, on September 1, 1798. Lyon was wrongly arrested and later won a malicious prosecution case against his accusers. In his triumph, Lyon commissioned a self-portrait, *Pat Lyon at the Forge*, by John Neagle. The cupola of the Walnut Street Jail, where Lyon was incarcerated, can be seen out the window. This version of the portrait (circa 1829) hangs in the Philadelphia Academy of Fine Arts. (Courtesy of the Library of Congress)

In the summer of 1863, sixteen-year-old Jesse James started fighting with Confederate guerrillas, known as bushwhackers, in his native Missouri, a border state caught between Union and Confederate loyalties. In this photo, he is wearing a homemade guerrilla shirt; its large breast pockets held ammunition for the six-shot revolver that was the bushwhackers' weapon of choice. After the war, James applied many of the techniques he mastered as a bushwhacker—planning, surprise, and precision—to robbing nearly a dozen banks starting in 1866, when he was nineteen, and continuing until one of his gang members, Bob Ford, assassinated him in 1882, when he was thirty-four. Politics motivated many of the robberies James carried out with his older brother, Frank, and the Younger brothers. (Courtesy of the Library of Congress)

Butch Cassidy and his partner, the Sundance Kid, were out-of-work cowboys who turned to bank robbery in the West as members of the Wild Bunch, or the Hole-in-the-Wall Gang, which Cassidy headed. He was a charming and intelligent thief whose failed attempt, with the Sundance Kid, to resettle in Bolivia became stuff of legend. Early in his career, Cassidy, who grew up in Utah as Robert Leroy Parker, was convicted of stealing a five-dollar horse and sentenced in 1894 to two years at the Wyoming State Penitentiary, in Laramie, where this photo was taken. Detectives with the Pinkerton agency later mounted the photo on cards as they searched for Cassidy and the Sundance Kid, otherwise known as Harry Longabaugh, a sure shot originally from Pennsylvania. The photo also appeared in newspapers nationwide. (Courtesy of the Library of Congress)

John Dillinger (center), the bane of the Federal Bureau of Investigation and the nation's first Public Enemy Number One, enjoyed a celebrity status usually reserved for movie stars. On January 30, 1934, he was awaiting prosecution at the Crown Point Jail in his native Indiana when he posed for eager photographers with the two public officials who were supposed to bring him to justice: Lake County Sheriff Lillian Holley (far left) and the county's prosecuting attorney, Robert G. Estill. Some who have studied Dillinger's career theorize that in this picture he is purposely holding the fingers on his right hand in the shape of a gun. The photo infuriated U.S. Attorney General Homer S. Cummings and ended the political careers of Holley and Estill. A month after the photo was taken, Dillinger broke out of the jail in his boldest escape, using a fake gun he had carved out of wood and dyed with black shoe polish. He was thirty years old at the time. Five months later, FBI agents would gun him down in Chicago. (Courtesy of Everett Collection Inc./ Alamy)

Growing up poor near Dallas, Texas, Bonnie Parker dreamed of being a poet or a Broadway starlet. She and her boyfriend, Clyde Barrow, terrorized the American Southwest in the mid-1930s as one of the most notorious duos in the history of American crime. Bonnie and Clyde's twisted genius rested not so much in their crimes and how they executed them, but rather in their understanding of the relationship between fame and crime, including bank robbery. In their quest for fame, Bonnie and Clyde were careless: This photo, which they took and which police discovered in a raid of one of their hideouts, shows the license plate of their getaway car. (Courtesy of the Federal Bureau of Investigation)

By the time he first met Bonnie Parker at a party in Dallas, Texas, in January 1930, Clyde Barrow, an aspiring saxophone player, already had a long record for burglary, car theft, and breaking out of prison. Barrow, whom historians generally believe was born on March 24, 1909 (two years earlier than what is listed on this identification card), was twenty years old when he was charged in this case on March 2, 1930. Four years later, during a crime spree that included bank robbery, Barrow's unprovoked killing of two police officers near Dallas on Easter Sunday 1934 proved his vicious character. When an armed posse killed Bonnie and Clyde on May 23, 1934, in Louisiana, the two went down together, just as she had predicted. (Courtesy of the Federal Bureau of Investigation)

In the mid-1930s, FBI Director J. Edgar Hoover launched a war on bank robbers and gangsters with the approval of President Franklin D. Roosevelt and U.S. Attorney General Homer S. Cummings. Roosevelt's anticrime legislation rivaled his New Deal economic reforms as the most aggressive actions his administration took to relieve the country during the Great Depression. Hoover's targeting of bank robberies increased the FBI's stature and led to many of the innovations that modernized the agency. (Courtesy of the Library of Congress)

Willie Sutton's innumerable disguises and calm demeanor made him one of the most prolific bank robbers of his era, particularly in the 1950s. He said he got his biggest thrill, after robbing banks, from breaking out of prison. Sutton denied saying the remark so often attributed to him—that he robbed banks because "that's where the money is"—but he embraced its sentiment and incorporated it into the title of his 1976 memoir, *Where the Money Was*. (Courtesy of the Federal Bureau of Investigation)

Newspaper heiress Patty Hearst helps rob the Hibernia Bank branch in the Sunset District of San Francisco, on April 15, 1974. Her participation in the heist with members of the leftist Symbionese Liberation Army captivated Americans as they tried to figure out whether she had acted voluntarily or under duress, as she later claimed. Hearst, known by her SLA name of "Tania," is shown here with SLA leader Donald DeFreeze, or "Cinque." At the age of twenty-two, Hearst in 1976 was convicted of armed bank robbery and a firearms charge, and she was sentenced to seven years in federal prison. President Jimmy Carter commuted her sentence in 1979, after she had served twenty-two months, and President Bill Clinton pardoned her in January 2001, on his last day in office. (Courtesy of the Federal Bureau of Investigation)

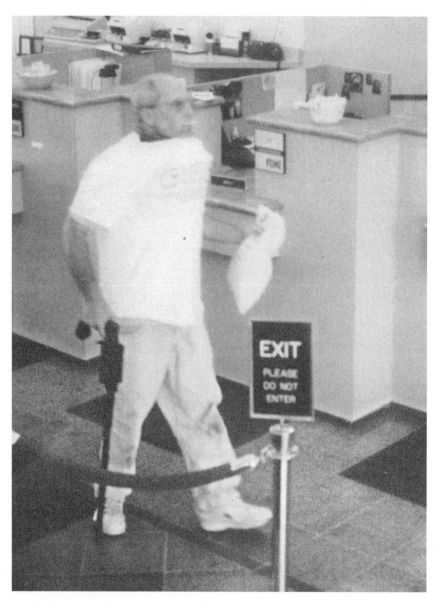

Brian Wells, a forty-six-year-old pizza delivery driver, wears a live bomb around his neck as he robs a PNC Bank branch south of Erie, Pennsylvania, on August 28, 2003. Wells is sucking on a lollipop as he carries a bag of cash in one hand and a gun shaped like a cane in the other. The Pizza Bomber case, which the FBI elevated to Major Case 203, confounded investigators who tried to determine whether Wells, who died in a bomb blast later that day, was forced to rob the bank or was part of the strange plot. The FBI unraveled the scheme after four years of investigation and determined that Wells was a willing participant—to a degree. (Courtesy of the Federal Bureau of Investigation)

6

LONE WOLVES

Willie Sutton, the Great Brink's Robbery, and a Thief Found Dead

Once the Great Depression ended, bank robbery would never again frighten the United States to such a degree. The new federal anticrime laws had an effect, particularly if the statistics from 1933—that robbers that year struck almost two banks a day—can be believed. In 1934, the first year it compiled such data for bank robberies, the FBI recorded twelve bank robberies from May 18 until the end of the fiscal year (September 30).[1] The fiscal year numbers were 114 and 70, respectively, in 1935 and 1936. The number of bank robberies dropped to 54 in 1937 and rose to 90 in 1938 before reaching 133 and 146 in 1939 and 1940, respectively.[2] From there, the number of bank robberies dropped significantly—the lowest number of recorded bank robberies on record for a full fiscal year was 17 in 1944, though the number would hit 103 by 1951.[3]

The evidence is clear that the newly empowered FBI made an immediate difference in bringing serial bank robberies under control and restoring a sense of security at banks and other financial institutions.[4] More than anything, as Brian Burrough has written in his chronicle of the great crime wave of the Great Depression, "the manhunts for Dillinger and his peers introduced America to an idea that we take for granted today: that the federal government bears the ultimate responsibility for the nation's law and order."[5]

After the Dillinger days came to a close, bank robberies became notable not so much because of who committed them, but because of the details of the individual robberies, such as the amount stolen or the unusual methods the thieves used to get their booty. No longer would so many individual bank robbers get transformed into national celebrities so regularly. At the same time, never again would an FBI official, other than J. Edgar Hoover, who oversaw the national crime-fighting apparatus, achieve the level of stardom that Special Agent Melvin Purvis reached after Dillinger's death. Bank robbers would largely become anonymous even if the size of their heists were unprecedented, such as the $2.7 million stolen from the Brink's building, in Boston, in 1950.

The trend that put the bank robber in the background had one major exception: Willie "the Actor" Sutton.

Willie Sutton was also known as "Slick Willie," a nod to his ability to elude the FBI and other authorities, often by donning the various disguises—fake mustaches, dyed hair, the uniforms of a police officer, a postal worker, or a Western Union telegram deliveryman—that earned him the nickname "the Actor." During the twenty-five years he robbed banks, Willie Sutton was caught three times. He spent thirty-six years in prison, but still was believed to have stolen as much as $2 million, though the number of banks he robbed is difficult to verify. Some estimates have him knocking off as many as sixty banks in two and a half years alone.[6]

Sutton's skills as a thief undoubtedly elevated him to the rank of the most famous bank robber in America, particularly in 1950, when the FBI added him to its list of Ten Most Wanted fugitives, a crime-fighting tool Hoover created that year. But much like other well-known bank robbers before him, Sutton gained notoriety for his personality—his suave manner, his affection for fine tailored suits (a habit that contributed to his final capture), and his dislike of violence. He always carried a gun but was disinclined to use it; he relied on firmness and courteousness to create the fear and respect that caused so many bank employees to give him the money. "One victim said witnessing one of Sutton's robberies," according to the FBI, "was like being at the movies, except the usher had a gun."[7]

Sutton's life-affirming reason for robbing banks—"I was more alive when I was inside a bank, robbing it, than at any other time in my life"— suggests that he robbed banks because doing so gave him purpose. He enjoyed the thrill of the heist and the excitement of the chase. But like so many of his predecessors, Willie Sutton primarily robbed banks because he liked money and because—to paraphrase the renowned remark attributed to him—the banks had the money. Sutton was neither political, like Jesse James, nor prone to homicidal behavior, like Dillinger or Pretty Boy Floyd. Sutton, much like George Leslie and Herman Lamm, considered bank robbery a job—a lawless job, but a challenging and financially rewarding job nonetheless. Sutton was a crook sui generis, with his originality reflecting the times. When men in gray flannel suits were defining general American culture, Willie Sutton pioneered the role of bank robber as modern businessman. He was so successful that he was his own boss.

William Francis Sutton Jr. was born on June 30, 1901, in Irishtown, a tough neighborhood on the docks in Brooklyn, New York, known for its working-class, Irish families. He grew up neither poor nor in a family fraught with financial uncertainty. His father, as Sutton reflected, "was a hard-working blacksmith who earned fifteen dollars a week, which was not a bad salary in those days. A blacksmith at that time was like an automobile mechanic today. No matter how bad the times got, there was always a place somewhere for a good one."[8] Though members of Sutton's family were not lawbreakers, he grew up in an atmosphere of lawlessness, where Irish mobsters ran the rackets on the docks and, with no shame, burglars, robbers, and other crooks told tales about their crimes at the neighborhood bars and taverns. These characters influenced the ten-year-old Sutton, who admired their nice clothes and shined shoes. "They became my first heroes," Sutton recalled. Soon he and a neighborhood buddy were "planning our first burglary as if it were the most natural thing in the world."[9]

Sutton and his pal broke into a cash register at a small department store, but he did not immediately follow up his first-time heist with others. He did well in grade school, though he was caught stealing his teacher's lunch money, and dreamed of becoming a criminal defense lawyer. Sutton never went to high school—World War I intervened—and his plans for a law degree got permanently put on hold. In Sutton's mind, his eventual career was not much different from the career he would have liked. As he recalled,

The line between a bank robber and a lawyer is a very thin one, anyway. In robbing a bank I always planned the job carefully, leaving nothing to chance. It's the same thing in trying a case. "Preparation is everything," lawyers say. Once you're inside the bank, you have to see everything, guard yourself against everybody. While he is putting on his case, the lawyer has to be equally alert, equally on guard against anything the other side might throw at him. In both professions, it helps to be a little paranoid.

And whatever they might say in the law schools, it also helps to have a grudge against society. The criminal lawyer, like the criminal, is the enemy of Law and Order. The criminal attacks society head on; the lawyer is trying to set you free after you have been caught so that you can go out and steal some more. Whether he succeeds or not, he profits from your crime. The only way you can pay him is out of the money you have got away with at one time or another, everybody knows that. It isn't called his share of the loot, of course. It's called "the fee." But that's only because he has a license that entitles him to do what he's doing, and you haven't. [10]

Sutton's worldview was set before adulthood: Everyone is a criminal, in his or her own way. Sutton also grew to believe that the greatest honor among thieves is to abide by a code of silence and not rat anyone out. By the time he was seventeen, Sutton had no compunctions about stealing. He pilfered $16,000 from the office safe of his girlfriend's father. He was prosecuted and got a suspended sentence, as long as he promised not to see the girl again. He got a good job at a shipyard, where he was a "burner," who used an acetylene torch to cut through steel hulls. Sutton saw even this work as preparation for bank robbery, his true calling. He dreamed the hull was a bank vault, and that he was slicing into it to grab all the money inside. "I already knew a great deal about vaults and the inner workings of a bank," Sutton wrote about this time in his life. "I never doubted that I was going to be putting all this specialized knowledge to the best possible use."[11] He gained even more understanding of vaults and their vulnerabilities by studying them and using fake letterhead to write to steel companies in Pittsburgh to get free samples of the latest alloys.[12] Sutton had become an expert at "punching" safes, or drilling into them, at any number of jewelry stores, department stores, and other businesses he and his partners broke into in his early days as a professional criminal, when he worked jobs throughout the Northeast with a gang of thieves under the direction of a crook named Doc Tate. When he finally tried to rob his first bank, Sutton thought he was ready.

The job was a failure. Sutton's confidence was high; days earlier, he had robbed a jewelry store on Broadway during the day. On September 7, 1925, he and his partner Eddie Wilson tried to rob the First National Bank of Ozone Park, at 101st Avenue and Woodhaven Boulevard, in Queens, New York. In keeping with his strategy, Sutton cased the bank, but misjudged the thickness of the concrete floor in its cellar. He planned to break into the cellar at night, which he did; drill through the ceiling, which he tried to do; and climb through the hole in the ceiling and use a torch to cut into the bank vault above. The last stage never happened. Sutton and Wilson needed more time to drill through the ceiling than they expected. By the time they started trying to burn through the vault, bank employees had started to arrive for work. Sutton and Wilson fled and left behind their equipment, including an oxygen tank. Police traced it to Wilson, and he and Sutton were arrested and convicted in 1926. Wilson got ten years. Sutton got five to ten, which he initially served at the New York state prison at Sing Sing, and then at the state prison at Dannemora, near the Canadian border. He was twenty-five years old.

Sutton got out of prison in 1929 the typical way—he was released. Over the rest of his life, he would get out by escaping. He was sent back to Sing Sing in June 1931 for the robbery of a jewelry store, and broke out on December 11, 1932. He scaled the prison wall with a makeshift ladder. After fourteen months robbing banks, Sutton was caught and convicted again and sentenced to twenty-five to fifty years at the Eastern State Penitentiary, in Philadelphia. Sutton and eleven other inmates escaped by tunneling out on April 3, 1945. Philadelphia police apprehended Sutton the same day. He was convicted again and sentenced to life at the Philadelphia County Prison, in Holmesburg, Pennsylvania. He and four other inmates escaped on February 10, 1947, by dressing as prison guards and climbing over the prison walls on ladders. Sutton considered escaping from prison as much of a profession as robbing banks. He did both because he could, and because they gave him a charge. Sutton said he spent more time planning his prison escapes than his bank robberies, "if only because I spent so much more time inside, trying to get out, than outside, trying to get in."[13] He also wrote, "If any enterprising reporter had ever asked me why I broke out of jail, I suppose that's what I would have said: 'Because I was in.' But also, you know, because there's the thrill that comes from breaking out of jail, after years of the most meticulous planning, with everybody watching you, against all the odds, that is like nothing else in the world."[14]

In between the prison breaks were the bank robberies, and the constant running from the law. As did Dillinger, Sutton once went to an underground doctor to help him become invisible. He got a nose job. Once the swelling went down, Sutton got back to work robbing banks. Sutton had adopted his trademark technique of wearing disguises long before he got plastic surgery. In one of his heists—the robbery of the Corn Exchange Bank, at 543-545 West 110th Street, near Broadway, in Manhattan, around forty minutes after seven in the morning on July 8, 1933—Sutton dressed as a policeman. Once inside, he took out his gun and robbed the place, with Wilson and another man, Joseph Perlongo. They showed a sense of etiquette during the heist, when they held thirteen people captive but bound only the hands and feet of the men. The women were allowed to sit in chairs, though they eventually were herded into the bank's vault, with some unbound men, and locked in.[15] Sutton and the others got into the vault after foiling a security measure in which the bank's assistant manager, Paul Miller, and teller, August Melicher, each had half of the combination to the bank's vault. Sutton forced both men to open the vault, and the robbers got away with $23,835. The *New York Times* covered the robbery on its front page, declaring the use of "what appeared to be a carefully laid plan," though the police had not yet identified Sutton and the others as the robbers.[16] Sutton reasoned that the police immediately had to have known he was involved. "They always knew it was me. Every time I did a job, it was like leaving my calling card."[17] The robbery proved one of his most personally memorable. "The take came to something under thirty thousand dollars, which was far less than I expected," Sutton recalled. "On the other hand, it was one of the robberies I most enjoyed. You can't have everything."[18]

Sutton was caught for the final time on February 18, 1952, or five years and one month after he escaped from the Philadelphia County Prison. He had been living undetected in an eight-by-ten furnished room on Dean Street in Brooklyn, about four blocks from the borough's police headquarters. Sutton was on the lam for any number of crimes, including the robbery on March 9, 1950, of $63,942 from the Manufacturers Trust Company on Queens Boulevard in Long Island City. By now Sutton had been on the FBI's Ten Most Wanted list for nearly two years, and the FBI had circulated his photograph to police agencies as well as to tailors, given Sutton's well-known penchant for nice clothes. A twenty-four-year-old clothing salesman by the name of Arnold Schuster told police in Brooklyn he had seen Sutton on the subway the evening of February 18, 1952, and had followed him to a nearby service station. The police officers visited the gas station that night, learned that a man had purchased a car battery there, and found the man on a nearby street with the hood of his car up.

The man told police his name was Charles Gordon, but they continued to question him. When the patrolmen, Donald Shea and Joseph McClellan, told the man they wanted to get him fingerprinted, he confessed. "OK, you got me," he said. "I'm Willie Sutton."[19] Sutton seemed resigned to his capture. "I've been expecting it," he said.[20] Sutton made no attempts to flee, or to fight back, though the police found a gun in between his legs, held down, as Shea recalled, "by a ladies sanitary belt."[21] The New York City police commissioner, George P. Monaghan, was elated. "We've got Willie Sutton," he told the press. "Sutton was the most sought after criminal in the United States. We've caught the Babe Ruth of bank robbers."[22] Monaghan, on the spot, promoted Shea and McClellan, the two young police patrolmen, to detectives. Sutton held court with reporters, who questioned him about life on the run. It did not sound enchanting. "Extreme loneliness does things to a man," he said.

> I went to church at least once every week. I read a lot of psychology and psychiatry. I found it strange to change identity every time someone seemed to be catching up with me, and when a man changes his identity he begins to think more deeply. It's hard to be somebody different, over and over again. You're never sure of who's around you. In restaurants and other public places you study faces and actions—anyone might betray you. That study becomes a habit.[23]

Sutton saw his reputation as a thoughtful and likeable bandit plummet three weeks after his arrest. Arnold Schuster, who alerted the patrolmen to him, and whose role in Sutton's capture made the newspapers, was walking in his neighborhood when he was fatally shot: once in each eye and twice in the groin. The murder was never solved, but Sutton came under suspicion, despite his disavowals and his public statement that Schuster's death "sinks me."[24] Sutton witnessed the consequences. "With the murder of Arnold Schuster," he recalled, "the public's attitude toward me turned completely around. They had viewed me as a little guy who had outwitted the authorities without hurting anybody, and there was now a young man, a Coast Guard veteran, who had been gunned down in the street, gangster-style, because he had tried to be a good citizen. I could understand their attitude very well."[25]

At his trial for bank robbery following his arrest, Sutton felt like a pariah. He recalled that no one mentioned Schuster's name, but that "his ghost hung over the entire proceedings. When the prosecutor said, in his summation, 'He isn't Robin Hood, he's just a hood,' it had an entirely different meaning than it otherwise would have."[26] For all his fame, Willie "the Actor" Sutton's true identity, in the eyes of the law, was nothing more than a crook.

Sutton in 1952 was convicted of a bank robbery and sentenced to 30–120 years at the New York state prison at Attica. Ill from emphysema, he was released from prison on Christmas Eve of 1969. Sutton died at age seventy-eight in Spring Hill, Florida, north of St. Petersburg, on November 2, 1980, but not before he added to his fame. In addition to writing two books about his exploits, Sutton, in 1970, shot a television commercial for the new photo credit card program for a bank in New Britain, Connecticut.

Also during his lifetime, Sutton saw the maxim he said he never said—that he robbed banks because "that's where the money is"—transformed into a medical term. Sutton's Law, coined in 1960, refers to the theory that physicians should first explore their hunches, or what appears to be the obvious, when diagnosing an illness. Sutton, never known to have less than a healthy ego, enjoyed having a medical term named after him, even if he denied making the statement that inspired it.[27] And even if he indeed never said the phrase so often attributed to him (though he had no qualms about appropriating it for the title of one of his books), Sutton's criminal pragmatism embodied the phrase. He robbed banks because they were there, and they had the money.

Willie Sutton often complained that the authorities tried to blame him for bank robberies he did not commit. These included one of the largest robberies on record: the great Brink's robbery of January 17, 1950, when a gang of armed thieves stole a then-record $2.7 million in cash and securities from a Brink's armored car service counting house and garage in Boston.[28] It was known as the "crime of the century"[29] and "the most daring and lucrative job in crime annals."[30] With his cunning and industriousness, Sutton was an initial suspect, as reporters informed him when he was arrested in Brooklyn in February 1952. He denied any involvement, and said he had an alibi to prove his case.

Sutton was right. He had nothing to do with the Brink's robbery. It was the handiwork of a group of eleven Boston-area criminals who realized, as Jesse James had when he robbed trains in the 1800s, that after banks, the best targets for cash-rich robberies are the companies entrusted with shuttling the money to and from banks and other financial institutions. In one main respect, the robbery of an armored car is less dangerous for the thief than the robbery of a bank. The money inside a Brink's truck, unlike the cash stored at a bank, is often "completely untraceable; it's either new money going to a bank or old money going to a federal reserve depository to be destroyed."[31]

The Brink's job was so well planned and executed that it was also known as "the perfect crime."[32] Shortly before seven-thirty at night on January 17, 1950, seven men carrying guns and wearing Halloween-like masks—one was of Captain Marvel—as well as navy pea coats, gloves, and chauffer's hats (to look like Brink's employees), walked into the Brink's building at 165 Prince Street, in Boston's North End. They robbed it of $1,218,211.29 in cash and $1,557,183.83 in checks, money orders, and other securities, for a total haul of $2,775,395.12.[33] The group had considered robbing the Brink's garage three years earlier, when it was in a different location, and then spent at least a year planning the heist they carried out.

The crew got into the Prince Street building with ease. They had cased the place on the inside and outside for months, and they had the keys to all five of its doors. During their secretive trips, they had taken the doors' lock cylinders, replaced them, quickly had keys made to fit the original cylinders, then reinstalled those cylinders in the doors. The heist went smoothly. The seven robbers forced to the floor all five nighttime employees, who had been counting that day's deliveries, tied their hands behind their backs, and taped their mouths shut. The robbers loaded the loot into bags and left. No one fired a shot. The only evidence left behind was rope, adhesive tape, and a chauffer's cap. The heist took fifteen to eighteen minutes.

The investigation would last nearly six years—the statute of limitations for bank robbery—and cost the FBI $29 million to investigate.[34] The FBI and Boston police immediately suspected a number of local underworld figures, and their suspicions would prove correct in the end, but getting the evidence for indictments was difficult. The eleven men eventually identified in the heist had agreed not to talk, and none of them were known to be lavish spenders of the stolen money. High on the FBI's list from the start were Anthony Pino, a suspect in other major burglaries and robberies in Massachusetts; Joe McGinnis, a liquor store owner whom Pino said he was on with the night of the robbery; Joseph James "Specs" O'Keefe (so nicknamed for his predilection for horn-rimmed glasses[35]); and Stanley Gusciora (both O'Keefe and Gusciora were associates of Pino's). As did Pino, O'Keefe and Gusciora denied to the FBI that they had been part of the robbery. Their alibis, while far from impeccable, could not be undermined without more information.

It came from O'Keefe, who could not stay out of trouble. In June 1950, while heading to Missouri, ostensibly to visit the grave of Gusciora's brother, O'Keefe and Gusciora were arrested on burglary charges in the northcentral Pennsylvania town of Towanda. Both were convicted and sentenced to prison. While incarcerated, O'Keefe grew increasingly upset at what he believed was his associates' attempt to shortchange him from getting his share of the loot from the Brink's job. While out of prison, he unsuccessfully pressured his buddies in Boston to give him his money, an estimated $100,000. In June 1954, O'Keefe was nearly killed three times in what the FBI considered assassination attempts. Back in prison on January 6, 1956, this time in Massachusetts, an embittered O'Keefe finally decided to talk to the FBI. He said Pino came up with the plan to rob the Brink's building, and recruited him and the others. Five days before the expiration of the statute of limitations, the FBI charged O'Keefe, Pino, Gusciora, and their eight associates with bank robbery and related crimes. A state grand jury later indicted the eleven on similar charges, and they were prosecuted in state court.

Eight of the men were convicted and sentenced to life in prison in October 1956, though they served only about fourteen years[36]—except

McGinnis, who died of a fatal heart attack in prison in Massachusetts at age sixty-three on October 5, 1966. Two of the robbers, Gusciora and Joe Barfield, died of natural causes before trial. O'Keefe pleaded guilty, was the principal witness against his former associates, and had served only four years in prison when he was released in 1960.[37] But true freedom eluded O'Keefe for the rest of his life. One of the key perpetrators in one of the biggest bank robberies in American history never got his share of the loot. And, by arrangement with the FBI, he lived under assumed names in the Midwest and in Los Angeles to avoid gangland retribution.[38] O'Keefe contributed to a book about the Brink's job, but unlike the thief-turned-author Willie Sutton, O'Keefe was never able to cash in on his crime fully in the public marketplace. "I'm tired of not being myself," he told a reporter in 1975, on the twenty-fifth anniversary of the Brink's job. "It's a bitch living under a false name. It would be like coming out of a cave. I want to be Joseph J. O'Keefe."[39] O'Keefe died of natural causes at age sixty-seven on March 24, 1976, at a hospital in Los Angeles. He had been a driver for the movie star Cary Grant.[40]

Investigators recovered only about $58,000 of the $1,218,211.29 in cash stolen in the Brink's robbery, with about $52,000 of that found inside a wall of a Boston office building in 1956.[41] The undiscovered loot—a theme in notable bank robberies dating to the time of Jesse James—made the heist even more intriguing, and Hollywood saw the merits of the unprecedented character-driven tale. The best-known depiction was 1978's *The Brink's Job*, a comedy directed by William Friedkin (*The French Connection* and *The Exorcist*), starring Peter Falk as Anthony Pino and Warren Oates as Specs O'Keefe. The tagline on the movie poster was accurate, at least with regard to the once-in-a-lifetime nature of the heist: "The robbery nobody thought could happen by the guys nobody thought could pull it off."[42] From the very start, of course, the FBI and the police had suspected Pino, O'Keefe, and their buddies.

Two of the robbers, Thomas "Sandy" Richardson and John "Jazz" Maffie, were consultants on *The Brink's Job* movie, which was shot in Boston in 1978, and were sources for *Big Stick-Up at Brink's!*, the 1977 book on which the film was based. Richardson, who was seventy-one in 1978, said on the movie set that the eleven robbers split the $1.2 million in stolen cash, and that "I spent mine pretty quickly. I really don't know where it went, it just went."[43] Maffie, then sixty-seven years old, said he gambled away his $100,000. Richardson said he decided to work on the

movie for the money—"as compensation for the non-paying years"[44]—
and his attitude about the real Brink's job was wistful. He saw it as one of
those crimes no one tried anymore. "At least no one got hurt," Richardson
said. "These days, with all these drug users and violent crimes, it's ter-
rible."[45]

The making of the movie seemed to imitate life. One afternoon two
masked men broke into the cutting room in Boston and stole what they
thought was the print of *The Brink's Job*. They demanded a $1,000,000
ransom from Friedkin for the return of the print, but they never got the
money (and they were never charged, either). The stolen film turned out
to be the working print, not the final print, so the thieves' loot was
worthless. As Friedkin recalled, the theft of a print of a movie about an
enormous robbery was an irresistible story, and was in the news for days.
"The film was stolen for ransom!"[46]

Gerhard Arthur Puff's notoriety stems not from a film, but from his
appearance in a unique area of American jurisprudence—the place where
bank robbery involves murder and capital punishment. Puff was executed
in connection with the robbery of more than $62,000 from a bank in
Kansas in 1951. When he was on the lam in New York City, he murdered
an FBI agent who was searching for him.

The Federal Bank Robbery Act of 1934 provided for the death penalty
when a homicide occurred during the robbery or attempted robbery of a
bank or other financial institution with federal deposits or federally insured deposits—a provision that remains in effect today.[47] The first person executed under the Federal Bank Robbery Act was Anthony Chebatoris, a thirty-eight-year-old ex-convict who killed a truck driver during an
attempted armed robbery of the Chemical State Savings Bank in Midland,
Michigan, on September 29, 1937. Chebatoris shot the truck driver, Henry Porter, after mistaking him for a police officer, and Porter died twelve
days later. Chebatoris was found guilty in federal court, sentenced to die,
and hanged at a federal prison farm in Milan, Michigan, on July 8, 1938.
His execution occurred though Michigan had become the first state to
outlaw capital punishment, in 1846. The governor of Michigan in 1938,
Frank Murphy, unsuccessfully appealed to President Roosevelt to move
the execution to another state.[48]

Gerhard Arthur Puff was the last inmate executed under federal law in New York state, and he was the first person to be sentenced to die for killing an FBI agent in metropolitan New York. He fatally shot Special Agent Joseph J. Brock, forty-four years old, during a gun battle at the Congress Hotel, in Manhattan, on July 26, 1952. Puff unsuccessfully argued self-defense in a case that made him, at one time, one of the FBI's most wanted fugitives.[49] He had fled after he and his accomplice, George Arthur Heroux, held up the Johnson County National Bank and Trust Company of Prairie Village, Kansas, south of Kansas City, on October 25, 1951. Heroux and Puff got into the bank at about five minutes after eight in the morning by forcing an employee to open the door. One stood over the employees in the reception room while the other forced the cashier to open the vault. The two robbers wore coveralls and hunting caps with upturned earmuffs. They got away in a stolen car. No one was hurt.[50]

The bank robbery and the subsequent murder seemed inevitable for Puff, a German immigrant whose first conviction, for disorderly conduct, came when he was twenty years old and living with his family in Milwaukee, Wisconsin, in 1934. He was later convicted of stealing domestic animals, as well as assault of a prison guard, armed robbery, and escape. Puff was awaiting prosecution for another armed robbery when he got out of the Milwaukee County Jail on October 17, 1951, after "an unknown party, acting through a Chicago bondsman, posted $3,000 cash bail" for his release.[51] Eight days later, he and Heroux, who had been Puff's cellmate in prison, robbed the bank in Prairie Village, Kansas. Puff was not unemployable. The FBI reported that, when he was not in prison, he worked as a truck driver, farmhand, machinist, and printer. But Puff liked expensive cars and expensive clothes, and he liked to gamble. His penchant for crime and his need for money gave him reasons to be a bank robber.

Puff turned into a killer as he tried to stay out of prison. The FBI got a break in their search for the thirty-eight-year-old Puff on July 25, 1952, when agents found Heroux (who was also on the Bureau's list of Ten Most Wanted) in Miami, Florida. A tip from Heroux led the agents north, to the Congress Hotel in New York, where Brock and others set up surveillance on one of the lodgers in Room 904. Brock was stationed near a first-floor stairway when he confronted Puff, who shot Brock five times, including twice in the chest, and took his gun. Holding Brock's gun, and a gun of his own, Puff fired at other FBI agents as he ran through the hotel lobby. Outside, Puff continued shooting until agents, stationed behind parked cars, returned fire and hit him in the right leg.[52] Puff's slaying of Brock was "premeditated and wanton," U.S. Attorney J. Edward Lumbard told jurors in Puff's trial in U.S. District Court for the Southern District of New York. On May 15, 1953, Puff was convicted of first-degree murder and sentenced to die.[53] Heroux, in a separate case, was sentenced to forty years for bank robbery.

Gerhard Arthur Puff was executed in the electric chair at Sing Sing on August 12, 1954. Puff was forty years old and had spent nearly fifteen months on death row. "Known in Sing Sing as 'the lonely prisoner,'" the *New York Times* reported, "Puff never had a visitor during his long wait in the death house."[54]

The death of another bank robber in the 1950s was equally lonely, but also mysterious. The skeletal remains of Frederick Grant Dunn, a thief likened to Dillinger, were found in a farmer's field near the central Kansas town of Ellsworth on September 8, 1959. Dunn, fifty-three or fifty-four years old, had been on the run from the police and the FBI for about a year. He had been last seen fleeing a movie theater in Ellsworth, where he was an escapee from the jail in Lincoln County, to the north. The FBI had named him to its Ten Most Wanted list on June 17, 1958.

The discovery of Dunn's skull and other bones came as a relief to FBI Special Agent Mark Felt, who had been assigned to lead the investigation to find him. Felt—who would go on to be Deep Throat, the *Washington Post*'s inside source during the Watergate scandal of the early 1970s—had been feeling pressure from J. Edgar Hoover and his other superiors in Washington, D.C., to make Dunn's the latest name to disappear from the ranks of the Ten Most Wanted.[55] As Felt recalled, "Hoover expected the special agent in charge to become personally involved in Top 10 cases. He also expected favorable results within a reasonable period. But this time I could not produce. The case was making a mockery of the Top 10 program and, by association, me."[56]

While Dunn was eluding the FBI, his image was staring back at customers at post offices nationwide, in his FBI Most Wanted poster. He was shown as well groomed and wearing a trench coat, much like a businessman, but the FBI warned the public not to be fooled. The poster declared, "CAUTION: DUNN IS KNOWN TO HAVE CARRIED FIREARMS. HE REPORTEDLY HAS A VICIOUS TEMPER AND SHOULD BE CONSIDERED EXTREMELY DANGEROUS."[57]

Dunn had been worthy of watching well before the FBI got involved. He had held jobs as a shoemaker, railroad shop worker, and salesman, but spent the most time as a criminal. Born May 13, 1905, in Sioux City, Iowa, at nineteen years old, he was charged with breaking into a jewelry store in Yankton, South Dakota. He was paroled three years later and robbed a bank in Slater, Iowa. After getting released from that sentence, he robbed a bank in Sioux City, for which he received a life sentence. Dunn got an additional thirty years for breaking out of the jail in Sioux City and shooting a deputy sheriff. Authorities recaptured him the same day. The governor of Iowa, Clyde L. Herring, commuted Dunn's life sentence to forty years in 1933, and he was paroled on June 9, 1941, when he was thirty-seven years old. Felt credited Dunn's good record in prison and his "fastidious personal habits"—he always carried a red comb and a green toothbrush in prison—as helping him win parole.[58] "Prisoners who are well groomed and well behaved have a greater chance of striking parole boards as 'rehabilitated,'" Felt recalled.[59]

Dunn was on parole when he carried out what the authorities considered his most alarming bank robbery. He and two accomplices—Jimmy Hamilton, who had recently escaped from prison, and Eddie Anderson, a newly released inmate—robbed the First State Bank of Portis, Kansas, of $2,900 on July 2, 1941. After the bank cashier fired at them and injured at least one of the three, the trio fled in a stolen car and drove to an abandoned farmhouse, where two women with two other cars were waiting for them.[60] Less than two weeks earlier, on June 21, 1942, Dunn and Anderson were suspected of severely beating a man and robbing him of $1,100 in LeMars, Iowa. And three days after that, on June 23, 1942, Dunn and Anderson were suspected of helping Hamilton escape from a prison farm at Clarinda, Iowa.[61] The trio's crimes caused police officers in Iowa to fear the worst as they sought help from the police in other states, including Minnesota, to find Dunn, Anderson, and Hamilton after the robbery of the bank in Portis. "The members of this mob, are all bad and I believe, unless soon apprehended, will put John Dillinger to shame," the chief of the Iowa Bureau of Investigation, R. W. Nebergall, wrote to his counterpart in Minnesota on July 13, 1942.[62]

Nine days later, in Denver, Colorado, the FBI captured Dunn, Anderson, Hamilton, and the two women who helped them get away after the bank robbery in Portis. Dunn was convicted and got a fifteen-year sentence at the federal penitentiary at Leavenworth, Kansas, but was released in 1952 and—after going back to prison for violating his parole—again in 1957. "We just couldn't hold this guy," Felt recalled, "and he just wouldn't give up."[63] Dunn went back to work in 1958, when he was arrested for robbing a grocery store near Russell, Kansas, and was placed in the jail in Lincoln County. He escaped in a stolen pickup truck and drove to Ellsworth, Kansas, where he was last seen buying a sixty-cent ticket at a movie theater with a $100 bill. A suspicious clerk called the police, and a patrolman fired at Dunn before he fled into a snowstorm.[64]

Dunn was never again seen alive. How he got to the farmer's field, where his remains were discovered about a year later, is unknown. The FBI verified Dunn's identity by using dental records and other evidence, including a red comb and green toothbrush found with Dunn's skull and other bones.[65] The FBI closed Dunn's case on September 25, 1959.[66]

Another would-be Dillinger was finished, though other bank robbers throughout the United States would continue to strike—in what soon became increasing numbers.

7

COUNTERCULTURAL CHAOS

Clean-Cut Killers, Patty Hearst, and a *Dog Day Afternoon*

No bank robber had ever put on a performance like this. As many as 3,000 spectators, as well as more than 150 police officers and numerous federal agents and reporters, were looking at a twenty-seven-year-old, bisexual, Vietnam War veteran named John Stanley Wojtowicz (pronounced WAHT-a-Witz). He was negotiating with police outside the Chase Manhattan Bank branch on Avenue P and East Third Street, in the Flatbush section of Brooklyn, New York. Wojtowicz had just used a rifle to hold up the place with the help of an eighteen-year-old sidekick. The temperatures on this Tuesday afternoon—around three o'clock, or closing time, on August 22, 1972—reached the nineties, and Wojtowicz, with his mop of thick brown hair, was sweating in his white V-neck T-shirt.[1] The crowd cheered him on.

Wojtowicz, a former teller at another Chase Manhattan Bank branch, was an amateur bank robber, but one with a mission: He wanted to knock off this bank to get money to pay the $3,000 needed for a sex-change operation for the man he had married in a nonlegal ceremony several months earlier. Wojtowicz described the man as his wife—Ernest Aron, later Elizabeth D. Eden, who was being hospitalized as a mental patient for trying to commit suicide. The bank manager, Robert J. Barrett, had secretly tipped off his superiors about the heist in a phone call. Now Wojtowicz and his accomplice, Salvatore Natuarale, also armed, had to deal with Barrett and eight other hostages and the prospect of a difficult, if not impossible, getaway. Wojtowicz appeared to be stuck, and he let his larger audience—the whole of New York City—know of his frustration.

"Well, we're holding up a bank and we were on our way out when a stupid cop car pulled up," Wojtowicz told a reporter for WCBS in a telephone interview.[2]

Fourteen hours later, Natuarale would be dead, and Wojtowicz, known as "Little John," would surrender without a fight. This strange holdup eventually would inspire the 1975 crime movie *Dog Day Afternoon*, in which Al Pacino portrayed Sonny Wortzik, based on Wojtowicz. "Desperation that has turned seriously lunatic" is how one movie reviewer described the botched bank robbery and related events.[3]

The same description fit other bank robberies in the 1960s and 1970s, decades in which American society—at least the postwar society of the 1950s—seemed, for many, in turmoil and sliding toward lunacy. Unlikely candidates for banditry—a former college football captain, a newspaper heiress, a young New Yorker trying to cope with his sexual identity on a scorching mid-August afternoon—robbed banks in often celebrated fashion. And in other instances, the transformation was the other way around. One bank robber who seemed destined for permanent incarceration became a published author of crime fiction once he finally got out.

No matter what the fate of the thieves, some bank robberies in the 1960s and 1970s mirrored the times. They were heists with a cause, not heists solely for the cash. Bank robberies in the 1960s and 1970s reflected more general changes in America as well. As suburbanization created sprawl throughout the nation, the number of banks grew, to 30,958 in 1965, from 21,676 in 1955, and 18,881 in 1945.[4] The number of bank robberies increased, too. The FBI reported 89 bank robberies in 1950, followed by the 103 in 1951, 335 in 1955, 436 in 1960, 1,143 in 1965, and 2,040 in 1970.[5]

With the rise in robberies came a jump in the size of the loot: "Bank losses more than doubled between 1961 and 1966, climbing from $2 million to $4.8 million, then came close to doubling again in a single year, skyrocketing to $8.7 million in 1967."[6] The surge in bank robberies made them more commonplace for the public, with exceptions. A slaying or other violence during a heist remained rare, so that, as of 1966, "increasingly, it [was] taking the bloody and the bizarre to make bank robberies news."[7]

The characteristics of suburbia contributed to the rise in the number of bank robberies in the 1960s. So did the nature of the new banks that opened in the suburbs. While the banks of the eastern cities and Old West relied on their downtown locations as a security measure, the banks of the suburbs had no such protection. According to one analysis from 1967,

> The very nature of the location of these branches makes them more vulnerable to attack. Suburbia is relatively uncrowded, there is less police protection, and escape routes are generally more accessible and better concealed. Suburban informality has left its mark on bank architecture, making the temptation for the robber even more tantalizing. Generally the new branches have few security features and lack the structural safeguards of downtown banks. The extensive use of glass makes them look light, open, and inviting. Most of them have low, open service counters and drive-in teller windows.[8]

Bank robbery in the 1960s and 1970s was a product of conformity— the homogenization of America that the suburbs helped create. In some instances, bank robbery also was a product of the nonconformity and individuality that came to be trademarks of the two decades.

Once he got out of federal prison on parole, in 1976, Albert Frederick Nussbaum started writing crime fiction, including thrillers. He had plenty of experience. Nussbaum, born in Buffalo, New York, on April 9, 1934, had been sentenced to forty years in prison in February 1964. He had been convicted of being an accomplice in a bank robbery in which a security guard was shot to death in the theft of about $35,000 from the Lafayette National Bank, in Brooklyn on December 15, 1961.[9] Nussbaum was twenty-seven years old. His partner was a thirty-two-year-old named Bobby R. "Bad Eye" Wilcoxson, who got his nickname from his artificial eye. Wilcoxson had fired the Thompson submachine gun that had killed the bank guard, Henry Kraus. Nussbaum and Wilcoxson had met in early 1960, when they were inmates at a prison in Ohio. After the murder of Kraus, the two were placed on the FBI's Ten Most Wanted list. One of their bank robberies, in Washington, D.C., involved a bombing.

Nussbaum had turned to crime long before he met Wilcoxson. He was one of three children born into a stable family in Buffalo, and possessed an intellect strong enough that he worked as a locksmith, gunsmith, airplane mechanic, and pilot.[10] Guns fascinated Nussbaum, and when he was seventeen, carrying a loaded .32-caliber revolver, he was arrested for robbing a jewelry store in Buffalo. He was still in high school and got probation. He went into the army and for a time settled in California, where he was arrested on charges including possession of a machine gun. After he left California, where he again got probation, he found his way to a prison in Chillicothe, Ohio, where he and Wilcoxson bonded. Nussbaum was serving a five-year sentence for transporting a Thompson submachine gun; Wilcoxson was serving eighteen months for transporting a stolen car across state lines.[11]

The two were an unusual pair. Nussbaum looked like a family man or a salesman; Wilcoxson had a rough appearance, mainly because of his artificial eye. The two men, according to the FBI, "were a study in contrasts."[12] The intelligent Nussbaum read books on crime, electronics, and explosives, and used the money from the bank robberies to create businesses. He was "the brains," the FBI said, while Wilcoxson was "the brawn," providing the muscle and handling the weapons during the bank robberies.[13] Nussbaum, in one writer's account, "was the Executive Suite variety of bank robber. He was an avid bibliophile who had taken courses in rapid reading in order to accelerate his campaign of 'self-education.' . . . He liked to describe himself as a 'long-range thinker'; he was cautious and meticulous about details."[14]

In December 1960, the odd couple carried out the first of their eight bank robberies in Buffalo, where Nussbaum was living with his wife of six months. Wilcoxson used a sawed-off shotgun the FBI said Nussbaum hid in Wilcoxson's winter coat "by drilling a hole in the barrel and tying it around Wilcoxson's shoulder with a shoelace."[15] By some estimates, Nussbaum and Wilcoxson would net $100,000 robbing banks in Buffalo, and about $250,000 overall. Nussbaum and his young family—he and his wife would have a daughter—lived modestly off the earnings, the source of which his wife said she didn't know.[16] Nussbaum hoped the proceeds from the bank robberies would boost the finances of his legitimate business, the Unique Service Company, which specialized in small radios, walkie-talkies, and other electronics. "Knocking off banks is wrong," Nussbaum is reported to have said to his buddy Bobby Wilcoxson. "But how can I go straight unless I can lay my hands on some dough?"[17]

Nussbaum's wife, Alicia, was home alone regularly in Buffalo while her husband and Wilcoxson traveled and robbed banks. In a show of "Nussbaum's modernity," he often flew his own Navion airplane.[18] Nussbaum and Wilcoxson incorporated Nussbaum's homemade bombs into their routine in June 1961, when they targeted the branch of the Bank of Commerce near the army's Walter Reed Hospital in Washington, D.C. Nussbaum theorized that a bomb would act as a decoy for them to throw off the police and rob the bank swiftly.[19] Their two test runs terrorized the nation's capital: The first pipe bomb blew up a trash can near the White House on the night of June 15, 1961. The second bomb exploded in a telephone booth at Fifteenth Street and Massachusetts Avenue, about seven blocks north of the White House, at fifteen minutes after eight the next morning, as commuters rushed by. Nussbaum and Wilcoxson were ready for the real event on June 30. As they prepared to rob the Bank of Commerce, they placed their third pipe bomb on a stairway of a nearby building. It didn't go off. Nussbaum and Wilcoxson, who carried the Tommy gun, robbed the bank anyway. They got $19,682, rather than what they thought would be $50,000.[20]

Six months later, they were in New York City, where they robbed the bank in Brooklyn—their fifth heist—with a third man, Peter Columbus Curry Jr., whom Nussbaum also had met in prison. The holdup took about ninety seconds. It started at about a half past nine in the morning, around opening time, when twelve patrons were on line inside the bank. Nussbaum waited outside the bank in a station wagon as his partners went to work. Curry entered through a side door and, carrying a revolver and with another in his belt, vaulted the teller's counter, and ordered everyone to drop to the floor.[21] The robber later identified as Wilcoxson "burst through the main entrance"[22] with a Thompson submachine in his overcoat and two hand grenades and a pistol in his pockets.[23] He demanded quiet. A customer escaped, giving Kraus, the bank guard, a chance to reach for his gun. Wilcoxson had reason to be worried. He and Nussbaum, while planning the robbery, had become acquaintances with Kraus, who was known as "Wyatt Earp" for his boast that he would shoot any robbers of his bank.[24] Wilcoxson shot Kraus four times in the chest.

Wilcoxson acted with menace. "The machinegunner, who was wearing a trenchcoat in a capelike fashion over his right shoulder, moved farther into the bank," the *New York Times* reported on its front page, "and trained his gun on the customers and employes [*sic*] on the floor while his accomplice swept packages of bills into a canvas bag."[25] The heist featured heroism. A police patrolman, Salvatore Accardi, who had been on foot patrol, rushed into the bank and fired a single shot at Wilcoxson, who fired back. Accardi was wounded and would have died, had not one of the bullets "struck his shield and embedded itself in his overcoat."[26] In their haste, the robbers forgot $10,000, but they left an indelible impression with the FBI. Kraus, the bureau said, had been shot "in cold blood"[27] and died on the floor of the bank. Curry, Nussbaum, and Wilcoxson got into their getaway cars and fled.

The FBI's manhunt focused on Buffalo, where Nussbaum had returned. The tip to look there came from Curry, who was arrested in Brooklyn two weeks after the fatal bank robbery. The FBI found a cache of weapons, including a bazooka, antitank guns, and machine guns that Nussbaum and Wilcoxson had hidden in a barn outside Buffalo. The pair committed three more bank robberies—one in Pittsburgh and two in Philadelphia—before the FBI caught them. The FBI got the lead for Nussbaum's arrest from his mother-in-law.

Nussbaum met with his wife in Buffalo on the night of November 3, 1962, and unsuccessfully tried to persuade her to flee to South America with him and their young daughter.[28] When Alicia Nussbaum got home, FBI agents were waiting; her mother, worried, had called them. Alicia Nussbaum had agreed to meet her husband again later that night—now November 4, 1962—at the Statler Hilton in downtown Buffalo. The FBI followed her there, and arrested Nussbaum after a car chase in which the speeds reached one hundred miles per hour. Agents captured Wilcoxson six days later in Baltimore, where he had been living with his girlfriend and their young daughter. "Without firing a shot," according to one account, "the FBI had taken into custody the most dangerous and best-armed hoodlums since the gangster era of the Thirties."[29] By the time the two one-time partners were convicted and sentenced to prison (Wilcoxson got life, as did Curry), Nussbaum and Wilcoxson were, according to the FBI, "bitter enemies,"[30] with a dispute over money having fueled their rancor.

Albert Nussbaum aspired to be a writer long before he was incarcerated. While on the lam in the fall of 1962, he used the pseudonym Carl Fischer and made a call from Philadelphia to Dan J. Marlowe, an author he admired. Marlowe had achieved success with a crime novel about a bank robber, *The Name of the Game Is Death*, published in 1962. The phone call was the start of a lifelong friendship, which Nussbaum further cultivated when he left prison in 1976 and moved to California to work as a writer. Marlowe was one of his mentors.[31] Nussbaum, who died in 1996 at age sixty-one, was prolific, with his primary focus on crime and adventure stories. He also wrote essays, criticism, reviews, and television scripts, and published short stories in periodicals such as Alfred Hitchcock's *Mystery Magazine*. Nussbaum sometimes wrote under pseudonyms because he had so many pieces in one issue of a given publication.[32] Other periodicals that carried his work included *The American Scholar* and *Women's World*.

As a bank robber, Albert Nussbaum used disguises and fake names because he was on the other side of the law and on the run. As an author, he disguised his true identity because he was so successful in his new profession. "I do a lot of traveling by car," Nussbaum wrote in one of his short stories, "Collision," published in *Mystery Magazine* in March 1974. "In fact, since the airlines began searching passengers and their luggage, that's the only way I travel. I have secrets and I want to keep them."[33]

Duane Earl Pope appeared to be set for a job in May 1965, when he graduated from McPherson College, in central Kansas, with a degree in industrial arts. Pope, born on February 8, 1943, in the prairie village of Roxbury, Kansas, was the twenty-two-year-old son of a wheat farmer; he was the fourth of eight children, and the first of them to go to college. Pope attended McPherson College on a football scholarship and was a captain of the Bulldogs football team; known as "Poper," he made allconference at defensive end. His time in college resembled how he had spent high school, where, though shy, he played football, basketball, and baseball; ran track; sang in the glee club; and was president of the senior class at Roxbury High School. Twenty-five miles away from Roxbury was the six-hundred-student McPherson College, a career-oriented liberal arts school founded in 1887 and affiliated with a Protestant sect, the Church of the Brethren.[34] Once he graduated from college, Pope could marry his fiancée, Melinda, and return to Roxbury to work on his family farm or to coach or teach. He could easily make enough money to pay off his debts of $1,300.[35]

Based on his past, Pope's life after college would be quiet and reserved. Why would it be otherwise? Even Pope's college football coach had to prod him to be more aggressive, to hit harder. "I never saw him mad," the coach, Sid Smith, recalled. "He used to hit a guy with a block in practice and then grab him to keep him from falling. The only emotion he ever showed was this shy little grin. He kept things pretty much to himself."[36]

Five days after he graduated from college, Duane Pope committed what a spokesman for the American Bankers Association called "the bloodiest" bank robbery in modern times.[37] At eleven in the morning on June 4, 1965, after driving to Nebraska, he walked into the family-owned Farmers State Bank in Big Springs, an unincorporated town of about five hundred people in Deuel County, in the Nebraska panhandle, about four hundred miles northwest of Roxbury. Pope wore a sport coat, white shirt, and striped tie. Under his clothes was a breastplate fashioned from a bulldozer blade.[38] At six feet, two inches tall, and weighing 185 pounds, he looked like an imposing but clean-shaven salesman in a bank where the typical customers were farmers who wore blue jeans and other work clothes. Pope carried a briefcase; inside was a Ruger automatic pistol he had purchased a week earlier and a silencer he had made at McPherson College's industrial arts building.

The bank was empty of customers. Pope approached the president of the bank, seventy-seven-year-old Andreas "Andy" Kjeldgaard, and asked him about a loan. As Kjeldgaard started to help him, Pope walked around the counter, pulled out the Ruger, and ordered Kjeldgaard to take money from the cash drawer and put it in his briefcase. Kjeldgaard and his twenty-five-year-old nephew, Franklin Kjeldgaard, an assistant cashier, complied, as did another employee, thirty-five-year-old bookkeeper Lois Ann Hothan, whom Pope told to get money from the vault. Hothan returned only with a handful of one-dollar bills; a time lock was keeping the vault shut. Pope had $1,598 in cash—enough to pay his debts, but a small amount for a bank robbery. He was upset. "Lady," he said to Hothan, "don't play games with me."[39]

A clean getaway was likely. Pope faced little resistance. But he ordered the Kjeldgaards, Hothan, and the fourth bank employee, Glenn Hendrickson, a fifty-nine-year-old cashier, to lie down on the floor, face down. Starting with Andreas Kjeldgaard, he shot each of the four in the base of the head and the back. Only Frank Kjeldgaard survived, but was paralyzed. He sounded the bank alarm. Pope calmly walked out of the bank and toward his rental car. He passed a seventy-four-year-old wheat farmer, Otto Mauser, who was on his way in. Pope nodded. "Good morning," he told Mauser.[40]

Pope fled, though his close connection to his alma mater eventually drew him back home, and to the police and the FBI. He briefly visited his parents' house, where he left a note, and then traveled to San Diego; Tijuana, Mexico, where he watched a bullfight[41]; and Las Vegas, where he gambled. The FBI had placed him on the list of Ten Most Wanted; the poster highlighted the strangeness of the case. A photograph of a smiling Pope, his face angular and handsome, appeared under the headline that declared him a fugitive.

While Pope was on the lam, the president of McPherson College, Dr. Desmond Bittinger, appealed to him to surrender. "We would like you to know that we, your friends at McPherson, both faculty and students, continue to be your friends," Bittinger said in a statement released to the press on June 10, 1965. "We suggest and urge that you give yourself up to the proper police authorities at once."[42] Pope telephoned Bittinger and told him he was tired of running. "I heard your plea, Doctor, for me to give myself up and I decided this is the thing to do," Pope said. "I am going to turn myself in."[43] On June 11, Pope took a plane to Kansas City, Missouri, checked into a downtown hotel, and called police. As he left the hotel in a squad car, he cried.

Pope confessed to robbing the bank and killing Andreas Kjeldgaard, Hendrickson, and Hothan. He had no way out. Witnesses had seen him leave the bank in a 1965, light green Chevrolet Impala, whose plates authorities traced to a car rental agency in Salinas, Kansas. Pope had signed his own name to the rental papers on June 3, 1965, the day before he robbed the bank. During the robbery, Frank Kjeldgaard, the lone survivor, never lost consciousness and, seated in a wheelchair, testified against Pope at trial. The way Pope robbed the bank—wearing conspicuous clothing, doing nothing to disguise his identity—was so amateurish as to suggest that maybe he wanted to get caught or did not care. "He did everything wrong," recalled the Deuel County attorney, Robert E. Richards. "Picking the bank with a time lock. Wearing those clothes. Advertising his own name. Not wearing a mask. And killing to wipe out the witnesses. Killing is the last thing a pro wants to do."[44]

Why Duane Earl Pope robbed the Farmers State Bank and slaughtered three people remains a mystery. Pope told investigators he pulled off the heist because he was in debt and wanted to get married. At his federal trial, in U.S. District Court in Lincoln, Nebraska, in November 1965, U.S. Attorney Theodore L. Richling presented evidence that Pope had thought about robbing the bank a year earlier, in 1964, when he was in Big Springs working during the harvest season and asked a friend if the bank had ever been held up. Pope, the government contended, showed no signs of mental infirmity or mental illness, but had "a compulsion to kill, nurtured by long-repressed hostilities."[45] The defense team, which included Robert B. Crosby, a former governor of Nebraska, argued that Pope was temporarily insane and "overtaken by mental illness,"[46] such as schizophrenia.

On December 3, 1965, the jury convicted Pope of all the charges against him, six counts related to bank robbery. Because murder alone is not a federal crime, Pope (as were Nussbaum and Wilcoxson) was convicted of a bank robbery involving a murder. Pope twice was sentenced to die in the electric chair: once as the result of the verdict in federal court, and again, in January 1970, when he was convicted in a state court in Nebraska. Both death sentences were overturned on appeal. Pope, who was seventy-one in 2014, is serving a life sentence at the federal penitentiary at Leavenworth, Kansas.

The triple murder and bank robbery in Big Springs has become no less baffling over time. Abuse Pope suffered as a boy, from a stern father, might have caused him eventually to lose control, said one author, Noel Grove, who covered the slayings as a young reporter for the *Hutchinson News*, in Kansas. Grove, who wrote a 2008 book on Pope's case, also believes a head injury Pope suffered as a young child affected his judgment as an adult.[47] In many respects, what others said about Pope's case in 1965 remains accurate today. No one really knows why the quiet, former college football star launched "a Horatio Alger story with a sick ending"[48] when he turned into a bank robber and a killer. "A week ago Sunday night he stood on the platform and I gave him his diploma," Merlin E. Frantz, the dean of academic affairs at McPherson College, said of Pope six days after the bank robbery at Big Springs. "How, in three or four days, can he go from a fine gentleman to a murderer? Something had to slip a cog somewhere."[49]

Jesse James rode again on April 15, 1974, when a group of armed thieves held up the Hibernia Bank branch at 1450 Noriega Street in San Francisco. One of the robbers was a twenty-year-old who went by the name "Tania," though until two months earlier she was known by her given name: Patricia Campbell Hearst, heir to a newspaper fortune. The spirit of Jesse James imbued the bank robbery because this was a heist that was about more than money. As the James brothers did when they held up the Clay County Savings Association in February 1866, Hearst and four of her fellow gang members targeted the Hibernia Bank not so much for the riches it held, but for what it represented. Hearst's group, the radical, leftist Symbionese Liberation Army (SLA), wanted to create revolution, and robbing a bank was one way the SLA could prove its control over the American system it wanted to overthrow. The robbery, during which Hearst carried a sawed-off M1 carbine assault rifle slung over her shoulder with a strap, netted about $10,000.

The haul from the heist was immeasurable for Patty Hearst, whom the SLA kidnapped on February 4, 1974. Fifty-nine days before the robbery she had embraced the SLA and adopted the name Tania, after a comrade who fought alongside the revolutionary Che Guevara in Bolivia.[50] "The spoils of war from the Hibernia Bank operation included much more than the money taken from the bank," Hearst recalled, in a tone made arch by hindsight.

> It was the victory itself, the successful blow against the capitalist system. In the aftermath, the SLA soldiers were gripped by an irrepressible exhilaration as they recounted their battlefield exploits. The sense of self-satisfaction and self-importance was unmistakable. The bagful of green bills, spread out on the floor in front of us, was treated rather casually as merely a business transaction. Expropriations were a necessity of life in the course of a revolution.[51]

The SLA's robbery of the Hibernia Bank, with Hearst in tow, captured and contributed to the tumult of the early 1970s. The Vietnam War, Watergate, and an energy crisis had wrenched a nation still reeling from the youth movement and antiwar furor of the 1960s. Patty Hearst clutching that rifle—an image caught on surveillance cameras and broadcast across a stunned nation—confirmed that the old order had faded and that nothing in America was sacred or secure. Just months earlier, Hearst, whose grandfather was billionaire publisher William Randolph Hearst and whose father was Randolph A. Hearst, a scion to the family fortune, was a little-known art history major at the University of California at Berkeley. When she entered the Hibernia Bank as Tania, Hearst had changed, as the United States had changed. A member of America's high society was now a bandit. A bank—a repository of money, of which her family had plenty—was her victim.

Patricia Campbell Hearst was born February 24, 1954, in San Francisco, home of her grandfather's flagship newspaper, the *Examiner*. She grew up among great wealth, a child who was welcome at the Hearst Castle, the landmark at the family ranch in San Simeon. She graduated as a straight-A student from Menlo College, south of San Francisco, and went on to graduate school at Berkeley, a bastion of campus unrest and militant radicalism in the 1960s. Hearst moved in with a fellow graduate student, Steven Weed, whom she met when he was twenty-three and a college graduate, and she was seventeen and in high school. They rented a sunny duplex at No. 4 2603 Benvenue Street in the city of Berkeley, where they got engaged in December 1973, and were to marry in June 1974. Whatever careers they had planned, Hearst would never want for money. "Wouldn't it be lovely," she recalled, "if I could write that we lived happily ever after?"[52]

The leader of the Symbionese Liberation Army, its self-styled "general field marshal," was a felon and prison escapee whose real name was Donald David DeFreeze, but whose new name, Cinque Mtume, or Cin, captured his cause. It was an amalgamation of the name of Joseph Cinque, who led the revolt on the slave ship *Amistad* in 1839, and "mtume," the Swahili word for apostle or disciple.[53] DeFreeze was thirty years old in early 1974, about a year after he founded the SLA, whose name incorporated the word "symbiosis," the biological term that refers to organisms coexisting in a mutually beneficial fashion. The SLA originated with the work of a black inmate organization meant to teach prisoners about political science and black heritage. Under DeFreeze, who was African American, the SLA became an organization aimed at destroying everything Cinque disliked, including racism and monogamy.[54] Using hollow-point bullets tipped with cyanide, members of the SLA in November 6, 1973, assassinated Marcus Foster, the first black superintendent in the history of Oakland, California, who had somehow disappointed De-Freeze. "The SLA had declared war on the United States," Hearst recalled DeFreeze telling her, "and this was a revolution of the poor and oppressed people against fascist Amerikkka."[55] The SLA's motto was "Death to the fascist insect that preys on the life of the people." DeFreeze was the only black member; SLA's other members, who numbered about ten, were white and upper middle class. In the view of the FBI, they were all domestic terrorists.

The SLA kidnapped Patty Hearst from the Berkeley duplex she shared with Steven Weed on February 4, 1974. It was an act of brutal strategy. After two SLA members, Russell Little (known as Osceola by the SLA) and Joe Remiro (Bo), were arrested for the slaying of Foster, the organization sought leverage to negotiate with the authorities for their release. The SLA targeted Hearst as a human bargaining chip after one of their members, as part of her regular job at the University of California at Berkeley, gained access to student records. The kidnapping also occurred months after the announcement of the Hearst-Weed engagement, including their address, had appeared in the newspapers. The kidnapping gave the SLA—a fringe group among the radical left—a platform to espouse its bizarre and violent views. The day of the kidnapping, Cinque sent a communiqué to the media about Hearst's abduction, or what he called a warrant for her arrest. The message described her as a "prisoner of war": "Patricia Campbell Hearst—daughter of Randolph A. Hearst, corporate enemy of the people."[56]

The ransom negotiations with the Hearst family had stalled by the time the SLA decided to achieve its next public relations coup by robbing a bank. Hearst's father had agreed to an SLA demand and had spent $2 million to feed the hungry in the San Francisco Bay area. That was too little for Cinque and his comrades; they wanted $6 million in ransom, an amount the Hearsts said outstripped their means. By then, in one of a series of recorded messages the SLA released to the media, Patty Hearst had announced that she was now "Tania" and a member of the SLA. "I have been given the choice of one: being released in a safe area, or two: joining the forces of the Symbionese Liberation Army and fighting for my freedom and the freedom of all oppressed people," she said in the recording. "I have chosen to stay and fight."[57]

As a soldier under Cinque's command, Hearst would be part of the bank robbery, which he believed would bring in thousands of dollars to help fund the SLA; the group would benefit from the spoils of the same capitalist institution it would prey upon. The SLA never referred to their target as a bank or their plan as a robbery. The heist was an "action," or an "appropriation," or a "combat operation," and the bank was always "the bakery" because "that is where the bread is."[58] The group studied the layouts and locations of banks—"it's the escape routes that are important," Cinque said, according to Hearst[59]—before picking the Sunset District branch of Hibernia Bank, on Noriega Street. The selection resonated with Patty Hearst. Its president was the father of one of Hearst's few close friends, Patricia Tobin, whose family had founded Hibernia Bank in 1859.

The surveillance photo of Patty Hearst inside the Hibernia Bank on April 15, 1974, is as iconic as the picture of John Dillinger smirking with the district attorney and the sheriff at the Crown Point Jail in Indiana. Hearst, wearing a long dark coat and waving her SLA-issued M1 rifle, is seen shouting as she and four of her fellow radicals take over the lobby: DeFreeze, Patricia Michelle Soltysik (known as Zoya by the SLA), Nancy Ling Perry (Fahizah), and Camilla Christine Hall (Gabi). DeFreeze, holding a rifle and a submachine gun, threatened a security guard, Ed Shea. The five SLA members stormed in about twenty minutes to ten in the morning. The other SLA members waited outside, in two cars.

"This is a holdup!" DeFreeze shouted. "The first motherfucker who don't lay down on the floor gets shot in the head."[60] Perry yelled, "SLA, SLA," while Soltysik, as Hearst recalled, vaulted "beautifully" over the counter and kicked at the tellers. Hearst, according to her recollection, shouted, "This is Tania . . . Patricia Hearst."

While waiting for Soltysik, Hearst at one point checked her watch, as if to make sure the heist was going as planned. The robbery took a little more than a minute. Soltysik completed it by jumping back over the counter with a bag of money stuffed under her jacket. Hearst and the other SLA members followed her out the door, and they fled. Outside, apparently in a panic, the gang shot two bystanders, Peter Markoff, fifty-nine years old, and Eugene Brannan, seventy years old, who both survived. Immediately after the robbery the FBI used the bank surveillance photos to identify DeFreeze and the other SLA members as suspects, and within a week issued a wanted poster with their names, including Patricia Campbell Hearst.

The most intriguing aspect of the robbery of the Hibernia Bank was whether its most famous participant was also a willing participant. The FBI first sought Patty Hearst as a material witness to the robbery, and not as a participant, because "there is reason to believe that she may have not been acting under her own free will,"[61] said the U.S. Attorney for the Northern District of California, James L. Browning Jr., who filed bank robbery charges against the others. "There's never been another case in the annals of legal history where the victim of a kidnapping has turned up in the middle of a robbery,"[62] Browning said. The FBI speculated, based on the surveillance photos, that the other members of the SLA had pointed their guns at Hearst during the holdup, and that she was under duress.[63] But Hearst indicated in a postrobbery recorded communiqué, which the SLA released to the media on April 24, 1974, that she knew what she was doing and that she had willingly helped rob the bank. She referred to herself as "Tania," said "my comrades and I expropriated $10,660.02" from the bank, and called the idea of her being brainwashed—her parents' contention—"ridiculous to the point of being beyond belief."[64] She referred to her mother and father as "the pig Hearsts." She called Steven Weed her "ex-fiancé," "a sexist pig," and a "clown," and said she was not coerced into robbing the bank. "I was positioned so that I could hold customers and bank personnel who were on the floor," Hearst said on the audio recording. "My gun was loaded and at no time did any of my comrades intentionally point their guns at me."[65] Said Hearst's father, Randolph A. Hearst, in response, "No matter what she says, we still love her. The girl we've known all her life would not say something like that of her own free will."[66]

In her memoir, published in 1982, Patty Hearst recalled that, before the heist, she had thought the planning of the bank robbery was a dream, "that it could not be really happening."[67] She said she was aware of the public speculation that she had been brainwashed into becoming a member of the SLA, and she said she worried her life would be at risk if

Cinque and the others truly thought that she had been coerced and had not chosen entirely on her own to join them and rob the bank. "And what did I think?" Hearst recalled.

> I was so intent upon convincing Cin and the others of my sincerity, I wished the speculation would end and would not endanger my new-found "freedom." I wanted the SLA to believe in me completely, and to that end I told myself I would accept whatever they told me, and do whatever I had to do to survive. In any event, I had my assignment. I would go into the bank with the others. [68]

The prosecutor at Patty Hearst's trial was James L. Browning Jr., the U.S. attorney who initially charged her only as a material witness, because he believed she might have been forced to help commit the bank robbery. When Heart went on trial, in U.S. District Court in San Francisco, in February 1976, Browning argued that the evidence was indisputable that Hearst participated in the bank robbery of her own free will. He cited, among other information, Hearst's activities in the bank and the testimony of a bank customer, Zigurd Berzins, who said he saw a woman he identified as Hearst scramble on the sidewalk to pick up loose ammunition clips and rounds she and the other robbers had apparently dropped as they entered the bank. "Rarely has so much evidence been available to a jury of a defendant's intent to participate in a bank robbery," Browning said in his closing argument. [69] Hearst's lawyer, the well-known F. Lee Bailey, countered that Hearst helped hold up the bank because she feared for her life if she refused. He said the SLA members physically and sexually abused her, and she was helpless to break free of them, even when she was left alone. "It is a case about dying or surviving—that is all Patricia Campbell Hearst thought about," Bailey said in his closing argument.

By the time of the trial, the SLA had ceased to exist in its original format. DeFreeze and five other members—Soltysik, Hall, Perry, Angela Atwood, and Willie Wolfe—were killed in a televised gunfight with the police in an apartment in the Compton section of Los Angeles on May 17, 1974. The day before, Hearst had unwittingly helped tip off the police that the SLA had migrated to Los Angeles from San Francisco. She had shot up the outside of a sporting goods store in Los Angeles, to distract the authorities from two SLA members, Emily and Bill Harris, who had been suspected of shoplifting inside. The Harrises and Hearst were absent from the apartment during the firefight that killed DeFreeze and the others, and the trio soon became part of a reformed SLA, with Bill Harris as the new general field marshal. The tactics remained the same—urban guerrilla warfare, including bombings and bank robbery. Four SLA members on April 21, 1975, held up the Crocker National Bank in Carmichael, California, near Sacramento. A shotgun blast killed Myrna Opsahl, a forty-two-year-old mother of two who was at the bank to make a deposit for her church.[70] Hearst later said she drove a getaway car.

Hearst continued to stay with the Harrises and other SLA members, and she remained committed to their cause. After conducting surveillance on the Harrises, on September 18, 1975, the FBI arrested them, Hearst, and another SLA member, Wendy Yoshimura, at apartments where they were hiding in the San Francisco area. Inside Hearst's apartment agents found the M1 rifle she used to rob the Hibernia Bank. Hearst also had a gun in her pocket. When asked her occupation when she was booked, she replied, "Urban guerilla."[71] Her apprehension made the cover of *Time* magazine.

The fascination intensified with Hearst's trial. It featured a spectacle of wealth, family tension, and domestic terrorism, while exploring such philosophical and moral questions as under what circumstances fear or duress can justify a crime. The jurors sided with Browning and the government's case and rejected Hearst's defense of coercion—that she was too afraid to flee her kidnappers for the nineteen months she was with the SLA. The defense's explanation resembled the "Stockholm Syndrome," the phenomenon in which a kidnapping victim eventually sympathizes with his or her captors. After a trial that stretched over two months, and at which she invoked the Fifth Amendment during her testimony, Hearst was convicted on March 20, 1976, of armed bank robbery and use of a firearm to commit a felony. On September 24, 1976, Hearst, twenty-two years old, was sentenced to seven years in federal prison—a sentence longer than the typical punishment for a bank robber, and a sentence longer than what Browning requested. U.S. District Court Judge William H. Orrick said he could not overlook the seriousness of Hearst's crimes. "Miss Hearst," he said, "the violent nature of your conduct cannot be condoned. Violence is unacceptable and will not be tolerated."[72]

Browning, who wanted a sentence of six years, asked the judge to consider any penalty as a deterrent to a generation gone out of control. "Rebellious youth who become revolutionaries, for whatever reason, and voluntarily commit criminal acts will be punished," Browning said. Patty Hearst, described as "appearing thinner and more wan than usual," said nothing.[73]

Three days after Hearst was sentenced, Bill and Emily Harris pleaded guilty to kidnapping her, and each served eight years in prison. Nearly seventeen years later, in February 2003, the SLA returned to court. Bill Harris and Emily Harris, who had remarried and was now known as Emily Montague, and two other SLA members, Sara Jane Olson (formerly Kathy Soliah) and Mike Bortin, were sentenced to six to eight years in state prison for the murder of Myrna Opsahl during the 1975 bank robbery of the Crocker National Bank in Carmichael. The four pleaded guilty to second-degree murder; Montague admitted to firing the shotgun that killed Opsahl. Hearst was never prosecuted for that bank robbery. She got immunity in exchange for her testimony at the only trial in the case, which occurred in 1976. It ended with the acquittal of the lone defendant at that time, Stephen Soliah, the brother of Kathy Soliah.

Legally, Patty Hearst can no longer be considered a bank robber. President Jimmy Carter commuted her sentence in the Hibernia Bank case on February 1, 1979, and she was released from prison after serving twenty-two months. President Bill Clinton pardoned Hearst on January 20, 2001, his final day in office. After Hearst left prison, in 1979, she married a former San Francisco police officer, Bernard L. Shaw.[74] He had worked as one of her bodyguards after she was released on bail following her conviction and while she awaited sentencing. Hearst became a mother of two children and, in the years after her release, went on to act in movies and on television. She wrote her memoir, originally called *Every Secret Thing* and later *Patty Hearst: Her Own Story*, made into a 1988 movie, *Patty Hearst*. She dedicated the book to her mother and father.

The book's publication, in 1982, set off extensive news coverage, as the public thirsted for Patty Hearst's version of what was going through her mind when she was in the Symbionese Liberation Army and when she robbed the Hibernia Bank. In an interview that preceded the book's publication, Hearst told Barbara Walters of ABC News that she was too scared to renounce her captors. One of Walters's questions underscored the incongruity of the moment: Patty Hearst was now married and the mother of a six-month old daughter, though once she had been at the center of bank robbery that detractors said illustrated the worst of youth-driven radicalism in the United States. Walters asked Hearst what she would tell her daughter about her bank-robbing past. "I haven't thought about it yet," Hearst replied. "Maybe I won't tell her anything. Maybe I'll just let her find out about it for herself, like sex."[75]

By the time Patty Hearst had released her memoir and gone on her publicity tour, John Stanley Wojtowicz had been out of prison for three years. He was released in 1978, after serving six years of the twenty-year sentence he had received after pleading guilty to one count of armed bank robbery in the spectacle that was the holdup of the Chase Manhattan Bank branch in Brooklyn on August 22, 1972. That heist had ended the following day, at about four in the morning, in a limousine headed to John F. Kennedy International Airport.

As Wojtowicz had demanded, the limousine carried him; his accomplice, Salvatore Natuarale; and seven of the hostages from the bank. Wojtowicz had hoped to get on a plane and fly to Denmark for the sex-change operation for Ernest Aron. An FBI agent was driving the van, as Wojtowicz knew. He did not know that the special agent, James Murphy, had worked out a plan with another special agent, Richard J. Baker, who met the limousine on the tarmac. After Murphy uttered a code—"Will there be food on the plane?"—and Baker answered in the affirmative, Murphy turned and shot Natuarale in the chest, killing him. The FBI arrested Wojtowicz, and the hostages were safe. The FBI recovered the loot: $38,000 in cash and $175,000 in traveler's checks.[76]

The circus-like atmosphere that had surrounded the bank robbery obscured the reality that it could have turned violent. Wojtowicz appeared unhinged, and he was volatile. The hostages would say later that Wojtowicz treated them kindly. Wojtowicz and Natuarale had pizza delivered and tossed $2,000 outside the bank to pay for it; FBI agents descended on the sidewalk to pick up the cash. Wojtowicz stood outside and negotiated with the police. The crowd cheered. Wojtowicz's gay friends arrived at the scene and kissed him. The crowd cheered. Wojtowicz remained defiant. "The Supreme Court will let me get away with this," he said. "There's no death penalty. It's ridiculous. I can shoot everyone here, then throw my gun down and walk out and they can't put me in the electric chair."[77] He told the WCBS reporter that he "was more scared than the hostages—I'm really nervous."[78]

The robbery started as a three-man venture, with the impetus for the crime coming from Wojtowicz's love for a fourth, Ernest Aron. Wojtowicz, who had no criminal record, led the plot, with assistance from Natuarale, who was a petty criminal also known as Donald Matterson, and their twenty-one-year-old friend, Robert A. Westenberg. For inspiration, the three before the robbery went to a theater in Times Square to watch *The Godfather*. That film's conflicted protagonist, the gangster Michael Corleone, was played by Al Pacino, who three years later would play the character modeled after Wojtowicz in *Dog Day Afternoon*.[79] Wojtowicz, Natuarale, and Westenberg then went to Brooklyn, where they entered the branch of the Chase Manhattan Bank and got past the lone security guard, Calvin Jones, who was held hostage for three hours and released. Westenberg got scared and fled when a police car approached the bank.[80] He later pleaded guilty to conspiracy and was sentenced to two years in federal prison.

Aron, though not initially present at the scene, loomed over the entire ordeal. Wojtowicz, who described Aron as a woman trapped in a man's body, said Aron had tried to commit suicide several times because of the inability to afford a sex-change operation. So Wojtowicz, desperate to find the money, and with his personal life in turmoil (he was separated from his legal wife, a woman), robbed the bank. He told WCBS he got the idea for a bank heist "while drinking with a Chase Manhattan executive at a gay bar downtown"[81]—a scenario the bank said was unlikely.[82] Whatever its origin, the bank robbery was a crime of passion for Wojtowicz. "Love is a very strange thing," he told U.S. District Judge Anthony J. Travia at his sentencing on April 23, 1973. "Some people feel it more deeply than others. I loved my wife, Carmen; I love my son, my daughter, my mother; and I love Ernie. Ernie is very, very important to me, and I'd do anything to save him."[83]

The bank robbery failed to save the relationship between Wojtowicz and Aron. Wojtowicz remained alienated from his estranged wife, his new spouse, and society in general. As the newspaper accounts reflected, his sexual orientation made him a misfit. At the time, the gay rights movement was just beginning to emerge and the American Psychiatric Association still classified homosexuality as a mental disorder.[84] "At various times during the evening [of the bank robbery]," the *New York Times* reported, "Mr. Wojtowicz' mother and a Paulist priest who works with homosexual groups were brought to the scene to plead with the gunmen to surrender. They were unsuccessful."[85] Wojtowicz's sense of rejection grew when the police brought Aron to the scene, wearing his hospital coat. Wojtowicz had told police he would release a hostage in exchange for Aron's appearance at the scene of the bank robbery. Upon his arrival, Aron spoke to Wojtowicz in person and over the phone, and told police he wanted nothing to do with him. Aron said he feared Wojtowicz might kill him.[86] Yet even after Aron rebuffed him, Wojtowicz held on to hope that his plan to fund the sex-change operation might work. He got in the limousine with the FBI to go meet a plane he thought was destined to fly him to Denmark.

John Wojtowicz achieved something of his goal in the end. He got $7,500 for the movie rights to his story, and gave $2,500 of it to Aron, who paid for the sex-change operation and became Elizabeth D. Eden. After the procedure, she refused to visit Wojtowicz, who went on to marry, in a nonlegal ceremony, another man, whom he met in prison.[87] Eden died of pneumonia related to AIDS on September 29, 1987.[88] She was forty-one.

Wojtowicz died of cancer at age sixty in 2006. He never stopped identifying himself as the person who held up the bank on that hot August afternoon in a bizarre crime in a turbulent time—the person whose life story became the basis for *Dog Day Afternoon*, an Oscar-winning movie (for best original screenplay), directed by Sidney Lumet, whose *Serpico*, from 1973, also starred Al Pacino and was set in a gritty New York City in the 1960s and early 1970s. Wojtowicz became known as "the Dog" in prison, because fellow inmates mispronounced his name.[89] After he was freed he once applied for a job as a security guard and used *Dog Day Afternoon* as a reference.[90] "When the movie came out, that became the essence of his life," his psychiatrist, Eugene Lowenkopf, said in a 2014 documentary, *The Dog*. "He then became the Dog."[91]

Wojtowicz initially called the film "a piece of garbage" that made him feel "exploited," but he praised Pacino's portrayal of his character as "an unbelievable performance" deserving of the Academy Award for best actor.[92] The one performance that most impressed Wojtowicz, however, was his own. "There was only one star," he recalled, "and that was me."[93]

8

STRIKING BACK, STRIKING BIG

Boosted Bank Security and Record-Breaking Hauls

John Dillinger was long gone on March 31, 1968, when the press reported J. Edgar Hoover's warnings about bank robbery's renewed threat to American society. Hoover was focusing not on a single thief or a gang, but on thousands of thieves. Their crimes had driven up the number of bank robberies in 1967 to a new high of 1,730, compared to 1,164 the year before; when bank burglaries and larcenies were also considered, the figure in 1967 was 2,551 and 1,871 in 1966.[1] Hoover blamed suburbia for the rise, and he targeted the bank robbers. He accused them of being "usually obsessed with the desire for 'easy money' or in desperate need of money," and said they were copycats, "undoubtedly influenced by news of others who have taken the risk and, if not successful, have escaped punishment through legal loopholes or judicial technicalities."[2] But Hoover, writing in a monthly publication of the FBI, also faulted the banks. "In all too many instances," Hoover wrote, "banks have neglected to apply imaginative leadership in thwarting robbery and in safeguarding banking facilities."[3]

As usual, the release of Hoover's remarks was strategic. The next day, the Senate Banking Committee was set to hear testimony from Fred M. Vinson, the U.S. assistant attorney general who headed the Criminal Division at the Department of Justice. Vinson was scheduled to push for a bill to improve bank security—legislation that President Lyndon B. Johnson had called for just two months earlier, in "To Insure the Public Safety," his special message to Congress on crime and law enforcement. "We must bring modern crime detection and protective equipment into our banks," Johnson said on February 7, 1968.

> Robberies of financial institutions have increased continuously in the past decade.
>
> In 1955 there were 526 robberies committed against financial institutions protected by Federal law. In 1966 there were 1,871 such offenses—an increase of about 250%.
>
> Silent alarms and camera systems now exist that can both deter these crimes and aid in investigation and prosecution. Yet many financial institutions have not yet installed them.[4]

The result of Johnson's pressure, Hoover's outcry, and Vinson's testimony was the Bank Protection Act of 1968, which Johnson signed on July 9, 1968. The act required the Federal Reserve, Federal Deposit Insurance Corporation, and other federal agencies to develop rules for federally insured banks and other financial institutions "with respect to the installation, maintenance, and operation of security devices and procedures, reasonable in cost, to discourage robberies, burglaries, and larcenies."[5] The law set a minimum of regulations. The rules required each institution to hire a security officer to develop an antirobbery plan, and they required each institution to establish procedures for opening and closing the building, for keeping all currency safe, for training employees on how to act before and after a bank robbery, for maintaining and operating security devices, and for identifying suspects in bank robberies. Among the required security devices, according to the regulations, were a vault, lighting for the bank at night, and an alarm system.

The safeguards seemed generic and slight, especially in light of media reports that the growing throng of bank robbers was turning to tools worthy of the space age. "They may equip themselves with short-wave radios for monitoring police calls, magnetic drill presses, oxyacetylene torches and radioactive materials (a radium source placed behind a safe while an X-ray plate is held against the combination lock will reveal the lock's tumbler arrangement)," according to one account. Even more worrisome, the account continued, was that "some burglars are said to be searching for lasers small enough to be portable yet strong enough to penetrate vault steel."[6] As for the banks, the same report urged them to adopt high-tech safeguards, such as "supersensitive microphones hidden in vaults [that] can detect the slightest sound or vibration against the outer walls and initially relay an alarm to police."[7]

Though they might have been based more on fantasy, these proposed safeguards, like the Bank Protection Act of 1968, pointed to the reality that many banks were unprepared, especially in small towns. One FBI survey "showed a significant percentage of banking institutions without even the crudest burglar alarms."[8] Some financial executives said the bank robbery threat was overblown because the overall economic loss in such crimes was so small. Others in the banking industry cautioned that an increase in bank robberies was sure to send a bank's insurance premiums higher. "The small expense of equipping institutions with preventative devices is in the long run probably cheaper than increased insurance costs," one commentator wrote.[9]

With no choice but to follow the Bank Protection Act of 1968, banks responded with security advances that continue, in updated forms, today. They include alarms, surveillance systems, bait money—bills that are marked or have their serial numbers cataloged—and dye packs, which are fastened to stacks of bills and explode when the money is handled. Bait money, alarms, dye packs, and electronic surveillance are designed to catch a robber after a heist occurs. Some banks have adopted more proactive measures, meant to prevent bank robberies or to limit the losses from heists. These measures include restricting the amount of cash in a teller's drawer; installing "bandit barriers," or sections of bullet-proof glass between customers and bank employees; and installing what are known as "man catchers" or "man traps"—vestibules, common in Europe but rarely used in the United States, in which bank employees can let customers in one at a time while also scanning them for weapons.[10]

Banks also typically require tellers and other employees to take a passive approach to bank robbers. Rather than resist, tellers are taught to hand over the money and, in some cases, help move the heist along, to get the robber out of the bank as quickly as possible and to avoid any gunfire or other violence. "It's just another financial transaction," according to one industry consultant. "Your job is to help me rob the bank."[11] The presence of armed guards and other high-profile security measures, such as man catchers, would undoubtedly thwart more bank robberies and prevent tellers from being put in such dangerous situations. Over the years, however, many banks have been reluctant to add guards and other protections. Some banks worry that more security measures or resistance from tellers could boost the risk of violence and hostage taking. Others fear creating a fortress-like atmosphere, including the use of bullet-proof glass to shield tellers, will upset bank customers "who value an environment that appears not to need such obvious security devices."[12]

Money is also a factor. Looking at bank robberies from a cost-benefit analysis, banks often consider increases in security of little benefit when compared to the small amounts of money robbers usually steal and the unlikely chance that a bank will get hit multiple times in a year. Most bank losses are insured, which gives banks, for some observers, less reason to spend thousands of dollars on bandit barriers and other security innovations that may never pay for themselves. This comment on the industry from 1966, two years before Congress passed the Bank Protection Act of 1968, has persisted: "Bankers, for all their traditional conservatism, play the odds on security."[13]

Through the years, other patterns have remained. Violence and bloodshed have stayed rare during bank robberies, and the nearly 60 percent clearance rate for bank robbery—which was as high as 80 percent in 1976—puts most thieves in prison.[14] Because most bank robbers work alone and are not professionals, the cases against them are frequently ironclad. When "robbers are arrested, multiple witnesses, surveillance images, and physical evidence contribute to high prosecution and conviction rates."[15] But for all the demands on Capitol Hill in the late 1960s that the banks had to act to reduce bank robbery, the heists continued, for a time. "The United States experienced a dramatic increase in bank robberies between 1965 and 1975, when the number of crimes quadrupled from 847 to 3,517," according to a comprehensive Department of Justice study from 2007. "Despite the enactment of the federal Bank Protection Act of 1968, robberies continued to rise through the early 1990s and the peak of 9,388 in 1991."[16] Then they started their steady decline.

The frequency of bank robberies typically tracks trends for crime in general; when the overall crime rate drops, as it has since the mid-1990s, so does the rate for bank robberies. The rise in Internet financial crimes is another factor behind the decrease in bank robberies, but so are increased security measures (when implemented) and stricter federal sentencing guidelines for bank robbers. Wells Fargo reported that robberies at its banks in Southern California dropped by more than 70 percent after it installed the bullet-proof bandit barriers at more than one hundred banks[17]—a decrease that shows the long-term effects of the Bank Protection Act of 1968. Starting in 1987, new federal sentencing guidelines allowed judges to add more time to a bank robber's sentence because of a prior record or use of a gun during the heist. Serial bank robbers could no longer get caught, serve a short sentence, and get out to rob again. "Once you get caught now, you are going to get hammered," one former FBI agent said of the new laws. [18]

The Bank Protection Act of 1968 and the changes that followed limited bank robberies but did nothing to eliminate heists, including those that were extremely lucrative, extremely violent, or both. Ten years after the act's passage, a thief committed what was then the largest bank theft in the United States—without ever touching the money. His was a crime not of the space age, but of the early information age.

Stanley Mark Rifkin's robbery of $10.2 million from the Security Pacific National Bank in Los Angeles started with his heist of a computer code. Rifkin, a thirty-two-year-old computer consultant who lived in nearby Sepulveda, had access to the bank because he worked there. He knew the secret code for the bank's wire transactions was posted in the wire transfer room. He walked into the room and memorized the code on October 25, 1978. At thirty-five minutes after four in the afternoon that same day, he wired $10.2 million from Security Pacific National Bank to the Irving Trust Company in New York City. And then Rifkin wired $8 million from there to Russelmaz, the Swiss bank account for the Soviet Union's official diamond broker in Zurich. [19]

Though not a traditional bank robbery—Rifkin used no force or threats to get the money—his heist was considered the largest bank robbery in the United States at that time. He also committed another federal crime: He defrauded the bank via the Fed Wire, or the Federal Reserve Communication System, which member banks used to transfer money in what were routine business transactions. Security National Bank certainly thought nothing of the $10.2 million transfer at the start. The bank discovered the theft eight days after it occurred, and only after the FBI reported it. The amount stolen was small; it was nothing to worry about for a bank whose wire transactions amounted to $20 billion in a week. [20] Rifkin embarrassed the bank nonetheless. Using nothing more than his memory and his understanding of the wire system, he stole an enormous amount of money and escaped with no one immediately realizing it was gone.

Rifkin likely would have stayed on the lam longer if he had not laundered $8 million of the stolen money in diamonds. The day after the robbery, he flew to Switzerland and used the money in the bank account to buy nineteen pounds of diamonds, or 43,200 carats. He spread the jewels on the bed in his hotel room in Luxembourg, where he had visited after leaving Switzerland. The quantity stunned him. "I was aghast," he recalled. "I didn't have the slightest idea what to do."[21] Rifkin returned to California and started arranging to sell the diamonds. He mentioned the robbery of the Security National Bank to one of his customers, who contacted the FBI. Agents arrested him at the house of a friend in Carlsbad, California, where they also found as many as fifty jeweler's envelopes filled with diamonds worth more than $8 million.[22] "I guess you want the diamonds," Rifkin said to the agents.[23]

Rifkin was indicted on the charges of interstate transportation of stolen property, wire fraud, entering a bank to commit a felony, and smuggling. While out on bail awaiting prosecution in U.S. District Court in Los Angeles, he was arrested in an FBI sting. He told an undercover FBI agent that he wanted to transfer as much as $50 million from the Union Bank in Los Angeles to the Bank of America in San Francisco. The FBI charged Rifkin with attempted theft, which put pressure on him to end both cases in a deal. He pleaded guilty to two counts of wire fraud in the $10.2 million robbery, and the government dropped the other case. Rifkin faced a maximum of ten years in prison at his sentencing on March 26, 1979. He wanted probation; he said he would give lectures to bank officials on how to prevent computer fraud. U.S. District Court Judge Matthew Byrne gave him eight years in prison and said Rifkin needed psychiatric help to help him figure out why he forfeited a successful career as a computer consultant to steal $10.2 million and use it to buy and sell diamonds.[24]

Rifkin described himself as having something of a split personality. "I feel there are two me's," he told the judge. "One rational and one not."[25] He said the rational Stanley Mark Rifkin was not always able to suppress his irrational doppelganger. Rifkin's lawyer asked for mercy, and described his client as a brilliant computer analyst who had "an unconscious, merciless desire to destroy himself."[26] Judge Byrne, while acknowledging Rifkin's mental issues, was unimpressed with the pleas for leniency. By attempting the second wire fraud, he said, Rifkin had shown "total disregard for the law."[27]

Though Rifkin got eight years, he was paroled after three. He went to work as a computer expert at the nonprofit American Association for the Advancement of Science. Unlike other big-time bank robbers, he never wrote a book, and he stayed out of trouble. His loot—all those diamonds—ended up with Security Pacific National Bank, which sold them for $6.5 million to a diamond broker. Soon the once-stolen stones were on sale in California department stores, under a brand name that hinted at their larcenous past. "Hot Ice," the diamonds were called.[28]

Stanley Mark Rifkin's haul stood as the record for robberies in the United States until 1997, when $18.9 million was stolen from an armored car company in Los Angeles. Before and after that landmark heist, the 1990s were filled with other bank robberies of significance, including one that ended in one of the bloodiest police shootouts in the history of Los Angeles. The high-profile heists kept bank robbery entrenched in popular culture. The situation recalled the defense a lawyer presented a decade earlier, in 1981, in the case of one of the youngest bank robbers on record. The lawyer represented a television-loving nine-year-old named Robert who was accused of pointing a toy gun at a teller at the New York Bank for Savings, in midtown Manhattan, and demanding money in late February 1981. The lawyer said the youth spent the day before the robbery watching shows such as *Adam 12*, *The Rockford Files*, and *Hogan's Heroes*. "Robert," the lawyer said, "is a victim of shows that are on television, depicting violence and breaking the law. Robert is also the victim of a broken family and Robert is a victim of the environment around him."[29]

The political environment influenced bank robbery in the 1990s. A four-man robbery gang known as the Aryan Republican Army struck at a time when Timothy J. McVeigh's bombing of the Alfred P. Murrah Federal Building in Oklahoma City on April 19, 1995, made the nation all too aware of the threat of domestic terrorism. The Aryan Republican Army attempted to finance its planned violent and radical revolution with the proceeds from twenty-two bank robberies carried out in the Midwest in 1994 and 1995. The leader of the band of Aryan Republican Army bank robbers, also called the Midwestern Bank Bandits, was Peter K. Langan, a white supremacist who was thirty-eight years old when he went on trial in U.S. District Court in Columbus, Ohio, in January 1997, on charges that he robbed two banks—an eighth of the sixteen bank robberies the FBI said he committed in seven states. [30]

Langan, known as Commander Pedro, was convicted and sentenced to life plus additional time in federal prison on December 18, 1998. He got life without parole for placing a pipe bomb inside a bank in 1994 and another thirty-five years for other charges, including two bank robberies and the assault of federal agents. Langan and his fellow robbers had taunted investigators. After one heist, they left behind a lunch box with a Hostess Twinkie and a pipe bomb inside. At another, a robber dressed as Santa Claus said, "Ho, ho, get down on the floor," to the bank customers, and left behind a present—a bomb in a Santa hat. [31]

The gang culture that thrived in the United States in the early 1990s, particularly in the South-Central section of Los Angeles, also manifested itself in bank robberies. In 1993, two reputed members of the Rollin' 60s Crips—Robert Sheldon "Casper" Brown, twenty-three years old, and twenty-four-year-old Donzell Lamar "C-Dog" Thompson—were indicted on charges they trained high school students to use high-powered rifles to commit as many as five armed bank robberies a day over four years in the late 1980s and early 1990s, with Brown implicated in a record 175 heists. [32] Brown pleaded guilty to five of the bank robberies and on November 1, 1993, was sentenced to thirty years in federal prison. Thompson pleaded guilty to two of the robberies and got twenty-five years. Federal prosecutors, in their sentencing memorandum, likened Brown and Thompson to Fagin, the character in Charles Dickens's *Oliver Twist* who teaches street urchins to become pickpockets in Victorian London and lives off what they make on the street. Brown and Thompson's young crews were products of South-Central. Like Fagin, the pair committed none of the crimes themselves. Their young henchmen were accused of firing twenty bullets in the bank robberies and assaulting fifteen bank employees and five customers. "Dickens invented Fagin as the exploiter and debaucher of youth to inspire horror and revulsion in his Victorian audience," wrote assistant U.S. attorneys John Shepard Wiley Jr. and Michael Reese Davis. "Brown and Thompson inspire the same horror and revulsion today. The difference is that Fagin is only fiction." [33]

Brown and Thompson commanded their minions in a city that long had been considered the bank robbery capital of the world. In the early 1990s, 29 percent of all bank robberies in the United States occurred in Los Angeles.[34] The large number of financial institutions (3,500 in 1992), the large number of people (9.1 million in Los Angeles County alone in 1992), and the ribbons of getaway-ready freeways combined to make bank robbery a daily event in the seven counties that the FBI's Los Angeles office covers in Southern California.[35] So did the longer banking hours, sometimes lax security, and the availability of weapons.[36] In 1992, when the number of bank robberies hit an all-time record 2,641 in the Los Angeles area, sixty bank robberies happened in one week, and twenty-eight in one day—in the same year that the Chicago area had a total of ninety-five bank robberies, a record for that city.[37] One characteristic of the bank robbery boom in Los Angeles in 1992 was the proliferation of "takeover" robberies. The bandits, often members of armed street gangs, put aside the once-common method of handing a teller a note and instead took the bank's money by force. "The bank robberies we have are just astronomical, and the violence we have is skyrocketing," an FBI agent in Los Angeles said in August 1992. "When I talk to other [agents] from across the country and tell them our bank robbery stats, the numbers are so unbelievable they think I've been drinking."[38]

The arrests of Robert Brown and Donzell Thompson in 1993 helped check the trend. The number of bank robberies in Southern California dropped by 28 percent in 1993 compared to 1992.[39] Brown's connection to 175 heists outdid the previous record of sixty-four bank robberies committed by one person—Edwin Chambers Dotson, called the "Yankee Bandit," because of his New York Yankees baseball cap, who struck in Southern California in 1983 and 1984.[40] "Brown and Thompson worked relentlessly to make Southern California more violent, more traumatizing, more forbidding, more deadly, more laden with fear and loss and pain and grief," the federal prosecutors wrote in their sentencing memo. "Their harm to others was daily, sometimes even hourly. Their violence continued for years. It ranged from the merely shattering to the completely lethal."[41]

Bank robbery sprees were not limited to Southern California in the 1990s. In Washington State, a handsome drug dealer and former surfer named William Scott "Hollywood" Scurlock used masks, including those of former American presidents, and elaborate and heavy pancake make-

up—hence his nickname—to rob fifteen banks in the Seattle area between 1992 and 1996. He and his two accomplices netted nearly $2.3
million until the forty-one-year-old Scurlock shot himself in the head
during a gunfight with police on Thanksgiving Day, November 28,
1996—the day after the trio robbed a Seafirst Bank branch in North
Seattle of $1.08 million.

Scurlock appeared to be an unlikely criminal. He grew up as the son of
a Baptist minister in Reston, Virginia, moved to Hawaii, where he surfed,
and then headed to the Pacific Northwest to attend Evergreen State College in Olympia, Washington, where he studied organic chemistry and
biochemistry. Scurlock, who had curly hair and an athletic build, and
looked like the actor Mel Gibson, was also a free spirit, divorced, child-
less, and a womanizer. Though he traded in drugs, he ostensibly worked
as a carpenter and lived in a three-story tree house, more than sixty feet
off the ground, he built near Olympia on nineteen acres facing Mount
Rainier. One of Scurlock's cousins referred to him as a hippie.[42] In Scurlock's bedroom in the tree house, over the king-size bed, hung a copy of a
painting of Robin Hood by the American artist N. C. Wyeth.[43]

Scurlock had no major crimes on his record, though he had made
hundreds of thousands of dollars dealing crystal methamphetamine. After
his business partner was murdered, Scurlock got out of the drug trade and
turned to bank robbery for income.[44] His inspiration came from a descen-
dant, Doc Scurlock, who rode with the outlaw Billy the Kid, and from the
movies.[45] He became fixated in 1991 with *Point Break*, starring Patrick
Swayze as Bodhi, a surfer-turned-bank-robber who leads a gang of laid-
back thieves called the Ex-Presidents. During the heists they wear latex
masks of Presidents Lyndon B. Johnson, Richard Nixon, Jimmy Carter,
and Ronald Reagan. Bodhi and his crew—pursued by Johnny Utah, a
rookie undercover FBI special agent played by Keanu Reeves—come off
as offbeat heroes as they victimize banks, the symbols of the capitalist
system. They are not after money; their robberies last only ninety seconds, and they take money from the tellers' drawers and never the vault.
Scurlock, who spent his life veering off different paths, liked what he
saw. As crime author Ann Rule has written, "At some point, and no one
can say when, William Scott Scurlock, thirty-nine years old and at the
end of his financial tether, visualized himself standing in place of Patrick
Swayze. In his mind, he stepped into the movie and became its hero."[46]

Scurlock got away with so many bank robberies because of his make-up and his planning, but he could not remain disguised forever. At their last bank robbery, at the Seafirst Bank branch in North Seattle, Scurlock and his two accomplices—his longtime friends Steve Meyers, of New Orleans, and Mark Biggins, of Oxnard, California—showed up shortly before closing time. A bank employee recognized one of the three as the "Hollywood" bank robber—he had a fake mustache and a fake chin[47]— from photographs taken of him from previous bank robberies. The bank employee twice activated a silent alarm. The chase for Hollywood was on. Meyers and Biggins were wounded in the manhunt, later pleaded guilty to bank robbery charges, and on May 14, 1997, were each sentenced to twenty-one years and three months in federal prison. Meyers was forty-seven years old and Biggins forty-three.

Scurlock ended his role in his final heist by shooting himself. A police dragnet flushed him into a residential neighborhood, where he hid in a camper for about twenty-four hours until he committed suicide. He had been discovered in the camper, alive, by two brothers, who, while visiting their eighty-five-year-old mother for Thanksgiving, checked her camper out of concern for the search for the last of the three robbers wanted in the heist of the Seafirst Bank branch. The brothers spotted Scurlock and called police. Officers fired away, and found Scurlock dead.[48] That same day, the FBI searched Scurlock's tree house, his regular house, and a barn on his property. The agents found two sawed-off shotguns, a 9-millimeter Luger pistol, rifles, a silencer, boxes of ammunition, a fake beard, a fake mustache, other makeup, a police scanner, two-way radios, a brown fedora, passports, airline tickets, and $20,402 in cash.[49] Scurlock's involvement in bank robberies baffled his friends, but he was prepared, at the time of his death, to carry out many more.

Investigators recovered all the $1.08 million stolen in Scurlock's final bank robbery, and speculated that he might have spent much of his other loot on travel.[50] Most stunning was the amount he took and the number of banks he robbed. Both those factors, a top FBI official said after Scurlock's death, made the tree-house dweller "one of the most prolific bank robbers in the history of the United States."[51]

Emil Dechebal Matasareanu and Larry Eugene Phillips Jr. were more heavily armed than infantry soldiers—and certainly more heavily armed than the police—when they stormed into the Bank of America branch on Laurel Canyon Boulevard, in the North Hollywood neighborhood of Los Angeles, at a quarter after nine in the morning on February 27, 1997. The two friends were dressed in all black, including ski masks, and wore body armor on their chests and strips of Kevlar around their arms and legs. Each carried assault rifles similar to AK-47s, loaded with one hundred rounds, as well as pistols and another thirty rounds of ammunition. They entered the bank hoping to get away with as much as $750,000; the branch was flush with cash for the Friday payday.

The two got $300,000, but never escaped alive. They were killed in what became known as the North Hollywood shootout, a robbery and forty-four-minute gunfight with police that terrified Southern California with scenes bloodier than anything in a movie. The heist became embedded in the lore of Los Angeles and changed how police across the United States responded to violent incidents. After the North Hollywood shootout, the police could be confident they could rush to a bank robbery or shooting with as much firepower as the criminals.

The robbery in North Hollywood was not the first for Phillips, who was twenty-six years old, and Matasareanu, who was thirty. After the two were killed, the FBI named them as suspects in two earlier holdups, which netted the bandits about $1.5 million: the May 2, 1996, robbery of the San Fernando Valley branch of Bank of America, and the May 31, 1996, robbery of the Bank of America branch in Van Nuys. In both heists, which were near North Hollywood, the heavily armed robbers donned dark ski masks and opened fire inside the banks; a pregnant employee was injured in the second case.[52] Three years earlier, in 1993, Phillips and Matasareanu were already stockpiling weapons. Police in Glendale, a suburb of Los Angeles, pulled over the pair for speeding on October 23, 1993, and inside the rented car found an arsenal: two 9-millimeter pistols, two AK-47s, two .45-caliber guns, two homemade bombs, six smoke grenades, three machine guns, two bulletproof vests, a gas mask, six holsters, wigs, ski masks, two police radio scanners, about 2,800 rounds of ammunition, and a stopwatch.[53] Matasareanu and Phillips, who appeared equipped for a bank robbery, told the police they were driving to a shooting area in the San Gabriel Mountains called "Kentucky."[54] They were arrested, got plea deals, and each served less than four months in prison.

Phillips was the more dominating of the two. He fantasized about being rich, and would drive around affluent neighborhoods and imagine himself inside the spacious homes. He idolized Michael Milken, of junk bond infamy; Barry Minkow, a financial whiz kid whose business, ZZZZ Best Company, collapsed in fraud; and the characters in *The Godfather* movies. Phillips wanted to have so much money that he could spend $100 bills "by the handful," and his ideal crime was the robbery of $5.8 million from a Lufthansa jet at New York's John F. Kennedy International Airport on December 11, 1978—a daring haul that inspired another mob saga, 1990's *Goodfellas*.[55] "He wanted to live the American dream," Phillips's half brother recalled. "He decided to go about it the wrong way."[56]

Phillips found a malleable confederate in Emil Matasareanu, a Romanian-born immigrant who had arrived in the United States in 1977 and became a naturalized citizen in 1988. He grew up with his family in suburban Los Angeles, where he was teased for being overweight.[57] Matasareanu got a degree from DeVry Institute of Technology, and ran a computer consulting business that later fell apart. His marriage, his finances, and his health had all collapsed around the time he joined with Phillips, a fellow bodybuilder, and targeted banks. Matasareanu's wife and family, which included two sons, five years old and eighteen months old when he died, left for Romania six months before the North Hollywood shootout. He also had undergone recent surgery for epilepsy, apparently brought on by a blocked artery and the stress from the failure of his computer business.[58]

Matasareanu's main source of income was Dechebal Inc., a home for developmentally disabled residents that he and his mother ran in Pasadena. In 1995 the state suspended the license of his mother, Valerie Nicolescu, based on allegations of improper treatment of two of the residents. The home soon closed, leaving Matasareanu without a steady income. His financial situation improved after the first of the two bank robberies in May 1996. He and his wife, who was then with him, rented a large house in the San Gabriel Valley. Matasareanu soon needed more money, and, as his mother recalled, he was despondent over the disintegration of their business and his marriage. "His actions were more like suicide," she said after the fatal bank robbery. "I'm sorry that he died this way but he exchanged his life for nothing."[59] Of Larry Phillips Jr., she said, he "was a bad guy who got my son."[60]

Phillips and Matasareanu, looking like they were ready for war, opened fire as soon as they got into the Bank of America branch in North Hollywood on February 27, 1997. They had driven up in their getaway car, a Chevrolet Celebrity sedan, and might have been feeling calmer than usual when they headed into the bank; police said they might have taken phenobarbitals to ease their nerves.[61] The success of their heist was in doubt even before they pulled their triggers. Two Los Angeles Police Department officers on patrol saw them walk into the bank, and the officers called for backup for a possible robbery.[62]

Inside, Phillips and Matasareanu blasted through the tellers' windows—eliminating the bandit barriers—and got inside the vault, still firing. They shoved $300,000 into a cart and went for the door. Someone in the bank had activated the alarm, so by the time Phillips and Matasareanu got outside, at half past nine, fifteen minutes after they had arrived, police had surrounded the bank. Eventually three hundred law-enforcement officials took up positions near the scene.

Phillips and Matasareanu kept firing. They sprayed as many as 1,100 rounds of armor-piercing bullets at the badly outgunned police, who emptied their weapons of 750 rounds. Five officers went to a nearby gun store, B&B Gun Shop, to get high-powered guns to match the arsenal of Phillips and Matasareanu. The two had with them, or in their getaway car, five fully automatic assault rifles, all of which were illegal to carry in California.[63] "They had some awesome firepower and we basically had nothing," one police officer recounted years later. "At times the biggest gun we had was a 9 mm pistol and a shotgun."[64] Eleven police officers and six civilians were injured in the firefight, which television news helicopters captured on film and broadcast live. The footage looked like something out of a war zone.

By twelve minutes before ten in the morning, Matasareanu had gotten into the getaway car while Phillips followed on foot, shooting away as his partner, driving slowly, urged him to get in. Police shot out the tires, but the pair of gunmen still attacked. "All our training was that we would respond with extra force and we expect them to surrender," one police officer said. "That never happened."[65] Three minutes later, at nine minutes before ten, still in a firefight with police, Phillips shot himself in the head. Matasareanu, now on foot, failed to hijack a pickup truck. Police closed in. For six minutes, until about ten o'clock, he and the officers exchanged fire. At six feet tall and 283 pounds, and wearing a bullet-proof vest strengthened by a steel plate, Matasareanu was hard to take down. Not until he ran out of ammunition did he stop firing. He had been shot twenty-nine times in the buttocks, arms, fingers, and, in what turned out to be the fatal wound, the left thigh. A police officer ran up to him, asked him his name, and asked him how many other gunmen were out there. Matasareanu replied that his name was Pete. He refused to give any other information. "Fuck you," he said. "Shoot me in the head."[66] Para-medics arrived at the scene at ten minutes after eleven, about seventy minutes after Matasareanu went down. By then, he had bled to death.

A lawsuit was one legacy of the North Hollywood shootout. An attor-ney for Matasareanu's two young sons claimed the police had "cold-bloodedly murdered" their father by refusing to get him medical atten-tion, though a mistrial was declared in the case in 2000, and a judge later dismissed the suit.[67] More lasting was the effect on the Los Angeles Police Department and police forces nationwide. At a time when the LAPD was still recovering from the 1991 riots over the beating of motor-ist Rodney King, the officers' handling of the shootout earned praise and raised morale.[68] Many of the officers were considered heroes; President Bill Clinton met with some of them to express the nation's gratitude. The North Hollywood shootout soon helped make the LAPD and other police forces more prepared—and more heavily armed. The California State Legislature passed a law that allowed police to carry assault rifles—which remained illegal for civilians—and other law enforcement agencies in other states also spent more money on training and more powerful weaponry. Never again, the police hoped, would officers be at a disad-vantage against bank robbers such as Larry Phillips Jr. and Emil Matasa-reanu, two homicidal misfits whose gunfight ended a bank robbery that was as brazen as any heist in the bank robbery capital of the world. The two were, in the words of one high-ranking LAPD officer, "demons, devils."[69]

Seven months later, and forty-five minutes southeast of North Holly-wood, the Los Angeles police were trying to solve the biggest armed robbery, in terms of cash stolen, in the nation's history. Like the Brink's job, this heist was not a traditional bank robbery, because the victim was not a bank, but it is still categorized as such. Before it was stolen, the money—all $18.9 million of it, most of it in twenty-dollar bills—was being sorted at the Dunbar Armored Car Company depot on Mateo Street in downtown Los Angeles; drivers were to distribute the cash to automatic teller machines at banks and other financial institutions throughout the city. Within minutes, the $18.9 million was gone—and as much as $10 million was never recovered.

Shortly after midnight on September 13, 1997, five armed men, wearing ski masks and dressed in black, entered the side door of the Dunbar depot, where a few workers were on the overnight shift. The robbery team, to try to establish alibis, had gathered a few hours earlier, on the evening of September 12, 1997, at a house party in Long Beach.[70] They were prepared when they slipped inside the depot. They had a key, a floor plan, and radio headsets to communicate with one another. They knew the habits of the late-night employees—including that some of them, while on break, would leave the vault open[71]—and the robbers had the benefit of surprise.

They corralled the depot's employees, ordered them to the floor, and bound their feet with duct tape. The bandits tied up more employees, got to the vault, and used bolt cutters to break open the padlocks on the metal cages that held the cash inside. They stuffed the money into carts, wheeled them to a loading dock, and headed to their getaway vehicle, a fourteen-foot U-Haul truck that one of the five had rented for the heist. Before they left, they smashed all the surveillance cameras inside the depot and took the cameras' videotapes. The robbers had grabbed more loot than even they had anticipated. They filled the cab of the U-Haul with stacks of cash, creating "a carpet of money that went all the way up to their thighs."[72] Soon, after stopping at one of the robber's apartments to change their clothes, the six were back at the party in Long Beach, acting as if nothing unusual had happened that night.

The robbers would not be arrested for another two years. The Los Angeles police and the FBI, later joined by criminal investigators with the Internal Revenue Service, had a suspect from the start. He was Allen Pace III, a twenty-eight-year old resident of Compton who, the day before the heist, had been fired as a safety officer at the Dunbar Armored Car Company, where he had been in charge of making sure other employees followed safety precautions, but had gotten into trouble for tampering with company vehicles.[73] Pace had a grudge, and he had the knowledge and experience (and the key) that would have allowed him and the other robbers to get in and out of the depot so easily, and with so much cash. One of the depot's employees said she recognized the voice of one of the robbers, which further pointed to Pace. Yet he and his accomplices were shrewd. To undermine speculation that an insider had pulled off the heist, they had made marks at the scene to suggest the robbers had forced their way in.[74] Pace and his confederates were also prudent. They did not spend money in outlandish ways. They kept away from one another. They said little as the police and FBI investigated a robbery that the authorities initially described as involving only "more than $1 million," to keep the heist from turning into a national story and sending the robbers into hiding.[75] The investigators wanted to keep watching Pace.

A small shard of plastic helped break the case. Hours after the robbery, while he combed the depot for clues, Los Angeles Police Detective John Licata, one of the two lead investigators on the case, spotted it on the floor of the depot's garage—"a tiny rectangle of amber-colored plastic that looked like it had come from a vehicle taillight."[76] The shard matched none of the lights of Dunbar's armored cars. Licata and the other lead investigator, FBI Special Agent John McEachern III, kept returning to the tiny piece of evidence as the robbery's first anniversary passed and the case remained open. Dunbar, based in Baltimore, and its insurer, Lloyd's of London, had put up a reward of $125,000 within days after the robbery, but that money produced no breakthroughs.

The investigation turned on the words of a police informant. That person came forward in 1998 and identified a man named Eugene Lamar Hill Jr. as being part of the plot. A fifteen-member task force, "Operation Dunrob," which McEachern headed, formed in October 1998 to run down the growing leads. The investigators discovered that Hill had rented a U-Haul truck the day before the robbery and returned it after the heist. The FBI crime lab, in Quantico, Virginia, said the plastic shard came from that same truck. The task force arrested Hill on September 22, 1999. Agents found him with a stack of money and money wrappers from the Dunbar depot. Hill confessed and identified his five co-conspirators, including their leader, Allen Pace III.

Police said Pace had told his buddies, his "rent-a-cop" friends, that they could make quick cash by robbing the depot, and he was right.[77] They gambled away some of the cash in Las Vegas, where one of them was from, and were believed to have spent other large amounts on businesses, homes, and cars; the robbers and others had set up fronts to launder the money. The robbers also burned some of the cash to avoid detection, because the serial numbers on much of the money had been sequenced, making the loot easier to trace. [78] Destroying some of the cash helped break the sequence.

The six bandits faced charges including conspiracy to commit robbery and using a gun in a crime of violence. Pace was almost alone in the end. Four of his five co-defendants cooperated, accepted plea deals in U.S. District Court in Los Angeles, and received sentences of seven to ten years. Pace and his other co-defendant, Erik Damon Boyd, who was twenty-nine years old, went to trial and were convicted on February 27, 2001. Pace testified that he had no role in the planning or execution of the robbery. He said one of the co-defendants had framed him "because I was messing with his wife." [79] Boyd got seventeen years in federal prison. Pace got twenty-four. "You were the employee who knew about [the money]," U.S. District Judge Lourdes Baird told Pace on June 18, 2001. "You were the one who got everyone involved." [80] Pace said nothing.

Pace and his co-defendants will be legally attached to the case long after they leave prison. Baird ordered each of them jointly responsible for paying $18.9 million in restitution to Dunbar and Lloyd's of London. Pace is scheduled to get out of prison on March 18, 2021. But the criminal investigation, in one respect, is unfinished: With $10 million of the stolen cash still missing, the possibility exists that others know where the money is or have been spending it. "If there are others out there, and the money's still out there," FBI agent McEachern said the day Pace was sentenced, "this ain't over." [81]

In its coverage of the sentencing of Allen Pace III, the *Los Angeles Times* ranked the $18.9 million robbery from the Dunbar Armored Car Company as the biggest of its kind—with qualifications. "Two recent heists in North Carolina and Florida equaled or surpassed the take from the Dunbar, but both of those were strictly inside jobs—not daring and violent armed robberies," the newspaper reported. "The FBI says more cash was taken in the Dunbar robbery than any other armed takeover robbery in American history." [82] In that regard, the Dunbar heist is the nation's largest armed robbery of cash, but the other two cases are equally noteworthy because of the amount of money stolen. Like the Dunbar heist, these robberies—again in the tradition of the train robberies of the Jameses and Youngers, and the Brink's job—did not target banks, but rather the companies that get the money to the banks.

On March 29, 1997, Philip Noel Johnson, a security guard at the Loomis, Fargo & Company's Southside depot, in Jacksonville, Florida, robbed his employer of nearly $19 million. Johnson made off with the nine hundred pounds of cash in a stolen Loomis, Fargo van after he kidnapped two fellow guards at gunpoint; one was later found unharmed in Johnson's house and the other was found handcuffed to a tree in the mountains of western North Carolina.[83] Johnson had driven to North Carolina, where he had hidden most of the money in a rented storage shed in tiny Mountain Home, south of Asheville. He abandoned the Loomis, Fargo van in Asheville, and went on the lam, including to Mexico. The FBI had tracked Johnson from Jacksonville to Asheville to Mexico. But they could not find him until August 30, 1997, when U.S. Customs agents arrested the thirty-three-year-old after he was taken off a bus heading from Mexico to Houston, Texas. Johnson had given the agents a different name, which a computer database recognized as an alias that Johnson had been using since he left Jacksonville.[84] The FBI found the stolen money in the storage shed in North Carolina on September 18, 2007, after someone discovered, in a refuse bin in Asheville, a copy of the money order Johnson had made out for the shed.[85] About $50,000 remained missing.

Johnson, who was embittered by his job at Loomis, Fargo, had planned the robbery for years. He pleaded guilty in 1998 to robbery, kidnapping, and money laundering, and on January 20, 1999, was sentenced to twenty-five years in prison in U.S. District Court in Jacksonville. He said he wanted to use the stolen money as a kind of ransom; he said he intended to return all but $1 million or $2 million to Loomis, Fargo if the company improved the working conditions and pay for its employees. If that plan failed, Johnson said, he planned to build medical clinics and houses for the poor in Central America. "I just wanted to get out of the situation of being a slave in America," Johnson said of his reasons for stealing from Loomis, Fargo. "Their employees are little more than slaves."[86] Speaking of his arrest, Johnson told the judge, "I just wanted to say that if I'd known this was going to happen, I would have found some kind of alternative. This is a waste of my life."[87]

David Scott Ghantt also blamed job dissatisfaction for his huge heist. He was a vault supervisor and driver at Loomis, Fargo's depot in Charlotte, North Carolina, when he stole $17 million from the vault on October 4, 1997. He carried out the heist—the third-largest of its kind in the United States—by propping open the vault and returning that night. Upon leaving, he took the tapes from two security cameras, but not the other sixteen, which recorded him with the cash. Ghantt was not working alone. Though married, he had planned the robbery with his girlfriend, Kelly Campbell, a former Loomis, Fargo employee, and her friend, a "small-time hustler" named Steve Chambers. [88]

Ghantt was looking to get rich, but he never did. "Your Honor, if I could undo what I did, I would," the twenty-nine-year-old said at his sentencing in U.S. District Court in Charlotte on April 29, 1999. "I was stuck in a go-nowhere job, and I wasn't happy with my life. I'm sorry." [89] Ghantt, who had no prior record and had been decorated for his service in the army during the Persian Gulf War, got seven and a half years in federal prison for his guilty plea to bank larceny and money laundering.

Ghantt had fled to Mexico immediately after the heist to stay clear of the authorities back home; the tapes on the security cameras had made him a suspect from the start. In North Carolina, his friends were spending the stolen cash as quickly as they could, which alerted the FBI and turned the case into a tale of backwoods avarice. Three weeks after the robbery, Steve Chambers and his wife, Michele, moved out of their mobile home and into a $635,000 mansion in a development called Cramer Mountain Country Club, about sixteen miles west of Charlotte. The couple paid cash for a BMW convertible and bought a three-and-a-half-carat diamond ring worth $43,000. Michele Chambers walked into a bank and tried to deposit $200,000. Loomis, Fargo wrappers were still on the money. [90] In all, Ghantt, the Chamberses, and some seventeen other people were convicted in the case, though most of them faced counts for money laundering done after the heist. At one point, the FBI said, some members of the gang wanted to kill Ghantt, fearing that, even in Mexico, he was a risk for spilling the scheme. A confidential informant, wearing a wire, helped the FBI further develop a case against the Chamberses and helped agents find Ghantt near the Mexican island resort of Cozumel, where he was arrested in March of 1998. The arrests of the others followed.

Michele Chambers and Steve Chambers, who were twenty-six and thirty-one years old when charged, respectively, also pleaded guilty. She got seven years and eight months in federal prison. Her husband, charged with getting others to open safety deposit boxes to store the stolen money, got eleven years and three months.[91] As part of the prosecution, the government seized and auctioned their house and other objects they and the others had purchased with the ill-gotten gains, of which all but $2 million was recovered. The items put up for auction included big-screen television sets, a velvet portrait of Elvis Presley, a Harley-Davidson motorcycle, and another piece of art, which had hung in the Chamberses' foyer. It was a portrait of a bulldog dressed as World War II hero General George S. Patton.[92] "Ever since the first arrest was made, it has taken on a type of folk-tale flavor," a U.S. marshal said of the case of the $17 million. "Let's face it: You're moving from a trailer in a field to the country club. It was very much *The Beverly Hillbillies*."[93]

North Carolina's involvement in two of the nation's largest cash robberies, both in the late 1990s, might seem unusual on its face. The state, unlike Missouri in the 1800s, had no reputation for lawlessness, and unlike Southern California, North Carolina had no historical claim to being the bank robbery capital of the world. Yet by 1998 and early 1999, North Carolina had become a hotbed for bank robbery. Even as the number of such heists continued to decline nationally, they rose to 289 in North Carolina in 1998, a jump of 38 percent from 1997.[94] The FBI's field office in Charlotte, which covers all of North Carolina, ranked fourth in the nation in 1998 in the number of bank robberies that it investigated—behind Los Angeles, San Francisco, and Seattle.[95]

The reasons for the increase in North Carolina included growth in both bank branches and population—the factors that had influenced the statistics for bank robbery since the early days of the United States. But another factor was at work: the personality of North Carolina, which, like other Southern states, takes pride in its hospitality. In 1999, bandit barriers were the exception in banks in North Carolina, as were other security measures such as armed guards, which had become more common elsewhere. Banks in North Carolina liked their relaxed atmosphere and niceties, and many bank robbers came to enjoy them as well. "You have to understand that we have a different way of doing things here," the president of the North Carolina Bankers Association said in May 1999.

"Customers don't want to be frightened or overly stressed by security. Some customers feel so welcome here that they carry the teller a card or cake on her birthday."[96] Said an FBI agent in Charlotte, "Bank robbery is a crime of opportunity. The banks in North Carolina have a lot of branches that pride themselves in being friendly."[97]

The overt friendliness was not on display in the heist of the $17 million from Loomis, Fargo in Charlotte in October 1997. Nor did it play a part in the $19 million robbery of the Loomis, Fargo depot in Jacksonville, Florida, in March 1997—a hit in which the money was hidden in North Carolina. But these two cases showed that the sleepy countryside of North Carolina was not immune to enormous thefts, just as the state as a whole was not protected from a bank robbery boom—even if it was a boom in which the bandits were mostly losing. Robbers were being caught 70 percent of the time in North Carolina, higher than the nationwide average of 60 percent.[98]

Bank robbery in the late 1990s in the United States was like bank robbery in the decades and centuries before—a crime that knew no limits or boundaries across the nation, whether in Los Angeles, New York, Charlotte, the Hell's Fringe area of Oklahoma, or Clay County, Missouri. Given a chance, and given the need for money, a bank robber could strike anywhere. No place was invulnerable. That trait of the bank robber would become horribly clear early in the new century, when one of the strangest heists in American history would occur in late August 2003, at a small bank branch in a nondescript shopping plaza in the northwestern corner of Pennsylvania.

9

ROBBERY AND REVERBERATIONS

Pizza Bomber, the Post-9/11 FBI, and Online Heists

The customer looked like something was wrong with his neck. When he walked into the PNC Bank branch just south of Erie, Pennsylvania, on August 28, 2003, the customer's chest bulged under his T-shirt and a metal collar was around his neck. The chief bank teller thought the contraption was a brace or a body cast—that the customer was suffering from a neck injury. The customer, who was of middle age but walked with a cane, stood in line and grabbed a Dum Dum lollipop from a basket on the counter. He walked up to the chief teller and handed her an envelope that contained a four-page note. It said the man had a bomb, that he wanted $250,000, and that the teller and everyone else in the bank had better cooperate, or the bomb would go off. "Act now, think later or you will die," the note read. The teller looked at the man, one of several customers in the bank at about a half past two in the afternoon on this Thursday leading into the Labor Day weekend. She told him the manager was at lunch, and that she herself could not get into the vault, so she could not give him $250,000. The man said he had no time to wait. He lifted his shirt. The bomb was locked around his neck. [1]

The bomb was real, and it was on a timer. That alone made this heist highly unusual. Bank robbers occasionally claim they are carrying bombs, but the devices are rarely live. An empty box, a set of radio antennae sticking out of a lunch bag, an assertion that a robber or a hostage has a bomb strapped to his or her chest: The FBI and police have encountered these kinds of scenarios over the years, but virtually never had the bandits' threats turned out to be true. This case outside Erie, an industrial city of about one hundred thousand people on Lake Erie, in northwestern Pennsylvania, was different. So different that the FBI gave it a name—COLLARBOMB—and elevated it to what is known as Major Case status, making its investigation a top priority that got more of the bureau's resources. In its first several weeks, a total of seventy-five federal agents and state and local police officers would work on Major Case 203. In 2003, some of the recent Major Case investigations had been for the terrorist attacks of September 11, 2001; the bombing during the Olympics in Atlanta on July 27, 1996; and the bombing in Oklahoma City on April 19, 1995. Like those cases, Major Case 203 was complex. Though officially classified as COLLARBOMB, it became known as the Pizza Bomber case, after the forty-six-year-old pizza deliveryman, a loner by the name of Brian Wells, who walked into the PNC Bank wearing the bomb locked to his neck. At eighteen minutes after three on that day, about forty minutes after Wells robbed the bank, the bomb exploded, killing him and triggering an FBI investigation that got stranger as it got longer. It lasted six years.

If the Pizza Bomber case was unusual because of the bomb, it was also something of an anomaly for another reason: The FBI investigated it, taking the lead with help from the federal Bureau of Alcohol, Tobacco, Firearms, and Explosives, and the Pennsylvania State Police. After 9/11, the FBI's priorities had changed. Counterterrorism took over as the preeminent concern; national security superseded law enforcement as the FBI's primary function.[2] The bureau's listing of its top ten priorities, in the years after 9/11, also reflected the shift. Counterterrorism moved into the top spot, followed by counterintelligence and counterespionage, and protecting the nation from cyber attacks.[3] Eighth on the list was combating significant violent crime—the same class of offenses that, under J. Edgar Hoover, helped mold the modern FBI, especially after the bureau needed to rehabilitate itself in light of its disastrous foray into domestic spying with the Palmer raids of 1919 and 1920. Bank robbery, perhaps the crime most responsible for giving the FBI its identity, became less of a priority for the bureau in the years after 9/11.

Even before terrorist attacks, the FBI had started to reprioritize its resources. The bureau introduced a "measured response" initiative to decide when its agents would investigate bank robberies.[4] The heist had to meet one of three criteria: It had to be a violent bank robbery in which, for example, a gun was displayed; it had to involve significant financial loss; or it had to be the work of serial bandits or "criminal organizations that cross jurisdictional boundaries."[5] This reprioritization intensified shortly after 9/11, as the FBI shifted five hundred of its agents from traditional law enforcement duties to counterterrorism, leaving fewer agents to investigate bank robberies, which the bureau had already deemphasized.[6] Between fiscal years 2000 and 2004, nearly 30 percent fewer FBI agents investigated bank robberies; an average of 316 agents handled such cases in 2000 compared to 225 in 2004.[7] The number of bank robbery investigations the FBI referred to the offices of U.S. attorneys also dropped, from 2,019 in fiscal 2000, to 1,809 in fiscal 2004—a decrease of about 10 percent.[8]

The FBI's new role did not go unnoticed. Its reduced response to bank robbery was among the most significant effects of its post-9/11 reorganization, a number of local police departments told the Inspector General's Office of the Department of Justice in a 2005 report on the FBI. For some departments, according to the report, the FBI's reduced response "created a marked void," increased the caseloads for local police, and exposed convicted bank robbers to state sentences frequently less severe than the federal penalties for bank robbery.[9] Some in the FBI responded that local and state authorities were fully capable of handling bank robbery cases on their own. Others said the FBI agents in some jurisdictions "continue to respond and investigate all bank robberies, although fewer agents are sent to investigate each incident than in the past. FBI officials in these districts said it was important to work these cases because it helped strengthen relationships with state and local partners."[10] The FBI, when it chose, could still have a role in solving bank robberies. But after 9/11, the crime and the bureau would no longer be as closely linked as they had been in the days of the G-men. By 2014, about half of the FBI's sixteen thousand agents and analysts were assigned to national security issues.[11] Also in 2014, the FBI was two years behind in releasing what had been one of its most widely publicized documents: its annual *Bank Crime Report*, which provided a variety of statistics from the year before. For the FBI, bank robbery's importance had faded.

When the Pizza Bomber heist occurred in the outskirts of Erie in August 2003, its significance was clear. At a time when the FBI was moving away from bank robberies, it had designated the Pizza Bomber case as one of the biggest in its history. Never before had a bomb killed a thief during a bank robbery. The FBI, at the start, had no idea what happened. The behavior of the bank robber, Brian Wells, was bizarre. Though he said he had a live time bomb locked to his neck, he acted with nonchalance. He waited in line in the bank, grabbed a lollipop, and, though he told the teller he had no time to wait, did not appear to be in a rush when he left with a canvas bag stuffed with $8,702—far less than $250,000 he had demanded. His clothing was odd. He wore an oversize white T-shirt with "GUESS Jeans" on the front— a knockoff that seemed to convey a taunt: Guess who did this? Wells drove away from the bank in his own car, a 1996 Geo Metro, but he did not speed off. He stopped at a McDonald's next to the bank, got out of the Geo, and picked up a rock that was in a flower garden where one of the restaurant's drive-through signs was posted. Taped to the bottom of the rock was a note. Wells took it, got back in his car, and drove away at a reasonable speed.

The state police stopped him from getting to wherever he was headed. Troopers pulled him over in the parking lot of an eyeglasses store several yards from the McDonald's; the store's parking lot opened onto one of the busiest roads in Erie County, which, if Wells had driven onto it, would have immediately taken him to the interstate. The troopers ordered Wells out of the car and cuffed his hands behind his back. He sat cross-legged near a police cruiser and pleaded with the troopers to help him. They stood by, realizing that the bomb, if it went off, could kill them if they got too close. The nearest bomb squad was stationed in the city of Erie, six miles to the north. Those officers were on their way, with no guarantee they would get there in time. Wells sounded desperate, but not frantic. He was cryptic in what happened to him—how he had ended up with a bomb around his neck—and gave few clues as to why he was a bank robber if he was supposed to be working as a pizza deliveryman. His job and his workplace, a nearby pizzeria, were two details he divulged as he sat in the parking lot.

Wells told the troopers the device was a bomb; it resembled a huge handcuff connected to a large metal box, which contained two pipe bombs, two kitchen timers, and enough batteries to supply the detonation charge when the timers counted down to zero. Wells said he had delivered pizzas to a spot near the bank, and a group of black men had accosted him there. One man fired a gun in the air, he said, and they all forced him to wear the bomb. Wells said one of his assailants gave him written instructions, which were in the Geo, and told him how and when he would rob the PNC Bank branch while wearing the bomb. Wells said his assailants told him he had about twenty minutes to rob the bank and another fifty minutes to follow the written instructions. Wells said the notes directed him where to drive after the robbery to retrieve keys he would use to defuse the bomb. "I don't know if I have enough time," Wells told the troopers of his present predicament. "I'm not lying." Wells refused to describe what his assailants were wearing or provide other information on what happened.

Wells asked for a cigarette. He asked for a priest. The bomb squad had yet to arrive, and he wanted to know who was going to unlock the device he had come to realize was about to kill him.

"It's gonna go off," Wells told the troopers. "I'm not lying."

At eighteen minutes after three o'clock, about forty minutes after Wells left the bank, the bomb went off. It tore a hole the size of a paperback into his chest. He died immediately, three minutes before the bomb squad arrived.

By that night, investigators with the FBI, ATF, and state police had pieced together what Wells was supposed to have done, but not why. By examining nine pages of notes—including the instructions Wells had given to the teller, the note he had retrieved from under the rock, and the notes he had in his car—the investigators determined Wells was to have followed the instructions to go on a kind of scavenger hunt: He would have made at least two stops to gather more notes and more clues on where to find the keys that would stop the bomb from ticking. The scheme was like something out of a Rube Goldberg cartoon. FBI Special Agent Jerry Clark, the lead investigator, quickly determined that Wells would have never survived, even if he had followed all the instructions without interruption. Bank robbery and money were clearly at the center of the scheme; yet Wells held on to the bag of cash, despite the possibility that he would die with it. Clark wondered whether Wells was supposed to have given the loot to someone, and the handoff never happened. Clark also wondered about Wells's role. Was he a bomb hostage, as he claimed, who was forced to wear the bomb and rob the bank? Or was he somehow involved? And why was the cane that Wells had carried into the bank really a homemade shotgun designed to look like a cane?

The mystery got more complicated. Three days after Wells was killed, his friend and fellow pizza deliveryman, Robert Pinetti, was found dead of an apparent drug overdose. Pinetti was forty-three years old and, like Wells, a recovering alcoholic. The FBI had interviewed Pinetti after Wells's death, but Pinetti died before agents could perform what was to be the critical follow-up interview. Another death stumped investigators three weeks later. Early in the morning of September 21, state police found the body of a dead man stuffed in a working freezer inside a garage attached to a house. The location of the house was intriguing—it sat at the start of a dirt road that led to a clearing where, the investigators had determined, Wells had made his final pizza delivery before he had the bomb locked to his neck.

The morbid find provided no immediate break in the Pizza Bomber case, though it presented a number of new leads. The body in the freezer was that of James Roden, a forty-five-year-old alcoholic who laid carpet. The person who told state police about Roden's body was the owner of the house where it was found—fifty-nine-year-old William A. Rothstein, an eccentric handyman, substitute teacher, and robotics enthusiast. He had telephoned the police to tell them he had helped stuff the body in the freezer at the request of his one-time fiancée, Marjorie Diehl-Armstrong. Rothstein said Diehl-Armstrong had fatally shot Roden, her boyfriend, in an argument at Diehl-Armstrong's house, in the city of Erie. Like Rothstein, who had a degree in electrical engineering, Diehl-Armstrong was bright; she had a master's degree in education. Also like Rothstein, Diehl-Armstrong had spent her life on the fringes of society. In Rothstein's case, his extreme arrogance prevented him from getting a steady job; he always insisted he was smarter than anyone else. Diehl-Armstrong's extreme narcissism kept her from fitting in and getting a job, but her more severe problem was her mental illness, including bipolar disorder.

Fifty-four years old in the summer of 2003, Diehl-Armstrong long had been well known to local law enforcement. Nearly twenty years earlier, on July 30, 1984, she had fatally shot another boyfriend, Robert Thomas, in a case that became infamous for the condition of Diehl-Armstrong's house, where police found the forty-three-year-old Thomas's body. The place was filled with hundreds of pounds of rotting government surplus cheese and butter. Diehl-Armstrong—then Marjorie Diehl—never denied she killed Thomas, but said she shot him six times in self-defense, because he had abused her. When she finally went to trial in 1988—the case was delayed for years as Diehl got mental health treatment so she would be competent for court—she was acquitted of the homicide charge. "I'm not going to get into any more trouble," she told the judge.

With the discovery of Roden's body in the freezer, Diehl-Armstrong once again was a suspect in a homicide investigation—one that seemed to have a connection to the Pizza Bomber case, at least for some. Clark and his partner in the case, ATF Special Agent Jason Wick, believed that the location of the freezer—in a house yards from where Wells made his final delivery—was more than a coincidence. Others in the FBI initially doubted a link, keeping the probe steered toward other angles, such as finding the African American men Wells said had accosted him. Another difficulty was the lack of access Clark and Wick had to Diehl-Armstrong. After her arrest in Roden's death, she was held at a state mental hospital, where her mental state prevented Clark and Wick from interviewing her. Diehl-Armstrong returned to the state mental hospital on January 7, 2005, after she pleaded guilty but mentally ill to third-degree murder and abuse of a corpse in Erie County Common Pleas Court, and was sentenced to seven to twenty years in state prison. "I'm not going to be in any more trouble," she told this judge.

The other main person of interest in the Pizza Bomber case, William Rothstein, was permanently unavailable. He died of cancer on July 30, 2004, three days after he had denied to Clark, in a deathbed interview, that he had been involved in the death of Wells. Clark believed Rothstein probably made the homemade bomb that killed Wells. Rothstein, with his experience in robotics and his various odd jobs, matched an FBI behavioralist's profile of the bomber. But investigators had been unable to glean any solid clues from the device, such as fingerprints, which would have pointed to Rothstein and prodded him to confess.

The big break for Clark and Wick came on April 27, 2005—nearly two years after Wells's death. They were finally able to interview Diehl-Armstrong, who had been moved to a regular prison. Clark and Wick interviewed Diehl-Armstrong a total of eight times, but by the summer of 2005, they had received enough information from her to develop several promising leads. She said Rothstein was involved in the fatal bombing of Wells, but she also said she had given Rothstein, at his request, two kitchen timers like those in the bomb. Diehl-Armstrong was careful not to implicate herself, though Clark and Wick soon heard from several of her fellow inmates that Diehl-Armstrong had told them she was part of the plot. She told the inmates she had killed Roden in mid-August 2003 because he had threatened to go to police over the Pizza Bomber plot. Those interviews, as well as the talks with Diehl-Armstrong, led Clark and Wick to interview one of Diehl-Armstrong's friends from Erie, Kenneth E. Barnes, a fifty-one-year-old drug dealer and a former television repairman with self-taught expertise in fixing computers. Like Rothstein and Diehl-Armstrong, Barnes was highly intelligent, but a criminal. "The fractured intellectuals" was how Clark and Wick described the trio.

Barnes's cooperation unraveled the plot. He said he knew a prostitute whom Wells often frequented, and that he let Wells and the prostitute use his house, where he sold crack, to have sex. With that bit of information, Clark and Wick were able to link Wells to Barnes, who was friends with Diehl-Armstrong, who was close friends with Rothstein. Wells no longer looked like an innocent victim, totally unaware of the scheme that had him rob a bank with a bomb locked to his neck. He was part of the plan. Barnes revealed more: He said that in the spring of 2003, Diehl-Armstrong had asked him to kill her elderly father, a former salesman, so that Diehl-Armstrong could get her inheritance of more than $1 million. Barnes said he wanted $250,000 to do the hit. Diehl-Armstrong did not have that much money, so she, Rothstein, and Barnes came up with the plan to rob the bank.

Wells had lied about the group of African American men he said forced him to wear the bomb. According to what Barnes told Clark and Wick—statements they corroborated through other sources—Wells agreed to be part of the plot and helped plan it. But he thought the bomb would be fake, Barnes said, and that he would use it as a prop to force the bank teller to turn over the money. Rothstein also had given Wells the cane gun to subdue the bank employees, if necessary. The day before the bank robbery, according to Barnes, he and the others outfitted Wells with a fake bomb as he reviewed what he was supposed to do the next day. Also present at the planning session, Barnes said, were Diehl-Armstrong, Rothstein, and Rothstein's housemate, Floyd A. Stockton Jr., a fifty-six-year-old fugitive on the lam from charges that he had raped a mentally disabled nineteen-year-old woman in Washington State in 2002.

Wells got a surprise the day of the bank robbery. When Rothstein and the others put the bomb around his neck, it was no longer a fake. He tried to flee, but Rothstein fired a gun in the air and Barnes tackled him. Wells went on to rob the bank, as planned, fearing that Rothstein would detonate the bomb if he refused. Wells had a hybrid role: He had agreed to rob the bank, hoping to get some of the proceeds, but always thought the bomb would be phony. When he realized otherwise, he tried to resist.

Others were involved as well, according to the evidence. Robert Pinetti, the fellow pizza deliveryman, had helped talk Wells into agreeing to the Pizza Bomber plot, and might have overdosed on a fatal drug mixture that was meant to kill him. Roden, whose body was found in the freezer, was supposed to have driven a car in the bank robbery, but Diehl-Armstrong killed him after he threatened to go to the police. And Rothstein was the most involved of all. Based on what Barnes and others said, he came up with the Pizza Bomber plot, made the bomb, and developed the elaborate ruse that would have sent Wells on the scavenger hunt after he held up the bank. If Wells was caught before the bomb went off, he was supposed to have told the police he was delivering pizzas, as he always did, until he was forced to wear a bomb and a rob a bank as a bomb hostage. Immediately after he robbed the bank, Wells was supposed to have given the money to Rothstein, but the exchange never occurred. Wells died with the loot.

For whatever reason, Wells, even until his death, stuck with a story that Rothstein and the others most likely told him to use: that a group of black men had accosted him. Wells's reluctance to break from that script, to tell the state police who was really behind the whole plot, convinced Clark and Wick that Wells mistakenly believed Rothstein and the others would have detonated the bomb from afar if he had turned them in to police. No matter what Wells did, however, he would have likely never escaped. The plan was too elaborate, and the bomb too lethal, for him to have survived. Rothstein, whom the FBI characterized as a kind of puppeteer, masterminded Wells's race against time with only one possible outcome: Wells's death. Rothstein was a sociopath who saw the bank robbery and the collar bomb and the scavenger hunt as stages in a game in which he could engineer another man's death.

Marjorie Diehl-Armstrong was the only person who went to trial in the Pizza Bomber case. On July 9, 2007, a grand jury in U.S. District Court in Erie indicted Barnes and her for the same three felonies: conspiracy to commit armed bank robbery, aiding and abetting an armed bank robbery involving a death, and aiding and abetting the use of a destructive device—the bomb—in a crime of violence. Barnes pleaded guilty and agreed to testify against Diehl-Armstrong at her trial. He was initially sentenced to forty-five years in federal prison, but had the sentence halved for his cooperation. The other surviving suspect in the Pizza Bomber case, Floyd Stockton, Rothstein's housemate, was never charged but was granted immunity in exchange for agreeing to testify against Diehl-Armstrong. He had a heart attack during the trial and, though he survived, he never took the stand.

A jury convicted Diehl-Armstrong on November 1, 2009. She testified at her three-week trial and claimed Rothstein framed her to be at spots connected to the Pizza Bomber case the day Wells was killed. One of the strongest pieces of evidence came from a UPS driver. He told Clark he saw Rothstein and Diehl-Armstrong at the pay phone from which the call was made for Wells to make his final pizza delivery—the delivery that ended with Rothstein, Barnes, and the others making him wear the bomb. The UPS driver observed Diehl-Armstrong and Rothstein at the pay phone at the same time the call came in to Wells's pizzeria.

Diehl-Armstrong shrugged off the phone call and other evidence as inconclusive, and was defiant during the trial and at sentencing. She faced a mandatory sentence of life plus thirty years when she appeared before U.S. District Judge Sean J. McLaughlin on February 28, 2010. Diehl-Armstrong said she was wrongly accused. "I didn't even know Brian Wells," she said. "I am not a crazed killer that goes around wanting to kill and injure people. I am not that type of woman. I never have been." McLaughlin recounted the evidence—how greed had driven Diehl-Armstrong, Rothstein, Barnes, and the others to misuse their considerable intelligence for nefarious means. Diehl-Armstrong and the others were misfits who came up with the weird bank robbery plot with no concern about whether Brian Wells lived or died. The Pizza Bomber case, McLaughlin said, was about murder as much as it was about money. No one had ever seen anything like it, with its strange cast of characters and its horrific conclusion. "Its bizarre nature, coupled with the equally bizarre and sociopathic personalities that perpetuated it, have tended to obscure what this case is really about," McLaughlin said. "And that is that this defendant and her conspirators sent a man to his certain death."

Four years later, in denying one of Diehl-Armstrong's appeals, another federal judge described her in terms that suggested she was one of the more dangerous criminals to take part in a bank robbery in some time. Diehl-Armstrong, U.S. Magistrate Judge Martin C. Carlson wrote, is "a serial killer" who was involved "in two calculated killings, murders marked by brutality, sadism, cruelty, and the morbid abuse of her victims, both living and dead."[12]

The Pizza Bomber case was, like the homemade bomb at the center of it, a one-off—a one-of-a-kind heist not expected to reoccur in Erie or anywhere else. The next major bank robbery in Erie was far less unique, but illustrative of what had become a trend in bank robbery in the United States through the 2000s and 2010s. On September 10, 2012, the Bucket List Bandit hit a bank in Erie, one of ten banks in nine states he was accused of holding up since June 21, 2012. The Bucket List Bandit was one of many serial bank robbers traveling to cities and towns throughout the country. These were crooks with a shtick—men and women who robbed banks in much the same way each time, often wearing the same clothes or employing the same mannerisms or, in the case of the Bucket List Bandit, conveying the same message at each stop.

Almost all infamous bank robbers who struck in the United States—from Jesse James to the Dalton Gang, to John Dillinger, to Bonnie and Clyde, to Willie Sutton, to Scott Scurlock—worked as serial bandits, knocking off one bank after another in a similar style. The serial bandits of the twenty-first century were different: They operated alone and were often less dangerous than their twentieth-century counterparts. Like their predecessors, however, these serial bank robbers were menacing enough to attract the attention of the FBI, which nicknamed them to elevate their public profiles and make them more vulnerable to capture. J. Edgar Hoover's FBI in the 1930s came up with Public Enemy Number One. Eight decades later, the bureau was coining nicknames like the Cell Phone Bandit, the Mad Hatter, and the Bucket List Bandit. Though some critics have said nicknaming bank robbers glorifies them, the FBI maintains that giving the suspects catchy titles engages the public and spurs tips. With the FBI's resources shifted toward counterterrorism after 9/11, advocates of the nicknames contend, the bureau increasingly needed the public's assistance to catch bank robbers. [13]

The Bucket List Bandit got his label because he told the tellers he was dying of cancer and had months to live—his bank robberies were the acts of a desperate thief trying to achieve as much as he could before his final demise. The Bucket List Bandit, middle-aged with a receding hairline and a mustache, each time showed the teller a note that demanded money; he sometimes said he had a gun, though he never displayed a firearm. He was calm throughout and, after indicating that he was terminally ill, usually walked out with loot. He asked for $5,000 in the heist in Erie, at a branch of the Huntington Bank, but made off with $4,080 and a red dye pack, which exploded when he left the building. As happened in the other bank robberies, surveillance cameras took photos. [14]

The Bucket List Bandit's real name was Michael Eugene Brewster, a fifty-four-year-old from Pensacola, Florida. His criminal career ended on September 12, 2012, two days after he robbed the bank in Erie. Police pulled him over in Roland, Oklahoma, near Tulsa, for running a stop sign. Police had no idea he was the Bucket List Bandit, but learned through computerized records with the National Crime Information Center (NCIC) that he was wanted in Pensacola for the theft of the car he was driving. After his arrest, police found out he was wanted on bank robbery charges. His crime spree had started when he robbed a Chase Bank branch in Colorado on June 21, 2012. Brewster later robbed banks in Arizona, Idaho, Utah, North Carolina, Florida, Tennessee, Illinois, and Missouri before robbing the bank in Erie. He got $33,858 overall. [15]

Brewster pleaded guilty to eleven felony counts of bank robbery and was sentenced in U.S. District Court in Erie on August 15, 2013. He acknowledged he had a long-term drinking problem, but also admitted that bank robbery was not on his bucket list, because he had none. The Bucket List Bandit did not have cancer or any other terminal illness. Brewster gave no reason for why he committed the heists, though a psychiatrist reported that the bank robberies excited Brewster. The Bucket List Bandit got no sympathy. U.S. District Judge Sean J. McLaughlin gave Brewster eleven years and three months in federal prison—the harshest sentence available under the federal sentencing guidelines, which accounted for the number of bank robberies and Brewster's criminal history. Brewster, the judge said, had terrorized bank tellers, and then falsely told them he was the one who was truly in fear of dying. "The impetus for the crime spree," McLaughlin said, "was simply greed, not grief."[16]

Though Brewster gave no motive for his work as the Bucket List Bandit, other serial bank robbers were known to steal for a cause, whether for drugs or for what they believed was their own survival. In the fall of 2003, a thief whom the media dubbed the Long Island Bank Robber held up ten banks in five towns in suburban New York City and got away with about $60,000. He was Stephen Trantel, a thirty-eight-year-old, self-employed commodities broker whose business suffered in the post-9/11 financial slowdown. Desperate for cash, Trantel studied the best methods for robbing a bank—he chose institutions without security guards, and avoided heists on Wednesdays, when, he noticed, most police officers cashed their checks[17]—and executed his first holdup on August 8, 2003.

Trantel, the son of a retired police officer, the son-in-law of a federal prosecutor, and the married father of two young sons, typically told tellers he had a gun, though he was unarmed, and wore a disguise that included a fake mustache. Police arrested him on November 28, 2003, after tracking him down using a fingerprint left behind on a demand note. The police matched the print to one in his records for a 1984 conviction for driving while intoxicated.[18] Trantel pleaded guilty to three felony counts of bank robbery in Nassau County Court and on May 27, 2004, was sentenced to nine years in prison.[19]

Until his arrest, even his wife had no idea Trantel was a professional bandit; she divorced him eight months after he went to prison. Trantel said he saw crime as the only way to prevent personal financial collapse. "The bottom line is that I just came to this epiphany that there's no other way," he once said. "If I want to hold onto everything, then I got to steal money."[20]

Other serial bank robbers got nicknames for how, rather than where, they pulled of their heists. In August 2000, the FBI in Los Angeles identified a thirty-six-year-old man as the Cell Phone Bandit, who had robbed "more than thirty banks from San Diego to Sacramento, jabbering away into his phone in the moments before the holdups."[21] The FBI said the robber's use of the phone might have been a ruse, but that he was also most likely armed. A month later, the Cell Phone Bandit was arrested in

Spokane, Washington, after he was accused of robbing a bank in Seattle.[22] His nickname did not retire with him.

Five years later, in suburban Washington, D.C., police and the FBI were searching for another Cell Phone Bandit—a nineteen-year-old community college student who, with her boyfriend, held up four banks in northern Virginia between October 12 and November 4, 2005. In three of the heists, the robber, Candice R. Martinez, was seen on surveillance video chatting calmly on her cell phone while a teller scrambled to comply with Martinez's demand note. Her boyfriend, David C. Williams, also nineteen years old, later admitted to being on the other end of the calls and driving the getaway car.[23] Authorities charged the pair on November 15, 2005, after an FBI agent spotted one of the cars used in the robberies. By then the two had stolen $48,620, which investigators said they used to buy a plasma screen television set, a car, and a $2,000 Chihuahua puppy that Martinez and Williams named Capone. The two each pleaded guilty to bank robbery charges in U.S. District Court in Alexandria, Virginia, and each was sentenced to twelve years in prison. At Martinez's sentencing, on March 3, 2006, a twenty-year-old teller spoke of how the holdup of her bank, in which no gun was used, traumatized her. The teller said she had to get counseling so she could continue to work. "Even if she had no intention of hurting me," the teller said, crying, "I didn't know that."[24] Despite the jaunty nickname, the Cell Phone Bandit was a danger.

Such was the case with numerous other serial bandits whose crimes earned them colorful monikers from the FBI. In 2007 in the Chicago area alone, agents were searching for as many as six serial bank robbers. The Time Bandit ordered his victims into the vault and told them to count to three hundred before they could move. The Paint-by-Numbers Bandit wore paint-speckled clothes. The Wheaton Bandit hit banks near that Chicago suburb. The Hard-Hat Bandit wore a yellow construction hat. The Fifteen-Second Bandit demanded cash from the tellers in that much time, which was five seconds more than the Ten-Second Bandit. And the Ten-Second Bandit was originally known as the Harry Caray Bandit, because he wore a wig, baseball cap, and oversize glasses that made him resemble Caray, the late beloved broadcaster of the Chicago Cubs. The Band-Aid Bandit, who used the plastic strips to cover a mole on his face, robbed thirty-nine banks in Florida from 2000 to 2006. The FBI in Los Angeles searched for the Bad Rug Bandit and the Paparazzi Bandit, who photographed the banks he robbed. The Duct Tape Bandit worked in

Kentucky. In Seattle, where the FBI office is known for concocting some of the catchiest nicknames, Attila the Bun wore her hair up during heists. And, also from the Chicago area, the Dr. Seuss Bandit struck twenty banks in 2006 and 2007 while he wore the striped stovepipe chapeau Seuss's Cat in the Hat made famous.[25]

Another robber with a penchant for unique headgear was the Hat Bandit, better known as the Mad Hatter. He held up eighteen banks in northern New Jersey from September 2006 to July 2007, netting a total of more than $60,000. He wore a different hat each time, including baseball caps, a knit cap, a fisherman's cap, and a hat with military insignia. Each topper helped disguise the Mad Hatter's face, which made him harder to catch—even though he and his hats were captured on bank surveillance video.[26] The person under the hats was James G. Madison, a fifty-year-old former machinist who, during the robberies, used demand notes and sometimes said he had a weapon, but never showed a gun.

Madison was on parole for pleading guilty in 1987 to manslaughter in the death of his girlfriend, whose body was found in a suitcase in a New Jersey river after she had been beaten to death with a lamp.[27] Madison said he robbed banks because he needed money for rent.[28] He was arrested on July 23, 2007, one day after a bank employee, during the robbery of her bank, got the license plate of the robber's getaway car, which belonged to Madison's new girlfriend. "Hopefully, his hat will be hanging in jail for a very long time," a prosecutor said after Madison's arrest.[29] Madison pleaded guilty in U.S. District Court in Newark to eighteen bank robberies and one attempted bank robbery, and on January 23, 2008, was sentenced to ten years in prison. Madison's nineteen crimes, federal authorities said, accounted for nearly 16 percent of the 120 bank robberies committed in New Jersey during his ten-month spree as the Mad Hatter.[30]

Age rather than apparel defined other serial bank robbers. The Grandpa Bandit, the Granddad Bandit, and the Geezer Bandit held up financial institutions well into late middle age and their golden years, as did the oldest known bank robber in the United States, J. L. Hunter "Red" Rountree, who died in federal prison at age ninety-two in 2004, a year after he committed his final heist. The FBI bestowed no nickname on Rountree, probably because he robbed only three banks during his criminal career, which began in 1998 when he was eighty-six years old—a time when most people are well into retirement.

Rountree was born on his family's farm near Brownsville, Texas, in December 1911, and he said he spent most of his professional life building a fortune as the head of Rountree Manufacturing Company, in Houston.[31] Rountree's wife died in 1986, and the next year, at age seventy-six, he married a thirty-one-year-old woman. He said he lost at least $500,000 putting her through drug rehabilitation programs, and claimed a bad loan from a bank in Corpus Christi, Texas, added to his problems and forced him into bankruptcy.[32] By 1998 Rountree had robbed the first of his three banks, the SouthTrust Bank in Biloxi, Mississippi, for which he was fined $260 and sentenced to three years of probation. The next year he robbed a NationsBank in Pensacola, and got three years in prison, where he was the oldest inmate incarcerated in Florida. A year after his release, he held up the First American Bank in Abilene, Texas, on August 12, 2003, and was sentenced to twelve and a half years in federal prison, a sentence long enough to guarantee he would never leave prison alive. He was in a wheelchair during his final stay.

Rountree had a routine when he robbed banks. He chose a bank he could drive to on a full tank of gas from his home, so the bank was somewhat far away; he arrived at the bank early, when the customers were few; and he stayed away from that city when he was done.[33] Rountree's last holdup, because of his age, had a touch of the surreal. He recounted that the teller blurted "Are you kidding?" when he demanded cash.[34] Rountree was not armed. He relayed the teller his intentions by giving her two envelopes, one of which had "robbery" written on it; the other, he said, was for the money. Despite the teller's disbelief, Rountree left with $1,999.[35] A bank employee saw the license plate of Rountree's car, and police pulled him over a half hour later.[36]

Until he was caught, Rountree enjoyed a kind of youthful exuberance he said the robberies created. His explanation for why he committed the crimes made him sound like Willie Sutton. "You want to know why I rob banks?" he said in a 2004 prison interview. "It's fun. I feel good, awful good. I feel good for sometimes days, for sometimes hours."[37] In another prison interview, in 2001, he mentioned the bad bank loan from years ago and sounded like his spiritual ancestors in crime—the bank robbery gangsters of the Great Depression, an era during which Rountree was in his twenties—offering another explanation for why he robbed banks. "A Corpus Christi bank that I'd done business with had forced me into bankruptcy. I have never liked banks since," Rountree said. "I decided I would get even. And I have."[38] Much like his forebears, he was also unrepentant. Asked in that same 2001 interview what he would do when he got out of prison, Rountree said, "I might rob another bank. I'm not saying I will or I won't. But, hey, I might need to."[39]

The Granddad Bandit and the Grandpa Bandit were both younger than Rountree. The Granddad Bandit, whose real name was Michael Francis Mara, was fifty-three years old on May 11, 2011, when he was sentenced in U.S. District Court in Richmond, Virginia, to twenty-five years in prison. Mara—called the Granddad Bandit because of his grandfatherly appearance, including a balding head and graying hair[40]—pleaded guilty to robbing two banks in the Richmond area and, as part of the plea, also admitted to robbing twenty-five banks in thirteen states between 2008 and 2010.[41] His total take was about $83,000. The FBI's nickname helped the bureau capture Mara, who was a grandfather with a lengthy prior record. In August 2010, the FBI put his photograph, from bank surveillance cameras, on billboards around the country and asked for the public's help in finding the Granddad Bandit. A week later, because of the billboards, the FBI got a tip that identified Mara as the suspect. Agents and the police surrounded his home in Baton Rouge, Louisiana, where they arrested him after a six-hour standoff on August 10, 2011.[42] Mara initially was not at home because he was robbing a bank in Charlotte, North Carolina.[43]

Mara typically used demand notes—the FBI found fifteen such notes, written on deposit slips, at his house[44]—and attracted little attention while he waited to rob a bank. "If he was standing behind you in the teller line while you're waiting for teller service you wouldn't give him a second look," an FBI agent said after his arrest. "He blends well with people, and his look reminds you of the fatherly granddad."[45]

The Grandpa Bandit's crimes were limited to Oregon. He was Ferrell Lee Brier, who was sixty-one years old on October 13, 2011, when he was sentenced in U.S. District Court in Eugene to thirteen years and two months in prison. Brier pleaded guilty to robbing seven banks in Oregon between October 2009 and May 2010. His take was $33,422.[46] Authorities said he was armed with a .45-caliber Smith & Wesson pistol but used demand notes, though at least twice he opened his jacket to display the gun tucked in his waistband. Brier's last robbery was of the Umpqua Bank, in Eugene, on May 3, 2011. Police identified him as the robber and arrested him at the home of an exotic dancer; investigators said he used the money from the bank robberies to pay for exotic dancers and prostitutes.[47] The FBI said Brier gave police one reason he robbed the bank in Eugene: "stupidity."[48]

The Geezer Bandit is the last in the trio of bank robbers notorious for their ages—still on the loose in 2015, wanted for robbing as many as sixteen banks, many near San Diego, since August 28, 2009. He looks old: Bank surveillance photos show a man, usually wearing a cap or hat, with a wrinkled face. The FBI has pegged the Geezer Bandit's age at between sixty and seventy, but he might not be a geezer after all.[49] The FBI believes he might have worn a synthetic mask, possibly designed for special effects, to conceal his true age and identity. In one of his early robberies, the Geezer Bandit had a small oxygen tank on his back, with a tube from the tank connected to a nosepiece. But in one of his later robberies, he sprinted from the scene.[50] The Geezer Bandit has flashed guns at tellers; the FBI has warned he is dangerous, and put up a $20,000 reward for information that leads to his arrest. The attention has turned the Geezer Bandit into a minor celebrity.[51] His wrinkled face has appeared on T-shirts, and he is the subject of several Facebook pages. As of late 2014, one of the pages had more than 14,270 "likes"—making the Geezer Bandit, for his fans, something of an ageless folk hero.[52]

No matter what the age of the Geezer Bandit, he is engaged in a line of work that is on the decline, and possibly dying, as the number of bank robberies in the United States continues to decline from the all-time high of 9,388 in 1991. The number of bank robberies per hundred bank branches has plummeted, from just over than 10 in 2000 to 4.47 in 2012.[53] And the amount of loot stolen has decreased, from a total of $77,096,405 in 2003—a figure that includes money and other valuables also stolen in bank burglaries and larcenies—to $38,343,502 in 2011.[54] For individual bank robbers, the crime no longer pays as it used to: The average take per bank robbery was $3,542 in 2013, down from $4,767 a decade earlier.[55]

The robbers have not vanished. They have migrated from banks to the Internet, where they can remain largely anonymous—no bank surveillance photos, no nicknames, no shootouts with the FBI and the police. More than anything, even more than improved bank security, the rise in online financial fraud has contributed to the decrease in the number of bank robbers. The risk of getting caught is lower on the Internet, and the takes are greater. In 2000, the first year it started compiling cases of Internet fraud, the FBI recorded 16,838 complaints.[56] By 2013, that number had grown to 262,813, with the total amount lost in Internet fraud that year reaching $781,841,611—close to double the $404 million the FBI said was lost in all 345,031 robberies recorded in the United States that year, including bank robberies.[57]

If Jesse James or John Dillinger or Bonnie and Clyde were alive in the 2010s, they probably would be stealing their money by using computer keystrokes rather than guns. To paraphrase what Willie Sutton might have said, more thieves are going online because, in the wired world, that is where the money is. These shadowy cyber bandits are America's newest public enemies.

AFTERWORD

By late 2014, a masked man had robbed three banks in Northern California within six months. The frequency and severity of the crimes—the at-large thief showed a gun in two cases—was enough for the FBI to get involved, and to coin a nickname. The FBI dubbed the robber the Bad Breath Bandit because he wore a disposable paper face mask during each heist.[1]

The nickname is memorable, and humorous, but also pathetic. A bank robber named after an element of personal hygiene seems not so much a brazen thief as a parody, a kind of twisted and undeserving heir to the legacy of Jesse James, Butch Cassidy, George Leslie, Harvey Bailey, Pretty Boy Floyd, and John Dillinger. To say that James and his descendants in crime displayed a higher degree of cunning and sophistication than the Bad Breath Bandit is not to glorify James and the others, but to point to a reality: By the early twenty-first century, the dethroning of the bank robber as the king of American thieves was all but complete.

No one should mourn the decline of the bank robber in the United States. To do so would to be like those misguided apologists for the Mafia, who rue the dismantling of organized crime and the sense of order they claim it supposedly brought to the mean streets of cities throughout the country. No bank teller should have to wonder whether the person standing in line is going to point a gun in his or her face. No bank customer should have to worry about getting caught in the crossfire. No city or town should have to fear the tragedy that a drug-addled and desperate bank robber can leave behind.

But being captivated by the likes of a Jesse James, a Willie Sutton, a John Dillinger, a John Stanley Wojtowicz, or a Marjorie Diehl-Armstrong also is understandable. Though criminals, they embodied their times and often exploited the weaknesses of the nation whose banks they plundered. They are fascinating because they are as complex as the country that bred them—whether in the aftermath of the Civil War, in the depths of the Great Depression, or in the turbulence of the 1960s and 1970s. "There is no typical bank robbery or method of solution," J. Edgar Hoover, that sworn enemy of bank robbers, once wrote, "just as there is no single person you could point to and say he is a typical bank robber."[2]

Much as Willie Sutton did, Hoover also captured why bank robbery always will be part of American culture—even as the king of thieves is left to grasp for his crown. "Banks," Hoover wrote, "are an almost irresistible attraction for that element of our society which seeks unearned money."[3]

NOTES

I. BREAKING IN

1. L. R. Kirchner, *Robbing Banks: An American History, 1831–1999* (Rockville Centre, NY: Sarpedon, 2000), 12.

2. Rick Beard, "When the Rebels Invaded Vermont," *New York Times*, October 17, 2014, http://opinionator.blogs.nytimes.com/2014/10/17/when-the-rebels-invaded-vermont/?mabReward=RI%3A11&action=click&pgtype=Homepage&region=CColumn&module=Recommendation&src=rechp&WT.nav=RecEngine&_r=0.

3. Thomas Lloyd, *Robbery of the Bank of Pennsylvania in 1798. The Trial in the Supreme Court of the State of Pennsylvania* (Philadelphia, 1808), 1, http://babel.hathitrust.org/cgi/pt?id=nyp.33433075955637.

4. The case is known today as "The Great Bank Heist of 1798," Carpenters' Hall, accessed March 26, 2014, http://www.ushistory.org/carpentershall/visit/bank.htm.

5. Lloyd, *Robbery of the Bank of Pennsylvania*, 4. See also Ron Avery, "America's First Bank Robbery," Carpenters' Hall, accessed March 26, 2014, http://www.ushistory.org/carpentershall/history/robbery.htm.

6. Lloyd, *Robbery of the Bank of Pennsylvania*, 13.

7. Ibid., 8.

8. Negley K. Teeters, *The Cradle of the Penitentiary: The Walnut Street Jail at Philadelphia, 1773–1835* (Philadelphia: Pennsylvania Prison Society, 1955), 39.

9. Avery, "America's First Bank Robbery."

10. Brearley B. Karsch, research volunteer, Carpenters' Hall, e-mail to the authors, March 12, 2014, citing Managing Committee minutes of Carpenters' Hall, January 21, 1799.

11. Lloyd, *Robbery of the Bank of Pennsylvania*, 183.

12. Bruce W. Chambers, "The Pythagorean Puzzle of Patrick Lyon," *The Art Bulletin* 58, no. 2 (1976): 227.

13. Patrick Lyon, *The Narrative of Patrick Lyon Who Suffered Three Months Severe Imprisonment in Philadelphia Gaol on Merely a Vague Suspicion of Being Concerned in a Robbery of the Bank of Pennsylvania With his Remarks Thereon* (Philadelphia, 1799), 3, 4. Eighteenth Century Collections Online, Gale, CIC Penn State University, accessed March 30, 2014.

14. "The Right to Right Wrongs," Historical Society of Pennsylvania, accessed March 26, 2014, http://www2.hsp.org/exhibits/anvil/loa04.html.

15. Bray Hammond, *Banks and Politics in America from the Revolution to the Civil War* (Princeton, NJ: Princeton University Press, 1957), 164.

16. Gerald C. Fischer, *American Banking Structure* (New York: Columbia University Press, 1968), 15.

17. Margaret G. Myers, *A Financial History of the United States* (New York: Columbia University Press, 1970), 163.

18. Fischer, *American Banking Structure*, 27.

19. Ibid., 28.

20. Henry Ruth and Kevin R. Reitz, *The Challenge of Crime: Rethinking Our Response* (Cambridge, MA: Harvard University Press, 2003), 15.

21. Ruth and Reitz, *The Challenge of Crime*, 9–10.

22. Saabira Chaudhuri, "U.S. Banks Prune More Branches: Migration to Mobile, Online Services Has Lenders Closing Local Outposts," *Wall Street Journal*, January 27, 2014, accessed March 17, 2014, http://online.wsj.com/news/articles/SB10001424052702303277704579347223157745640.

23. Deborah Lamm Weisel, "The Problem of Bank Robbery," *Problem-Oriented Guides for Police, Problem-Specific Guides Series*, no. 48, U.S. Department of Justice, Office of Community Oriented Police Services (2007): 2–3, 8, http://www.cops.usdoj.gov/Publications/e03071267.pdf.

24. These numbers include sixty bank burglaries and twelve bank larcenies in which money is taken without force. The financial institutions the statistics cover are federally insured commercial banks, mutual savings banks, credit unions, savings and loan associations, and armored carrier companies. All statistics from the Federal Bureau of Investigation (FBI), *Reports and Publications: Bank Crime Statistics: Bank Crime Reports*, accessed July 5, 2014, http://www.fbi.gov/stats-services/publications/bank-crime-statistics-2011/bank-crime-statistics-2011. See also "Issue of Interest: Bank Robberies," American Bankers Associa-

tion, accessed July 5, 2014, http://www.aba.com/Press/Pages/BankRobbery_
Issue.aspx.

25. FBI, *Crime in the United States 2003*, 34, http://www.fbi.gov/about-us/
cjis/ucr/crime-in-the-u.s/2003/03sec2.pdf; "Crime in the United States 2013,"
FBI, http://www.fbi.gov/about-us/cjis/ucr/crime-in-the-u.s/2013/crime-in-the-
u.s.-2013/tables/table-23/table_23_offense_analysis_number_and_percent_
change_2012-2013.xls.

26. FBI, "Crime in the United States 2013."

27. Weisel, "The Problem of Bank Robbery," 9.

28. FBI, *Reports and Publications: Bank Crime Statistics.*

29. D. A. Johnston, "Psychological Observations of Bank Robbery,"
American Journal of Psychiatry 135, no. 11 (1978): 1377.

30. Ibid.

31. James F. Haran and John M. Martin, "The Armed Urban Bank Robber:
A Profile," *Federal Probation* 48, no. 47 (1984): 49.

32. FBI, *Reports and Publications: Bank Crime Statistics.*

33. Ibid.

34. Steve Cocheo, "The Bank Robber, the Quote, and the Final Irony," *ABA
Banking Journal* 89, no. 3 (1997): 71–72. Cocheo provides an insightful analysis
of the remark forever tied to Willie Sutton.

35. Willie Sutton with Edward Linn, *Where the Money Was* (New York:
Viking Press, 1976), 121.

36. Jeff Nilsson, "America's First Bank Robbery," *Saturday Evening Post*,
March 16, 2013, http://www.saturdayeveningpost.com/2013/03/16/archives/
post-perspective/first-bank-robbery-in-united-states.html. Nilsson considers the
City Bank robbery the nation's first bank robbery, though the Carpenters' Hall
case, which he does not mention, clearly preceded it.

37. Ibid.

38. "Robbery of the City Bank," *Workingman's Advocate*, May 14, 1831.

39. Nilsson, "America's First Bank Robbery."

40. "Robbery of the City Bank."

41. "City Bank Robber Taken," *Atkinson's Saturday Evening Post*, April 2,
1831.

42. Ibid.

43. "Robbery of the City Bank."

44. Nilsson, "America's First Bank Robbery."

45. Ibid.

46. Bryan Burrough, *Public Enemies: America's Greatest Crime Wave and
the Birth of the FBI, 1933–34* (New York: Penguin Press, 2004), 15.

2. THE ORIGINAL OUTLAW

1. T. J. Stiles, *Jesse James: Last Rebel of the Civil War* (New York: Alfred A. Knopf, 2002), 173.

2. Ibid., 6. Stiles's entire book, a masterful biography, details the Jameses' political motivations.

3. Ibid., 334. See also Mark Lee Gardner, *Shot All to Hell: Jesse James, the Northfield Raid, and the Wild West's Greatest Escape* (New York: William Morrow, 2013), frontispiece.

4. Stiles, *Jesse James*, 206.

5. "The Malden Murder; Arrest of the Culprit Green," *New York Times*, February 14, 1864.

6. L. R. Kirchner, *Robbing Banks: An American History, 1831–1999* (Rockville Centre, NY: Sarpedon, 2000), 20.

7. Ibid., 15, 21.

8. Stiles, *Jesse James*, 393.

9. Richard Maxwell Brown, "Western Violence: Structure, Values, Myth," *Western Historical Quarterly* 24, no. 1 (1993), 8.

10. Ibid.

11. Stiles, *Jesse James*, 233.

12. Ibid., 211.

13. James D. Horan, *Desperate Men: The James Gang and the Wild Bunch*, rev. ed. (1949; repr., Lincoln: University of Nebraska Press, 1997), 8. Horan is among the writers who attribute Jesse James's constant blinking to granulated eyelids.

14. Stiles, *Jesse James*, 368.

15. Ibid., 245.

16. Ibid., 246.

17. Ibid.

18. "Jesse James' Bank Robberies," *American Experience: Jesse James*, Public Broadcasting System, 2005, accessed May 6, 2014, http://www.pbs.org/wgbh/americanexperience/features/general-article/james-robberies/.

19. William A. Settle Jr., *Jesse James Was His Name: Or, Fact and Fiction Concerning the Careers of the Notorious James Brothers of Missouri* (Columbia: University of Missouri Press, 1966), 88.

20. Kirchner, *Robbing Banks*, 15.

21. Lynne Pierson Doti and Larry Schweikart, *Banking in the American West: From the Gold Rush to Deregulation* (Norman: University of Oklahoma Press, 1991), 9.

22. Stiles, *Jesse James*, 90.

23. Ibid., 95.

24. Gardner, *Shot All to Hell*, 32–33.

25. Stiles, *Jesse James*, 122.

26. William A. Settle Jr., "The James Boys and Missouri Politics," *Missouri Historical Review* 36, no. 4 (1942): 414.

27. Settle, *Jesse James Was His Name*, 45, 46.

28. Stiles, *Jesse James*, 249.

29. Kirchner, *Robbing Banks*, 16.

30. Settle, "The James Boys and Missouri Politics," 416.

31. Ibid.

32. Stiles, *Jesse James*, 320.

33. Ibid., 324.

34. Ibid., 334.

35. Ibid., 378.

36. Settle, *Jesse James Was His Name*, 173, 174.

3. ROBBERY ON THE RANGE

1. James D. Horan, *Desperate Men: The James Gang and the Wild Bunch*, rev. ed. (1949; repr., Lincoln: University of Nebraska Press, 1997), 189.

2. *Butch Cassidy and the Sundance Kid* grossed $102,308,889, making it the 546th-highest-grossing movie of all time, and the 34th-highest when adjusted for inflation, according to www.boxofficemojo.com.

3. A number of authors spell Grat's full name as "Grattan." Federal records, however, list it as "Gratton." See the records for deputy U.S. marshals who worked at Fort Smith, Arkansas: http://www.nps.gov/fosm/historyculture/deputy-marshals-and-other-federal-court-employees.htm.

4. "Dalton Family History," Kansas Heritage Group, accessed May 28, 2014, http://www.kansasheritage.org/families/dalton.html.

5. Missouri also earned the sobriquet "poor old Missouri" because of the number of bandits in the state. See William A. Settle Jr., "The James Boys and Missouri Politics," *Missouri Historical Review* 36, no. 4 (1942): 414.

6. "Dalton Family History," Kansas Heritage Group.

7. Grant Foreman, *A History of Oklahoma* (Norman: University of Oklahoma Press, 1941), 353.

8. Ibid., 352.

9. Ibid., 354.

10. Carl L. Cannon, "The Old West Was Not Overrun by Bad Men; Emmet Dalton of the Famous Dalton Gang Explains Why Their Number Was Few," review of *When the Daltons Rode*, by Emmett Dalton, *New York Times*, February 1, 1931, Sunday Book Review.

11. "History—Deputies versus the Wild Bunch," U.S. Marshals Service, http://www.justice.gov/marshals/history/dalton/doolin-dalton.htm.

12. "Dalton Family History," Kansas Heritage Group.

13. Gary L. Roberts, "Dalton Gang," in *The New Encyclopedia of the American West* (New Haven, CT: Yale University Press, 1998), accessed June 4, 2104, http://ezproxy.gannon.edu/login?url=http://search.credoreference.com/content/entry/americanwest/dalton_gang/0. See also David Dary, "The Last Shoot-Out of the Dalton Gang," *Kansas City Star*, July 25, 1971, Sunday Magazine, accessed June 27, 2014, http://www.newspapers.com/newspage/51229635/.

14. Foreman, *A History of Oklahoma*, 355.

15. Harry Sinclair Drago, *Road Agents and Train Robbers: Half a Century of Western Banditry* (New York: Dodd, Mead, 1973), 209.

16. "Alila Train Robbery," *San Francisco Call*, March 5, 1891, accessed May 28, 2014, http://cdnc.ucr.edu/cgi-bin/cdnc?a=d&d=SFC18910305.1.3&e=-------en--20--1--txt-IN------.

17. Drago, however, questions whether the Daltons were involved in the Alila heist. See Drago, *Road Agents and Train Robbers*, 207.

18. Cannon, "The Old West Was Not Overrun by Bad Men."

19. T. J. Stiles, *Jesse James: Last Rebel of the Civil War* (New York: Alfred A. Knopf, 2002), 326.

20. Cannon, "The Old West Was Not Overrun by Bad Men."

21. A. B. McDonald, "Dalton Goes Back to Bandit Haunts," *New York Times*, May 10, 1931.

22. Ibid.

23. William Robbins, "Coffeyville Journal: Gunfight Defines a Town and a Family," *New York Times*, October 5, 1992.

24. Ibid.

25. Federal Writers' Project of the Work Projects Administration for the State of Kansas, *Kansas: A Guide to the Sunflower State* (New York: Viking Press, 1939), 173.

26. Robbins, "Coffeyville Journal: Gunfight Defines a Town and a Family."

27. McDonald, "Dalton Goes Back to Bandit Haunts."

28. Cannon, "The Old West Was Not Overrun by Bad Men."

29. Lynne Pierson Doti and Larry Schweikart, *Banking in the American West: From the Gold Rush to Deregulation* (Norman: University of Oklahoma Press, 1991), 39.

30. Federal Writers' Project of the Work Projects Administration for the State of Kansas, *Kansas: A Guide to the Sunflower State*, 175.

31. Robbins, "Coffeyville Journal: Gunfight Defines a Town and a Family."

32. Federal Writers' Project of the Work Projects Administration for the State of Kansas, *Kansas: A Guide to the Sunflower State*, 174.

33. Robbins, "Coffeyville Journal: Gunfight Defines a Town and a Family."

34. "Odd Happenings in a Week's News: Dalton Gang Spendthrifts," *New York Times*, May 3, 1931.

35. McDonald, "Dalton Goes Back to Bandit Haunts."

36. Ibid.

37. Russell E. Bearden, "Bill Doolin," in *The Encyclopedia of Arkansas History & Culture*, accessed June 4, 2014, http://www.encyclopediaofarkansas.net/encyclopedia/entry-detail.aspx?search=1&entryID=1632.

38. Thom Hatch, *The Last Outlaws: The Lives and Legends of Butch Cassidy and the Sundance Kid* (New York: New American Library, 2013), 162.

39. "History—Deputies versus the Wild Bunch."

40. L. R. Kirchner, *Robbing Banks: An American History, 1831–1999* (Rockville Centre, NY: Sarpedon, 2000), 31.

41. Bearden, "Bill Doolin." See also Drago, *Road Agents and Train Robbers*, 231.

42. Drago, *Road Agents and Train Robbers*, 231.

43. E. D. Nix to Judson Harmon, 30 July 1895, "History—Deputies versus the Wild Bunch."

44. Ibid.

45. Drago, *Road Agents and Train Robbers*, 235.

46. Nix to Harmon, 30 July 1895.

47. Ibid.

48. Ibid.

49. Ibid.

50. "Killing of Bill Doolin," National Park Service, Fort Smith, National Historic Site, http://www.nps.gov/fosm/historyculture/killing-of-bill-doolin.htm.

51. "Bill Doolin's Last Pistol Fight," *New York Times*, August 26, 1896.

52. Drago, *Road Agents and Train Robbers*, 243.

53. Ibid.

54. Herbert Asbury, *The Gangs of New York: An Informal History of the Underworld* (1927; repr., New York: Thunder's Mouth Press, 1998), 185–86.

55. George W. Walling, *Recollections of a New York Chief of Police* (1887; repr., Montclair, NJ: Patterson Smith, 1972), 278.

56. Asbury, *The Gangs of New York*, 187.

57. Walling, *Recollections of a New York Chief of Police*, 236.

58. Asbury, *The Gangs of New York*, 191.

59. J. North Conway, *King of Heists: The Sensational Bank Robbery of 1878 that Shocked America* (Guilford, CT: Lyons Press, 2009), 38.

60. Ibid., 39.

61. Asbury, *The Gangs of New York*, 191.

62. Conway, *King of Heists*, x.

63. Ibid., ix.

64. Ibid., 176.

65. Walling, *Recollections of a New York Chief of Police*, 280.

66. Conway, *King of Heists*, 170. See also Asbury, *The Gangs of New York*, 76.

67. Asbury, *The Gangs of New York*, 187.

68. Conway, *King of Heists*, 177.

69. Ibid., 36.

70. Ibid.

71. Ibid.

72. Conway, *King of Heists*, 184. Both Asbury and Walling have Leslie dying in 1884, but this is clearly a mistake, according to the *New York Times*, which reported Leslie's death after his body was found on June 4, 1878.

73. "A Great Bank Robbery," *New York Times*, October 28, 1878.

74. Ibid.

75. Ibid.

76. Conway, *King of Heists*, 192.

77. Ibid., 195.

78. Ibid., 185.

79. "On a Murder's Track," *New York Times*, June 8, 1878; "The Yonkers Murder," *New York Times*, June 11, 1878.

80. "The Yonkers Mystery," *New York Times*, June 9, 1878.

81. Ibid.

82. Conway, *King of Heists*, 186.

83. "Notable Burials," Cypress Hills Cemetery, http://cypresshillscemetery.org/timeline-2/notable-burials/.

84. Hatch, *The Last Outlaws*, 270.

85. Chapman's article is reprinted in Anne Meadows, *Digging Up Butch and Sundance* (New York: St. Martin's Press, 1994), 103.

86. Meadows, *Digging Up Butch and Sundance*, 104.

87. Hatch, *The Last Outlaws*, 34.

88. Horan, *Desperate Men*, 185.

89. Ibid., 189.

90. Hatch, *The Last Outlaws*, 49.

91. Ibid., 50.

92. Ibid., 106–7.

93. Ibid., 149.

94. Ibid., 61.

95. Ibid., 104.

96. Ibid.

97. Ibid., 184, 185.

98. Ibid., 214.

99. Drago, *Road Agents and Train Robbers*, 230.

100. Ibid., 230.

101. "Henry Starr," biography.com (website for A&E Television Networks' *Biography*), accessed June 28, 2104, http://www.biography.com/people/henry-starr-21247935.

102. Ibid.

103. Ibid.

104. "Bank Robber Starr Died with Family in Cell," Boone County Historical & Railroad Society, accessed June 28, 2014, http://www.bchrs.org/collections/historyqa/bank_robber_starr.html.

105. Mara Bovsun, "The Last 'Outlaw': End of Henry Starr's Era in Bank Heists," *New York Daily News*, August 20, 2010.

4. THE G-MEN GET GUNS

1. Curt Gentry, *J. Edgar Hoover: The Man and His Secrets* (New York: W. W. Norton, 1991), 172. The originator of the phrase "Public Enemy Number One," as it pertained to John Dillinger on the federal level, remains in dispute. Gentry, a meticulous biographer, attributes the usage unconditionally to J. Edgar Hoover, but notes the unsettled debate about who first came up with the general phrase "Public Enemy Number One." Other writers state that the U.S. attorney general at the time, Homer C. Cummings, first referred to Dillinger as Public Enemy Number One in an informal speech on June 22, 1934. The *New York Times*, however, has no record of the speech, nor does the Department of Justice. Clearly the phrase had started to become part of the vernacular. On June 24, 1934, in reporting on the $10,000 reward Cummings announced on June 23 for Dillinger's capture, as well as rewards for the capture of other outlaws, the *New York Times* wrote, "Cummings refrained from any mention of the men as 'public enemies,' as this phrase was deleted from the law by which Congress authorized the offer of rewards" ("U.S. Offers $10,000 to Get Dillinger"). The list of awards that Cummings announced put Dillinger at the top, at number one, which could have been a source of Public Enemy Number One. In addition, "newspapers began calling Dillinger 'Public Enemy Number One' because the law Cummings referred to was dubbed informally the 'Public Enemy Bill,'" according to Elliott J. Gorn, *Dillinger's Wild Ride: The Year that Made America's Public Enemy Number One* (Oxford: Oxford University Press, 2009), 123. Gorn notes on page 53 that, in Chicago at the end of 1933, "the Illinois state attorney general declared John Dillinger to be 'Public Enemy No. 1,' a phrase that had originated

with the Chicago Crime Commission." No matter what the phrase's origin, it is an American original, as was Dillinger.

2. Associated Press, "Drive Against 5,000 Known Bank Robbers Is Begun by Department of Justice Men," *New York Times*, April 6, 1935.

3. Ibid.

4. Ibid.

5. Ibid.

6. Ronald Kessler, *The Bureau: The Secret History of the FBI* (New York: St. Martin's Press, 2002), 10.

7. Rhodri Jeffreys-Jones, *The FBI* (New Haven, CT: Yale University Press, 2007), 2–3. Jeffreys-Jones provides an example of an early use of "special" among agents at the U.S. Mail Department in 1860.

8. Charles J. Bonaparte, *Annual Report of the Attorney General of the United States, 1907*, 9, http://www.fbi.gov/about-us/history/brief-history/docs_ar1907.

9. Ibid.

10. Tim Weiner, *Enemies: A History of the FBI* (New York: Random House, 2012), 11, quoting Congressman John J. Fitzgerald, a Democrat from New York, *Hearings of House Appropriations Committee on Deficiency Appropriations*, 59th Congress, 2nd Session (1907).

11. Charles J. Bonaparte, *Annual Report of the Attorney General of the United States, 1908*, 7, http://www.fbi.gov/about-us/history/brief-history/docs_ar1908.

12. Sanford J. Ungar, *FBI* (Boston: Atlantic-Little, Brown, 1975), 40.

13. Bonaparte, *Annual Report of the Attorney General of the United States, 1908*, 7.

14. Richard Gid Powers, *Secrecy and Power: The Life of J. Edgar Hoover* (New York: Free Press, 1987), 134.

15. Athan G. Theoharis, *The FBI & American Democracy: A Brief Critical History* (Lawrence: University Press of Kansas, 2004), 20.

16. Weiner, *Enemies*, 45. Weiner reports that authorities ended up releasing nine out of ten of the five thousand "subversives" whom agents jailed or detained.

17. Gentry, *J. Edgar Hoover*, 109, 117; Kessler, *The Bureau*, 17. Kessler refers to the "Bureau of Easy Virtue."

18. "President Demands War on Gangsters; Puts Duty on States," *New York Times*, November 26, 1930.

19. Allen H. Meltzer, *A History of the Federal Reserve, Volume 1: 1913–1951* (Chicago: University of Chicago Press, 2003), 433.

20. Donald R. Wells, *The Federal Reserve System: A History* (Jefferson, NC: McFarland, 2004), 2.

21. Bryan Burrough, *Public Enemies: America's Greatest Crime Wave and the Birth of the FBI, 1933–34* (New York: Penguin Press, 2004), 16–17.

22. Franklin D. Roosevelt, 3 Pub. Papers 242–43 (May 18, 1934), reprinted in *The Public Papers and Addresses of Franklin D. Roosevelt, Vol. 3*, 1934 (New York: Random House, 1938), 242–43, http://quod.lib.umich.edu/p/ppotpus/4925383.1934.001/7?page=root;size=100;view=image.

23. Don Whitehead, *The FBI Story: A Report to the People* (New York: Random House, 1956), 96. See also Associated Press, "'G Men' Soon to Guard Small Banks' Funds; Bill Gives Aid to All Insured Institutions," *New York Times*, August 2, 1935.

24. Homer C. Cummings, "A Twelve Point Program" (speech, Continental Congress of the Daughters of the American Revolution, Washington, DC, April 19, 1934), http://www.justice.gov/ag/aghistory/cummings/1934/04-19-1934b.pdf.

25. Burrough, *Public Enemies*, 16.

26. Thom Hatch, *The Last Outlaws: The Lives and Legends of Butch Cassidy and the Sundance Kid* (New York: New American Library, 2013), 174.

27. Roosevelt, 3 Pub. Papers 12–13 (May 18, 1934).

28. Cummings, "A Twelve Point Program."

29. Ibid.

30. "New Dillinger Killings Stir the President and He Asks Quick Action on Crime Bills," *New York Times*, April 24, 1934.

31. Committee on the Judiciary, *Bank Robbery*, H.R. REP. NO. 73-1461, at 1 (1934).

32. Ibid., 2.

33. Federal Bank Robbery Act of 1934, Pub. L. No. 73-235, 48 Stat. 783 (1934).

34. Committee on the Judiciary, *Amending the Bank-Robbery Statute*, H.R. REP. No. 75-1259, at 1–2 (1937).

35. Acts of May 18, 1934, Pub. L. Nos. 73-230, 231, 232, 233, 234, 48 Stat. 780-783 (1934).

36. Act of June 6, 1934, Pub. L. No. 73-295, 48 Stat. 910 (1934) (rewards); Act of June 18, 1934, Pub. L. No. 73-403, 48 Stat. 1008 (1934) (arrest powers and carrying of firearms); Act of June 26, 1934, Pub. L. No. 474, 48 Stat. 1236 (1934) (firearm regulation). The law regulating firearms was in Cummings's original Twelve Point Program; the others were not. Of the original twelve proposals, seven proceeded to become laws. One proposal failed to get out of committee, and "four were dropped, partly owing to objections raised in committee by advocates of States' rights who hesitated to grant increased power to the Federal Government." See "Roosevelt Opens Attack on Crime, Signing Six Bills as 'Challenge,'" *New York Times*, May 19, 1934.

37. Athan G. Theoharis, ed., *The FBI: A Comprehensive Reference Guide* (Phoenix, AZ: Oryx Press, 1999), 4.

38. Roosevelt, 3 Pub. Papers, 243.

39. Ibid.

40. Associated Press, "'G Men' Soon to Guard Small Banks' Funds."

41. "J. E. Hoover Shows 'Drain' of Rackets," *New York Times*, November 18, 1935.

5. MARQUEE MAYHEM

1. Richard Gid Powers, *Secrecy and Power: The Life of J. Edgar Hoover* (New York: Free Press, 1987), 200.

2. Elliott J. Gorn, *Dillinger's Wild Ride: The Year that Made America's Public Enemy Number One* (Oxford: Oxford University Press, 2009), 82.

3. Murray Schumach, *The Face on the Cutting Room Floor* (New York: William Morrow, 1964), 172.

4. L. R. Kirchner, *Robbing Banks: An American History, 1831–1999* (Rockville Centre, NY: Sarpedon, 2000), 46.

5. The term *FBI* will be used, starting in this chapter, also to refer to its predecessor agencies, the Bureau of Investigation and Division of Investigation. The use of FBI is meant to avoid undue confusion, as the predecessor agencies eventually became the FBI.

6. David Dary, for the Associated Press, "Once Famous Bank Robber Looks Back at 'Career,'" *Fort Scott* (KS) *Tribune*, November 12, 1973.

7. Ibid.

8. Newspaper Enterprise Association, "Smooth-Talking, Golf-Playing Harvey Bailey Deserts Farm to Be Bad Man No. 1," *Spokane* (WA) *Daily Chronicle*, September 19, 1933.

9. Bryan Burrough, *Public Enemies: America's Greatest Crime Wave and the Birth of the FBI, 1933–34* (New York: Penguin Press, 2004), 8.

10. Ibid., 18.

11. Ibid.

12. Dary, "Once Famous Bank Robber Looks Back at 'Career.'"

13. United Press International, "Closed National Bank in Lincoln Pays Off All of Its Obligations," *Daily Illini* (Urbana, Illinois), January 1, 1933. Other writers have put the amount stolen at $2,702,976.

14. Patrick Brophy, "Harvey Bailey—The Myth and the Reality," *Nevada* (MO) *Daily Mail*, June 19, 1986.

15. Ibid.

16. Burrough, *Public Enemies*, 46.

17. Ibid., 50.

18. Ibid., 61.

19. Powers, *Secrecy and Power*, 188.

20. Brophy, "Harvey Bailey—The Myth and the Reality." See also T. Lindsay Baker, "The Escape of Harvey Bailey," *Legacies: A History Journal for Dallas and North Central Texas* 18, no. 1 (2006): 4–10, http://texashistory.unt.edu/ark:/67531/metapth35088/m1/1/.

21. Dary, "Once Famous Bank Robber Looks Back at 'Career.'"

22. John Toland, *The Dillinger Days* (New York: Random House, 1963), 28.

23. Brophy, "Harvey Bailey—The Myth and the Reality."

24. Dary, "Once Famous Bank Robber Looks Back at 'Career.'"

25. Burrough, *Public Enemies*, 17.

26. Ibid., 17–18.

27. Walter Mittelstaedt, *Herman "Baron" Lamm, the Father of Modern Bank Robbery* (Jefferson, NC: McFarland, 2012), 1.

28. Ibid., 22. Mittelstaedt writes that Lamm was eighteen years old when Butch Cassidy died in South America: "The odds are very much against Lamm riding with Cassidy at any time in his career."

29. Burrough, *Public Enemies*, 18; Toland, *The Dillinger Days*, 29.

30. Curt Gentry, *J. Edgar Hoover: The Man and His Secrets* (New York: W. W. Norton, 1991), 168.

31. Dary Matera, *John Dillinger: The Life and Death of America's First Celebrity Criminal* (New York: Carroll & Graf, 2004), 11.

32. Toland, *The Dillinger Days*, 7.

33. Ibid., 10.

34. Matera, *John Dillinger*, 17.

35. Toland, *The Dillinger Days*, 11.

36. Matera, *John Dillinger*, 26.

37. Transcript, *American Experience: Public Enemy #1*, Public Broadcasting System, 2002, accessed July 31, 2014, http://www.pbs.org/wgbh/amex/dillinger/filmmore/pt.html.

38. Gorn, *Dillinger's Wild Ride*, 29–30. The remark is different in Matera's *John Dillinger*, which quotes Dillinger as saying, "Honey, this is a stickup. Get me the money," 56–57.

39. Gorn, *Dillinger's Wild Ride*, 29–30.

40. Ibid., x.

41. Burrough, *Public Enemies*, 225.

42. Gorn, *Dillinger's Wild Ride*, 57.

43. Ibid., 59.

44. Ibid., 63.

45. Ibid., 81.

46. Ibid., 73.

47. Toland, *The Dillinger Days*, 229.

48. Ibid., 237.

49. Ibid., 261.

50. Gorn, *Dillinger's Wild Ride*, 107.

51. "Dillinger Eludes Man-Hunt by 5,000," *New York Times*, April 25, 1934.

52. Burrough, *Public Enemies*, 231.

53. Gorn, *Dillinger's Wild Ride*, 26.

54. Burrough, *Public Enemies*, 103.

55. Ibid., 33.

56. Joe Popper, "Robber: In a Time and Place that Reviled Banks, Charles Arthur 'Pretty Boy' Floyd Shared His Loot and Became a Benefactor and Folk Hero," *Baltimore Sun*, January 16, 1999.

57. Robert Roper, "Just Tryin' to Make a Buck," review of *Pretty Boy: The Life and Times of Charles Arthur Floyd*, by Michael Wallis, *Los Angeles Times*, Sunday Book Review, April 19, 1992.

58. Michael Wallis, *Pretty Boy: The Life and Times of Charles Arthur Floyd* (New York: St. Martin's Press, 1992), 227.

59. Ibid., 187.

60. Burrough, *Public Enemies*, 20.

61. Ibid., 21.

62. Dan Morgan, "Pablo & Pretty Boy," *Washington Post*, December 12, 1993.

63. Wallis, *Pretty Boy*, 296.

64. Gorn, *Dillinger's Wild Ride*, xviii.

65. Burrough, *Public Enemies*, 225–26.

66. "Famous Cases & Criminals: Bonnie & Clyde," FBI, http://www.fbi.gov/about-us/history/famous-cases/bonnie-and-clyde. The FBI cites thirteen murders overall. For a list of the thirteen victims, see http://bonnieandclydehistory. blogspot.com/2010/01/bonnie-and-clyde-q-how-many-did-b-kill_6899.html.

67. *Bonnie and Clyde* was the fourth-highest grossing movie of 1967, according to the Internet Movie Database (IMDb), and it earned $50.7 million. See http://www.imdb.com/ and http://www.imdb.com/title/tt0061418/reviews-182.

68. Though a number of writers and historians list the year of Clyde Barrow's birth as March 24, 1909, debate persists over whether he was born instead on March 24, 1910. See Jeff Guinn, *Go Down Together: The True, Untold Story of Bonnie and Clyde* (New York: Simon & Schuster, 2009), 13.

69. Guinn, *Go Down Together*, 43.

70. Ibid., 87.

71. Ibid., 131.

72. Joe McGasko, "The Real Bonnie and Clyde: 9 Facts on the Outlawed Duo," biography.com (website for A&E Television Networks' *Biography*), De-

cember 5, 2013, accessed August 9, 2014, http://www.biography.com/news/
bonnie-and-clyde-9-facts-lifetime-movie-video.

73. McGasko, "The Real Bonnie and Clyde."

74. Emma Parker and Nell Barrow Cowan, *Fugitives: The Story of Clyde Barrow and Bonnie Parker as Told by Bonnie's Mother (Mrs. Emma Parker) and Clyde's Sister (Nell Barrow Cowan)*, ed. Jan I. Fortune (Dallas, TX: Ranger Press, 1934), 99.

75. Ibid., 242–45.

76. Guinn, *Go Down Together*, 5.

77. Luciano DiNardo, "The Massacre of Bonnie and Clyde," *Ottawa Citizen*, May 23, 2004.

78. Guinn, *Go Down Together*, photo pages, 26.

79. Gorn, *Dillinger's Wild Ride*, 133.

80. Toland, *The Dillinger Days*, 303.

81. Ibid., 310.

82. Gentry, *J. Edgar Hoover*, 173.

83. Anna Sage never avoided deportation. She was forced to return to Romania, where she died of liver failure in 1947. The U.S. Labor Department maintained that it alone had jurisdiction over immigration matters, and was not bound by Sage's deal with the Justice Department. See "People and Events: Dillinger's Betrayal," *American Experience: Public Enemy #1*, Public Broadcasting System, 2002, accessed August 9, 2014, http://www.pbs.org/wgbh/amex/dillinger/peopleevents/e_betrayal.htmlhttp://www.pbs.org/wgbh/amex/dillinger/filmmore/pt.html.

84. Toland, *The Dillinger Days*, 327.

85. Melvin Purvis died in 1960 at his home in North Carolina from a single bullet fired from the gun his fellow agents gave him when he resigned. The FBI ruled his death a suicide, but "it was later determined that Purvis may have been trying to remove a tracer bullet that was stuck in the pistol." See "People & Events: Melvin Purvis, 1903–1960," *American Experience: Public Enemy #1*, Public Broadcasting System, 2002, accessed August 9, 2014, http://www.pbs.org/wgbh/amex/dillinger/peopleevents/p_purvis.html.

86. Gentry, *J. Edgar Hoover*, 174.

87. Alvin Karpis died in Spain on August 26, 1979. He was seventy-two years old.

88. Powers, *Secrecy and Power*, 200–201.

89. Schumach, *The Face on the Cutting Room Floor*, 173.

90. Powers, *Secrecy and Power*, 201.

91. Mark Harris, *Pictures at a Revolution: Five Movies and the Birth of the New Hollywood* (New York: Penguin Press, 2008), 13.

92. Toland, *The Dillinger Days*, 39.

93. Harris, *Pictures at a Revolution*, 207–9.

6. LONE WOLVES

1. FBI, *Federal Bureau of Investigation Bank Crime Statistics for Federally Insured Financial Institutions July 1, 1973–December 31, 1973.* The report lists bank robberies going back to 1934. The figures listed here are for bank robberies only; in 1939, the FBI also started to record bank burglaries and bank larcenies. The authors received this report from FBI historian John Fox, PhD. The report provides what Fox found to be the earliest statistics for bank robbery as the FBI recorded them.

2. Ibid.

3. FBI, *Federal Bureau of Investigation Bank Crime Statistics.* The number rises to forty-eight with the addition of twenty-one bank burglaries and ten bank larcenies.

4. Bryan Burrough, *Public Enemies: America's Greatest Crime Wave and the Birth of the FBI, 1933–34* (New York: Penguin Press, 2014), 543–44.

5. Ibid., 545.

6. L. R. Kirchner, *Robbing Banks: An American History, 1831–1999* (Rockville Centre, NY: Sarpedon, 2000), 107.

7. "Famous Cases & Criminals: Willie Sutton," FBI, http://www.fbi.gov/about-us/history/famous-cases/willie-sutton.

8. Willie Sutton with Edward Linn, *Where the Money Was* (New York: Viking Press, 1976), 13.

9. Ibid., 23.

10. Ibid., 28.

11. Ibid., 37.

12. Ibid., 52.

13. Ibid., 121.

14. Ibid., 212.

15. "Gunmen Get $23,835 in Broadway Bank," *New York Times*, July 9, 1933.

16. Ibid.

17. Sutton with Linn, *Where the Money Was*, 145.

18. Ibid.

19. Lorena Mongelli, "Former Cop Recalls NYPD Arrest of Willie Sutton 60 Yrs. Later," *New York Post*, February 18, 2012.

20. Meyer Berger, "Sutton, Bank Thief, Captured in Street by Brooklyn Police," *New York Times*, February 19, 1952.

21. Mongelli, "Former Cop Recalls NYPD Arrest of Willie Sutton 60 Yrs. Later."

22. Sutton with Linn, *Where the Money Was*, 240.

23. Berger, "Sutton, Bank Thief, Captured in Street by Brooklyn Police."

24. Sutton with Linn, *Where the Money Was*, 246.

25. Ibid.

26. Ibid., 247.

27. Ibid., 119–21.

28. Though the Brink's counting house was not a bank, the suspects in the heist were charged with bank robbery, as the statute applied because the victim was a financial institution.

29. "Famous Cases & Criminals: The Brinks Robbery," FBI, http://www.fbi.gov/about-us/history/famous-cases/brinks-robbery.

30. Berger, "Sutton, Bank Thief, Captured in Street by Brooklyn Police."

31. Kirchner, *Robbing Banks*, 109–10.

32. "Famous Cases & Criminals: The Brinks Robbery."

33. Ibid.

34. Nancy Pomerene McMillan, "Brink's Is Robbed in Boston Again," *New York Times*, July 2, 1978.

35. Robert E. Tomasson, "Biggest Cash Robbery," *New York Times*, March 28, 1976.

36. McMillan, "Brink's Is Robbed in Boston Again."

37. Ibid.

38. William Buchanan, "Famous Brink's Job Still a Story to Remember," *Boston Globe*, January 17, 1980.

39. Robert E. Tomasson, "Specs O'Keefe, Informant in Brink's Robbery, Dies," *New York Times*, March 28, 1976.

40. McMillan, "Brink's Is Robbed in Boston Again."

41. "Famous Cases & Criminals: The Brinks Robbery."

42. For more on the movie *The Brink's Job*, see the Internet Movie Database, http://www.imdb.com/title/tt0077275/.

43. McMillan, "Brink's Is Robbed in Boston Again."

44. Ibid.

45. Ibid.

46. William Friedkin, *The Friedkin Connection* (New York: HarperCollins, 2013), 353–54.

47. Margaret A. Leaming, "An Occurrence at Milan—Michigan's Last Execution," *The Court Legacy*, no. 3 (1994), accessed September 6, 2014, http://www.fbamich.org/Portals/31/Documents/Newsletters/199404_Court_Legacy.pdf.

48. Ibid.

49. "Puff, Bank Robber, Is Sentenced to Death for Killing F.B.I. Man in Hotel Battle Here," *New York Times*, May 16, 1953.

50. "Famous Cases & Criminals: Gerhard Arthur Puff," FBI, http://www.fbi.gov/about-us/history/famous-cases/gerhard-authur-puff.

51. Ibid.

52. "Puff, Bank Robber, Is Sentenced to Death for Killing F.B.I. Man in Hotel Battle Here."

53. "Killing Called Wanton," *New York Times*, May 6, 1953.

54. "Puff Put to Death," *New York Times*, August 13, 1954.

55. Mark Felt and John O'Connor, *A G-Man's Life* (New York: PublicAffairs, 2006), 50.

56. Ibid., 52.

57. FBI, Most Wanted poster for Frederick Grant Dunn, included in collection of materials on Dunn in archives of the Minnesota Historical Society, 17, http://www2.mnhs.org/library/findaids/pubsaf08/pdf/pubsaf08-000013.pdf.

58. Felt and O'Connor, *A G-Man's Life*, 50.

59. Ibid.

60. "Sioux Cityans Held by FBI," *Sioux City Journal-Tribune* (IA), July 22, 1942, included in collection of materials on Dunn in archives of the Minnesota Historical Society, 16, http://www2.mnhs.org/library/findaids/pubsaf08/pdf/pubsaf08-000013.pdf.

61. Ibid.

62. R. H. Nebergall to Eldon Rowe, July 13, 1942, included in collection of materials on Dunn in archives of the Minnesota Historical Society, 13–14, http://www2.mnhs.org/library/findaids/pubsaf08/pdf/pubsaf08-000013.pdf.

63. Felt and O'Connor, *A G-Man's Life*, 51.

64. Ibid.

65. Ibid., 52.

66. Director, FBI, to William F. Proetz, no date listed, included in collection of materials on Dunn in archives of the Minnesota Historical Society, 24–25, http://www2.mnhs.org/library/findaids/pubsaf08/pdf/pubsaf08-000013.pdf.

7. COUNTERCULTURAL CHAOS

1. Emily S. Rueb, "A Botched Robbery that Went Hollywood," *City Room* (blog), *New York Times*, August 22, 2012, http://cityroom.blogs.nytimes.com/2012/08/22/a-botched-robbery-went-hollywood/?_r=0.

2. Ibid.

3. Vincent Canby, "Screen: Lumet's 'Dog Day Afternoon,'" *New York Times*, September 22, 1975.

4. U.S. Bureau of the Census, *Statistical Abstract of the United States: 1966* (Washington, DC: Government Printing Office, 1966), 449.

5. Federal Bureau of Investigation, *Federal Bureau of Investigation Bank Crime Statistics Federally Insured Financial Institutions July 1, 1973–December 31, 1973.* The authors received this report from FBI historian John Fox, PhD. All the figures here include banks, credit unions, and savings-and-loan institutions.

6. Carla W. Russell, "Bonnie and Clyde in the 1960's," *Federal Reserve Bank of Richmond Monthly Review*, August 1968, 8.

7. Charles and Bonnie Remsberg, "The Heisters Increase Their Haul," *New York Times Magazine*, January 16, 1966, 61.

8. Russell, "Bonnie and Clyde in the 1960's," 10.

9. Associated Press, "Suspect Seized in Bank Holdups," *New York Times*, November 5, 1962.

10. Charity Vogel, "The Nussbaum Case: The Strange but True Story of a Man Who Grew Up in Buffalo, Robbed Banks, Did Time and Ended Up Writing Crime Novels," *Buffalo News*, November 4, 2012.

11. Andrew Tully, *The FBI's Most Famous Cases* (New York: William Morrow, 1965), 61.

12. "FBI 100: An Odd Couple of Crime," FBI, February 19, 2008, http://www.fbi.gov/news/stories/2008/february/bankrobbers_021908.

13. Ibid.

14. Tully, *The FBI's Most Famous Cases*, 60.

15. "FBI 100: An Odd Couple of Crime."

16. Vogel, "The Nussbaum Case."

17. Tully, *The FBI's Most Famous Cases*, 62.

18. Ibid., 60.

19. Ibid., 59.

20. Ibid., 62.

21. "Bank Guard Killed in $35,000 Hold-Up," *New York Times*, December 16, 1961.

22. Ibid.

23. Ibid.

24. Tully, *The FBI's Most Famous Cases*, 66.

25. "Bank Guard Killed in $35,000 Hold-Up."

26. Ibid.

27. Ibid.

28. Vogel, "The Nussbaum Case."

29. Tully, *The FBI's Most Famous Cases*, 74.

30. "FBI 100: An Odd Couple of Crime."

31. Vogel, "The Nussbaum Case."

32. Ibid.

33. Al Nussbaum, "Collision," *Albert Nussbaum* (blog), October 5, 2014, http://www.albertnussbaum.com/?page_id=7.

34. Philip Benjamin, "Suspect in Killings Recalled as 'Quiet,'" *New York Times*, June 11, 1965. See also David Clouston, "Killer's Tale Topic for Former Hutch Reporter's Book," *Salina* (KS) *Journal*, November 30, 2008.

35. Bill Eddy, "1965 Robbery-Slaying Left Three Dead, One Paralyzed," *Lincoln* (NE) *Journal Star*, September 27, 2002.

36. Benjamin, "Suspect in Killings Recalled as 'Quiet.'"

37. United Press International, "Suspect Hunted in Bank Murders," *New York Times*, June 7, 1965.

38. Donald Janson, "Court Hears Confessions," *New York Times*, November 10, 1965.

39. United Press International, "How an All-American Boy Turned Into a Most Wanted Man," *Bulletin* (Bend, OR), June 16, 1965.

40. Frank Graham, "Big Springs Bank Robbery Recounted in New Book," *North Platte* (NE) *Bulletin*, December 4, 2008.

41. Ibid.

42. Adrielle Harvey, "Let Out and Locked Up: Days after 1965 Graduation, McPherson Alum Robs Bank, Kills Three," *McPherson College Spectator* (KS), December 12, 2008.

43. Ibid.

44. United Press International, "How an All-American Boy Turned Into a Most Wanted Man."

45. Donald Janson, "Killer of 3 in Bank in Nebraska Guilty; Sentenced to Chair," *New York Times*, December 4, 1965.

46. United Press International, "Duane Pope Called a Cold Mass Killer," *New York Times*, November 4, 1965.

47. Clouston, "Killer's Tale Topic for Former Hutch News Reporter's Book."

48. United Press International, "How an All-American Boy Turned Into a Most Wanted Man."

49. Benjamin, "Suspect in Killings Recalled as 'Quiet.'"

50. Patricia Campbell Hearst with Alvin Moscow, *Patty Hearst: Her Own Story*, originally published as *Every Secret Thing* (New York: Avon Books, 1988), 131.

51. Ibid., 163.

52. Ibid., 22.

53. Tim Findley, "A Symbionese Family Reunion," *New York Times*, January 28, 2002.

54. "The Rise and Fall of the Symbionese Liberation Army," *American Experience: Guerrilla: The Taking of Patty Hearst*, Public Broadcasting System,

2005, accessed October 5, 2014, http://www.pbs.org/wgbh/amex/guerrilla/peopleevents/e_kidnapping.html.

55. Hearst with Moscow, *Patty Hearst*, 41.

56. Ibid, 44.

57. Transcript, *American Experience: Guerrilla: The Taking of Patty Hearst*, http://www.pbs.org/wgbh/amex/guerrilla/filmmore/pt.html.

58. Hearst with Moscow, *Patty Hearst*, 137.

59. Ibid., 113.

60. Ibid., 160–61.

61. Earl Caldwell, "Patricia Hearst Placed at Bank Robbery," *New York Times*, April 16, 1974.

62. Ibid.

63. Ibid.

64. Wallace Turner, "Parents Hear Miss Hearst, on Tape, Call Them Pigs," *New York Times*, February 13, 1976.

65. Ibid.

66. Associated Press, "Patricia Hearst Denies Coercion, Scorns Family," *The Blade* (Toledo, OH), April 25, 1974.

67. Hearst with Moscow, *Patty Hearst*, 137.

68. Ibid., 140.

69. Wallace Turner, "Credibility of Miss Hearst Is Key Issue at Summation," *New York Times*, March 19, 1976.

70. Timeline, *American Experience: Guerrilla: The Taking of Patty Hearst*, http://www.pbs.org/wgbh/amex/guerrilla/timeline/index.html.

71. Ibid.

72. Lacey Fosburgh, "Patricia Hearst Gets Seven Years on Robbery Charge," *New York Times*, September 25, 1976.

73. Ibid.

74. Bernard Shaw died on December 17, 2013, at age sixty-eight.

75. Wallace Turner, "Patricia Hearst Says She 'Just Plain Couldn't' Flee Her Captors," *New York Times*, December 11, 1981.

76. "Robber Sentenced in Holdup to Pay for 'Sex Change,'" *New York Times*, April 24, 1973.

77. Frank J. Prial, "2 Hold 8 Hostages in a Bank in Brooklyn," *New York Times*, August 23, 1972.

78. Ibid.

79. Sam Roberts, "The 'Dog' Who Had His Day on Film," *New York Times*, August 4, 2014.

80. Murray Schumach, "3d Suspect Seized in Bizarre Holdup," *New York Times*, August 25, 1972.

81. Prial, "2 Hold 8 Hostages in a Bank in Brooklyn." See also Murray Schumach, "A Blighted 'Affair' Led to Bank Holdup," *New York Times*, August 24, 1972.

82. Schumach, "3d Suspect Seized in Bizarre Holdup."

83. "Robber Sentenced in Holdup to Pay for 'Sex Change.'"

84. Roberts, "The 'Dog' Who Had His Day on Film."

85. Prial, "2 Hold 8 Hostages in a Bank in Brooklyn."

86. Ibid.

87. Roberts, "The 'Dog' Who Had His Day on Film." See also Rueb, "A Botched Robbery that Went Hollywood." For Wojtowicz's relationship with his new spouse, see John Wojtowicz, "Real *Dog Day* Hero Tells His Story," *Jump Cut*, no. 15 (1977): 31–32.

88. "Elizabeth Eden, Transsexual Who Figured in 1975 Movie," *New York Times*, October 1, 1987.

89. Roberts, "The 'Dog' Who Had His Day on Film."

90. Ibid.

91. Ibid.

92. Rueb, "A Botched Robbery that Went Hollywood."

93. Roberts, "The 'Dog' Who Had His Day on Film."

8. STRIKING BACK, STRIKING BIG

1. Associated Press, "Bank Robberies Show Sharp Rise," *New York Times*, April 1, 1968. These annual numbers, which President Lyndon B. Johnson also referred to in a speech mentioned in this chapter, are different from the fiscal year numbers contained in *Federal Bureau of Investigation Bank Crime Statistics Federally Insured Financial Institutions July 1, 1973–December 31, 1973.* The authors received that report directly from the FBI historian John Fox, PhD. It lists the number of total bank robberies in fiscal 1967 as 1,470; it lists the total number of bank crimes—robberies, burglaries, and larcenies—as 2,259 in 1967. J. Edgar Hoover, as the authors state, puts the annual figures at 1,730 and 2,551, respectively. Whatever the figures, 1967 set a new record for bank robberies in the United States.

2. Ibid.

3. Ibid.

4. Lyndon B. Johnson, "Special Message to the Congress on Crime and Law Enforcement: 'To Insure the Public Safety,' February 7, 1968," in *Public Papers of the Presidents of the United States: Lyndon B. Johnson: 1968, Book I— January 1 to June 30, 1968*, 194–95 (Washington, DC: Government Printing Office, 1970).

5. Bank Protection Act of 1968, Pub. L. No. 90-389, 82 Stat. 294-295 (1968).

6. Charles and Bonnie Remsberg, "The Heisters Increase Their Haul," *New York Times Magazine*, January 16, 1966, 66.

7. Ibid., 61.

8. Ibid., 64.

9. Carla W. Russell, "Bonnie and Clyde in the 1960's," *Federal Reserve Bank of Richmond Monthly Review*, August 1968, 10.

10. Deborah Lamm Weisel, "The Problem of Bank Robbery," *Problem-Oriented Guides for Police, Problem-Specific Guides Series*, no. 48, U.S. Department of Justice, Office of Community Oriented Police Services (2007): 44–45, http://www.cops.usdoj.gov/Publications/e03071267.pdf.

11. John Hechinger, "FBI Presses Banks to Increase Security as Robberies Rise," *Wall Street Journal*, October 8, 2002.

12. Weisel, "The Problem of Bank Robbery," 12.

13. Remsberg and Remsberg, "The Heisters Increase Their Haul," 66.

14. Weisel, "The Problem of Bank Robbery," 10.

15. Ibid.

16. Weisel, "The Problem of Bank Robbery," 4.

17. Jack Nicas, "Crime That No Longer Pays," *Wall Street Journal*, February 4, 2013.

18. Ibid.

19. Neil Steinberg, "Computer Crimes Go Way Back," *Chicago Sun Times*, May 20, 2013; Pamela Hollie, "Police Recount Theft by Wire of $10 Million," *New York Times*, November 8, 1978.

20. Steinberg, "Computer Crimes Go Way Back."

21. Jay Becker, "Rifkin, A Documentary History," *Computer Law Journal* 2, no. 1 (1980): 475, http://repository.jmls.edu/cgi/viewcontent.cgi?article=1612&context=jitpl.

22. Hollie, "Police Recount Theft by Wire of $10 Million."

23. Becker, "Rifkin, A Documentary History," 478.

24. Robert Lindsay, "Computer Analyst Sentenced to 8 Years in Bank Theft," *New York Times*, March 27, 1979.

25. Becker, "Rifkin, A Documentary History," 483.

26. Lindsay, "Computer Analyst Sentenced to 8 Years in Bank Theft."

27. Ibid.

28. Steinberg, "Computer Crimes Go Way Back."

29. Dorothy J. Gaiter, "Lawyer Says 9-Year-Old Bank Robber Was Influenced by TV Crime," *New York Times*, March 2, 1981.

30. Jo Thomas, "Bank Robbery Trial Offers a Glimpse of Right-Wing World," *New York Times*, January 9, 1997.

31. Ibid.

32. Robert Reinhold, "Los Angeles 'Fagins' Admit to Series of Bank Robberies," *New York Times*, October 31, 1993.

33. Jesse Katz, "Pair Sentenced for Bank Holdups Using Youngsters," *Los Angeles Times*, November 2, 1993.

34. Ibid.

35. George de Lama, "Bank Robberies Like an Epidemic in L.A.," *Chicago Tribune*, August 16, 1992.

36. Victoria Kim, "Where Did All the Bandits Go?" *Los Angeles Times*, March 21, 2014.

37. De Lama, "Bank Robberies Like an Epidemic in L.A."

38. Ibid.

39. Katz, "Pair Sentenced for Bank Holdups Using Youngsters."

40. Reinhold, "Los Angeles 'Fagins' Admit to Series of Bank Robberies."

41. Katz, "Pair Sentenced for Bank Holdups Using Youngsters."

42. O. Casey Corr et al., "Scurlock: Known for Looks, Charm and His Big Tips," *Seattle Times*, November 30, 1996.

43. Ann Rule, *The End of the Dream* (New York: Pocket Books, 1999), 101.

44. Ibid., 118, 152, 159.

45. Ibid., 160.

46. Ibid., 159.

47. Ibid., 8.

48. Audra Ang, Associated Press, "FBI Study of Robberies Leads to 'Hollywood' Ending," *Spokesman-Review* (Spokane), December 1, 1996.

49. Lily Eng, "FBI Finds Rifles, Cash, Radios in Home of Bank Robber," *Seattle Times*, December 5, 1966.

50. Corr et al., "Scurlock: Known for Looks, Charm and His Big Tips."

51. Ang, "FBI Study of Robberies Leads to 'Hollywood' Ending."

52. "Bank Robbers Killed in Shootout Are Linked to Two Similar Cases," *New York Times*, March 3, 1997.

53. Ibid.

54. Doug Smith et al., "Chilling Portrait of Robber Emerges," *Los Angeles Times*, March 10, 1997.

55. Ibid.

56. Ibid.

57. Scott Lindlaw, "Bank Suspects Once Caught with Arsenal in Car," March 2, 1997, AP News Archive, http://www.apnewsarchive.com/1997/Bank-suspects-once-caught-with-arsenal-in-car/id-0db0d87ff079f05013c18290907ce765.

58. Ibid.

59. Ibid.

60. Ibid.

61. Rick Orlov, "North Hollywood Shootout, 15 Years Later," *Los Angeles Daily News*, February 26, 2012.

62. Ibid.

63. Smith et al., "Chilling Portrait of Robber Emerges."

64. Peter Prengaman, "LA Marks 10th Anniversary of Shootout," *Washington Post*, March 1, 2007.

65. Jaxon Van Derbeken, "Dying Bank Robber's Last Words to Police: 'Shoot Me in the Head,'" *Los Angeles Daily News*, April 18, 1997.

66. Ibid.

67. Prengaman, "LA Marks 10th Anniversary of Shootout."

68. Ibid.

69. Orlov, "North Hollywood Shootout, 15 Years Later."

70. David Rosenzweig, "2 Convicted in $18.9-Million Cash Robbery," *Los Angeles Times*, February 28, 2001.

71. Andrew Bridges, "Brains Behind Armed Cash Heist Sentenced," *St. Augustine Record* (FL), June 19, 2001.

72. Josh Meyer, "Lots of Loot on the Lam," *Los Angeles Times*, June 18, 2001.

73. Bridges, "Brains Behind Armed Cash Heist Sentenced."

74. Meyer, "Lots of Loot on the Lam."

75. Ibid.

76. Ibid.

77. Ibid.

78. Bridges, "Brains Behind Armed Cash Heist Sentenced."

79. Rosenzweig, "2 Convicted in $18.9-Million Cash Robbery."

80. Josh Meyer, "Leader of Heist Is Given 24 Years," *Los Angeles Times*, June 19, 2001.

81. Meyer, "Lots of Loot on the Lam."

82. Ibid.

83. Jim Schoettler, "Sobbing Robber Gets 25 Years for Loomis Heist," *Florida Times-Union* (Jacksonville), January 21, 1999.

84. Associated Press, "Suspect in Biggest U.S. Heist Arrested in Texas," *Los Angeles Times*, August 31, 1997.

85. "F.B.I. Finds Armored Car Cash," *New York Times*, September 19, 1997.

86. Schoettler, "Sobbing Robber Gets 25 Years for Loomis Heist."

87. Ibid.

88. Sue Anne Pressley (*Washington Post*), "Wild Spree Was Big Tip-Off— Big-Spending Bank Robbers Buy Ticket to Prison," *Seattle Times*, February 19, 1999.

89. Paul Nowell, "Thieves in $17M Heist Sentenced," April 30, 1999, AP News Archive, http://www.apnewsarchive.com/1999/Thieves-in-$17M-Heist-Sentenced/id-7054f8553ccc69ff0e50bdce2232d20b.

90. Pressley, "Wild Spree Was Big Tip-Off."

91. "Woman Gets 7 Years for Robbery," *Fayetteville Observer* (North Carolina), September 29, 1999, http://www.fayobserver.com/news/local/woman-gets-years-for-robbery/article_e63685a1-ebe7-538b-b32b-dcb7a72bcc7d.html?mode=jqm.

92. Ibid.

93. Ibid.

94. David J. Morrow, "Carolina Bank Robberies Show that Friendliness Carries a Price," *New York Times*, May 2, 1999.

95. Ibid.

96. Ibid.

97. Ibid.

98. Ibid.

9. ROBBERY AND REVERBERATIONS

1. All the information on the Pizza Bomber case is from Jerry Clark and Ed Palattella, *Pizza Bomber: The Untold Story of America's Most Shocking Bank Robbery* (New York: Berkley Books/Penguin, 2012).

2. John Hudson, "FBI Drops Law Enforcement as 'Primary' Mission," *The Cable* (blog), *Foreign Policy*, January 5, 2014, accessed October 23, 2014, http://thecable.foreignpolicy.com/posts/2014/01/05/fbi_drops_law_enforcement_as_primary_mission.

3. "Quick Facts," FBI, accessed November 22, 2014, http://www.fbi.gov/about-us/quick-facts.

4. U.S. Department of Justice, Office of the Inspector General, *The External Effects of the Federal Bureau of Investigation's Reprioritization Efforts*, September 2005, 87, http://www.justice.gov/oig/reports/FBI/a0537/final.pdf.

5. Ibid.

6. Ibid., i.

7. Ibid., 88.

8. Ibid.

9. Ibid., 90.

10. Ibid., 87.

11. Michael S. Schmidt, "At F.B.I., Change in Leaders Didn't Change Focus on Terror," *New York Times*, May 18, 2014.

12. *Diehl-Armstrong v. Pennsylvania Board of Probation and Parole, et al.*, Report and Recommendation, United States District Court for the Middle District of Pennsylvania, 1:13-CV-2302, April 7, 2014.

13. Gerry Smith, "Name That Robber: It Takes a Catchy Nickname to Catch a Bandit, FBI Says," *Chicago Tribune*, December 30, 2007.

14. Tim Hahn, "'Bucket List Bandit' Adds Erie to Bank Robbery Spree," *Erie Times-News* (PA), September 12, 2012, http://www.goerie.com/fbi-bucket-list-bandit-might-strike-again-updated-1-pm#.

15. Lisa Thompson, "'Bucket List Bandit' Gets 135 Months," *Erie Times-News*, August 16, 2013, http://www.goerie.com/article/20130816/NEWS02/308169944/'Bucket-List-Bandit'-gets-135-months#.

16. Ibid.

17. "My Banker Husband Was Actually a Bank Robber," Mirror.uk.co (website of London *Daily Mirror*), February 12, 2011, http://www.mirror.co.uk/news/uk-news/my-banker-husband-was-actually-a-bank-robber-112094.

18. Ibid.

19. "New York: Mineola: Guilty Plea in Robbery," *New York Times*, March 23, 2004.

20. "Wife of Suspected Bank Robber Tells All," cbs.news.com (website of CBS News), September 15, 2009, http://www.cbsnews.com/news/wife-of-bank-robber-tells-all/.

21. Josh Meyer, "FBI Identifies Alleged Cell Phone Bandit," *Los Angeles Times*, August 23, 2000.

22. Josh Meyer, "Suspected Cell Phone Bandit Caught in Spokane," *Los Angeles Times*, September 12, 2000.

23. Associated Press, "'Cell Phone Bandit' Sentenced to 12 Years for Bank Robbery," *USA Today*, March 3, 2006.

24. Ibid.

25. Smith, "Name That Robber."

26. Jonathan Miller and Nate Schweber, "Suspect Is Charged in a Bank Robbery Case of Many Hats," *New York Times*, July 24, 2007.

27. Ibid.

28. Associated Press, "Ex-Con: I'm the 'Mad Hatter' Bank Robber," *Washington Post*, August 28, 2007.

29. Miller and Schweber, "Suspect Is Charged in a Bank Robbery Case of Many Hats."

30. "'Hat Bandit' Gets 10 Years," 70nline.com (website of WABC-TV New York), January 24, 2008, http://7online.com/archive/5911550/.

31. Associated Press, "J. L. Hunter 'Red' Rountree, 92; Inmate Was Believed to Be Nation's Oldest Bank Robber," *Los Angeles Times*, November 23, 2004.

32. Reuters, "Oldest U.S. Bank Robber Gets 12 Years," cnn.com (website of CNN), January 23, 2004, http://www.cnn.com/2004/US/Southwest/01/23/oldest. bank.robber.reut/.

33. Ibid.

34. Associated Press, "J. L. Hunter 'Red' Rountree, 92; Inmate Was Believed to Be Nation's Oldest Bank Robber."

35. Associated Press, "Adrenaline Rush Never Gets Old for 92-Year-Old Bank Robber," *Lubbock Avalanche-Journal* (TX), March 28, 2004, http:// lubbockonline.com/stories/032804/sta_.shtml.

36. Reuters, "Oldest U.S. Bank Robber Gets 12 Years."

37. Associated Press, "J. L. Hunter 'Red' Rountree, 92; Inmate Was Believed to Be Nation's Oldest Bank Robber."

38. Reuters, "Oldest U.S. Bank Robber Gets 12 Years."

39. Jeff Kunerth, "89-Year-Old Bank Robber Not Sorry," *Orlando Sentinel*, February 4, 2001, http://articles.orlandosentinel.com/2001-02-04/news/010204 0077_1_rountree-inmate-red.

40. Associated Press, "'Granddad Bandit' Captured in Baton Rouge, FBI Says," *Times-Picayune* (New Orleans, LA), August 11, 2010, http://www.nola. com/crime/index.ssf/2010/08/granddad_bandit_captured_in_ba.html.

41. Associated Press, "'Granddad Bandit' Sentenced to 25 Years in Prison for String of Bank Robberies," *Post-Standard* (Syracuse, NY), May 11, 2011, http:// www.syracuse.com/news/index.ssf/2011/05/granddad_bandit_sentenced_to_2. html.

42. Associated Press, "'Granddad Bandit' Captured in Baton Rouge, FBI Says."

43. Associated Press, "'Granddad Bandit' Sentenced to 25 Years in Prison for String of Bank Robberies."

44. Ibid.

45. Associated Press, "'Granddad Bandit' Captured in Baton Rouge, FBI Says."

46. "'Grandpa Bandit' Sentenced to 13 Years by Federal Judge in Eugene for String of Robberies," *Oregonian* (Portland), October 13, 2011, http://www. oregonlive.com/pacific-northwest-news/index.ssf/2011/10/grandpa_bandit_ sentenced_to_13.html.

47. Ibid.

48. Associated Press, "Man Arrested in Eugene Accused as 'Grandpa Bandit,'" *Oregonian*, May 23, 2010, http://www.oregonlive.com/news/index.ssf/ 2010/05/man_arrested_in_eugene_accused.html.

49. FBI, San Diego Division, "Reward of $20,000 Offered in 'Geezer Bandit' Investigation," news release, December 2, 2011, http://www.fbi.gov/sandiego/ press-releases/2011/reward-of-20-000-offered-in-geezer-bandit-investigation-1.

50. Tony Perry, "Geezer Bandit May Not Be a Geezer," *Los Angeles Times*, December 23, 2011, http://articles.latimes.com/2011/dec/23/local/la-me-geezer-20111223.

51. Ibid.

52. Geezer Bandit's Facebook page, accessed November 12, 2014, https://www.facebook.com/pages/The-Geezer-Bandit/255201027167.

53. Jack Nicas, "Crime That No Longer Pays," *Wall Street Journal*, February 4, 2013.

54. "Reports and Publications: Bank Crime Statistics: Bank Crime Reports," FBI, accessed July 5, 2014, http://www.fbi.gov/stats-services/publications/bank-crime-statistics-2011/bank-crime-statistics-2011.

55. Federal Bureau of Investigation, *Crime in the United States 2003* (Washington, DC: Government Printing Office), 34, http://www.fbi.gov/about-us/cjis/ucr/crime-in-the-u.s/2003/03sec2.pdf; Federal Bureau of Investigation, *Crime in the United States 2013*, http://www.fbi.gov/about-us/cjis/ucr/crime-in-the-u.s/2013/crime-in-the-u.s.-2013/tables/table-23/table_23_offense_analysis_number_and_percent_change_2012-2013.xls.

56. Federal Bureau of Investigation, Internet Crime Complaint Center, *2013 Internet Crime Report*, 3, http://www.ic3.gov/media/annualreport/2013_IC3 Report.pdf.

57. Ibid.; Federal Bureau of Investigation, *Crime in the United States 2013*, http://www.fbi.gov/about-us/cjis/ucr/crime-in-the-u.s/2013/crime-in-the-u.s.-2013/violent-crime/robbery-topic-page.

AFTERWORD

1. "Wanted by the FBI: The Bad Breath Bandit," poster, FBI, accessed November 11, 2014, https://bankrobbers.fbi.gov/robbers-container/2014-11-14.1153334714.

2. J. Edgar Hoover, "A Look at Bank Robbery Statistics," *FBI Law Enforcement Bulletin*, April 1967, 1.

3. J. Edgar Hoover, *How Banks Can Help the FBI: A Booklet for the Information and Assistance of the Banking Institutions of America* (Washington, DC: Federal Bureau of Investigation, U.S. Department of Justice, November 1965), 1.

SELECTED BIBLIOGRAPHY

Asbury, Herbert. *The Gangs of New York: An Informal History of the Underworld.* 1927. Reprint, New York: Thunder's Mouth Press, 1998.

Banner, Stuart. *The Death Penalty: An American History.* Cambridge, MA: Harvard University Press, 2002.

Brown, Richard Maxwell. *No Duty to Retreat: Violence and Values in American History and Society.* New York and Oxford: Oxford University Press, 1991.

———. "Western Violence: Structure, Value, Myth." *Western Historical Quarterly* 24, no. 1 (1993): 4–20.

Burrough, Bryan. *Public Enemies: America's Greatest Crime Wave and the Birth of the FBI, 1933–34.* New York: Penguin Press, 2004.

Chambers, Bruce W. "The Pythagorean Puzzle of Patrick Lyon." *The Art Bulletin* 58, no. 2 (1976): 225–33.

Clark, Jerry, and Ed Palattella. *Pizza Bomber: The Untold Story of America's Most Shocking Bank Robbery.* New York: Berkley Books/Penguin, 2012.

Conway, J. North. *King of Heists: The Sensational Bank Robbery of 1878 that Shocked America.* Guilford, CT: Lyons Press, 2009.

Doti, Lynne Pierson, and Larry Schweikart. *Banking in the American West: From the Gold Rush to Deregulation.* Norman: University of Oklahoma Press, 1991.

Drago, Harry Sinclair. *Road Agents and Train Robbers: Half a Century of Western Banditry.* New York: Dodd, Mead, 1973.

Federal Writers' Project of the Work Projects Administration for the State of Kansas. *Kansas: A Guide to the Sunflower State.* New York: Viking Press, 1939.

Felt, Mark, and John O'Connor. *A G-Man's Life.* New York: PublicAffairs, 2006.

Fischer, Gerald C. *American Banking Structure.* New York: Columbia University Press, 1968.

Foreman, Grant. *A History of Oklahoma.* Norman: University of Oklahoma Press, 1941.

Friedkin, William. *The Friedkin Connection.* New York: HarperCollins, 2013.

Gardner, Mark Lee. *Shot All to Hell: Jesse James, the Northfield Raid, and the Wild West's Greatest Escape.* New York: William Morrow, 2013.

Gentry, Curt. *J. Edgar Hoover: The Man and His Secrets.* New York: W. W. Norton, 1991.

Gorn, Elliott J. *Dillinger's Wild Ride: The Year that Made America's Public Enemy Number One.* Oxford: Oxford University Press, 2009.

Guinn, Jeff. *Go Down Together: The True, Untold Story of Bonnie & Clyde.* New York: Simon & Schuster, 2009.

Hammond, Bray. *Banks and Politics in America from the Revolution to the Civil War.* Princeton, NJ: Princeton University Press, 1957.

Haran, James F., and John M. Martin. "The Armed Urban Bank Robber: A Profile." *Federal Probation* 48, no. 47 (1984): 47–53.

Harris, Mark. *Pictures at a Revolution: Five Movies and the Birth of the New Hollywood*. New York: Penguin Press, 2008.

Hatch, Thom. *The Last Outlaws: The Lives and Legends of Butch Cassidy and the Sundance Kid*. New York: New American Library, 2013.

Hearst, Patricia Campbell, with Alvin Moscow. *Patty Hearst: Her Own Story*. New York: Avon Books, 1988.

Horan, James D. *Desperate Men: The James Gang and the Wild Bunch*, rev. ed. 1949. Reprint, Lincoln: University of Nebraska Press, 1997.

Jeffreys-Jones, Rhodri. *The FBI*. New Haven, CT: Yale University Press, 2007.

Johnston, D. A. "Psychological Observations of Bank Robbery." *American Journal of Psychiatry* 135, no. 11 (1978): 1377–79. https://www.ncjrs.gov/App/Publications/abstract.aspx?ID=51895.

Kessler, Ronald. *The Bureau: The Secret History of the FBI*. New York: St. Martin's Press, 2002.

Kirchner, L. R. *Robbing Banks: An American History 1831–1999*. Rockville Centre, NY: Sarpedon, 2000.

Lloyd, Thomas. *Robbery of the Bank of Pennsylvania in 1798. The Trial in the Supreme Court of the State of Pennsylvania*. Philadelphia, 1808.

Love, Robertus. *The Rise and Fall of Jesse James*. New York: G. P. Putnam's Sons, 1926.

Lyon, Patrick. *The Narrative of Patrick Lyon Who Suffered Three Months Severe Imprisonment in Philadelphia Gaol on Merely a Vague Suspicion of Being Concerned in a Robbery of the Bank of Pennsylvania With his Remarks Thereon*. Philadelphia, 1799. Eighteenth Century Collections Online. Gale. CIC Penn State University. Accessed March 30, 2014.

Matera, Dary. *John Dillinger: The Life and Death of America's First Celebrity Criminal*. New York: Carroll & Graf, 2004.

Meadows, Anne. *Digging Up Butch and Sundance*. New York: St. Martin's Press, 1994.

Meltzer, Allen H. *A History of the Federal Reserve, Volume 1: 1913–1951*. Chicago: University of Chicago Press, 2003.

Mittelstaedt, Walter. *Herman "Baron" Lamm, the Father of Modern Bank Robbery*. Jefferson, NC: McFarland, 2012.

Myers, Margaret G. *A Financial History of the United States*. New York: Columbia University Press, 1970.

O'Reilly, Kenneth. "A New Deal for the FBI: The Roosevelt Administration, Crime Control and National Security." *Journal of American History* 69 (1982): 638–58. Accessed January 20, 2014. http://www.jstor.org/stable/1903141.

Parker, Emma, and Nell Barrow Cowan. *Fugitives: The Story of Clyde Barrow and Bonnie Parker as Told by Bonnie's Mother (Mrs. Emma Parker) and Clyde's Sister (Nell Barrow Cowan)*. Edited by Jan I. Fortune. Dallas, TX: Ranger Press, 1934.

Powers, Richard Gid. *Secrecy and Power: The Life of J. Edgar Hoover*. New York: Free Press, 1987.

———. *Broken: The Troubled Past and Uncertain Future of the FBI*. New York: Free Press, 2004.

Public Broadcasting System. *American Experience: Jesse James*. 2005. Accessed May 6, 2014. http://www.pbs.org/wgbh/americanexperience/features/general-article/james-robberies/.

Rule, Ann. *The End of the Dream*. New York: Pocket Books, 1999.

Ruth, Henry, and Kevin R. Reitz. *The Challenge of Crime: Rethinking Our Response*. Cambridge, MA: Harvard University Press, 2003.

Schumach, Murray. *The Face on the Cutting Room Floor*. New York: William Morrow, 1964.

Settle, William A., Jr. "The James Boys and Missouri Politics." *Missouri Historical Review* 36, no. 4 (1942): 412–29.

———. *Jesse James Was His Name: Or, Fact and Fiction Concerning the Careers of the Notorious James Brothers of Missouri*. Columbia: University of Missouri Press, 1966.

Stiles, T. J. *Jesse James: Last Rebel of the Civil War*. New York: Alfred A. Knopf, 2002.

Sutton, Willie, with Edward Linn. *Where the Money Was*. New York: Viking Press, 1976.

Teeters, Negley K. *The Cradle of the Penitentiary: The Walnut Street Jail at Philadelphia, 1773–1835.* Philadelphia: Pennsylvania Prison Society, 1955.

Theoharis, Athan G., ed. *The FBI: A Comprehensive Reference Guide.* Phoenix, AZ: Oryx Press, 1999.

———. *The FBI & American Democracy: A Brief Critical History.* Lawrence: University Press of Kansas, 2004.

Toland, John. *The Dillinger Days.* New York: Random House, 1963.

Tully, Andrew. *The F.B.I.'s Most Famous Cases.* New York: William Morrow, 1965.

Ungar, Sanford J. *FBI.* Boston: Atlantic-Little, Brown, 1975.

Walling, George W. *Recollections of a New York Chief of Police.* 1887. Reprint, Montclair, NJ: Patterson Smith, 1972.

Wallis, Michael. *Pretty Boy: The Life and Times of Charles Arthur Floyd.* New York: St. Martin's Press, 1992.

Weiner, Tim. *Enemies: A History of the FBI.* New York: Random House, 2012.

Weisel, Deborah Lamm. "The Problem of Bank Robbery." *Problem-Oriented Guides for Police, Problem-Specific Guides Series,* no. 48, U.S. Department of Justice, Office of Community Oriented Police Services (2007). http://www.cops.usdoj.gov/Publications/e03071267.pdf.

Wells, Donald R. *The Federal Reserve System: A History.* Jefferson, NC: McFarland, 2004.

Whitehead, Don. *The FBI Story: A Report to the People.* New York: Random House, 1956.

Yeatman, Ted P. *Frank and Jesse James: The Story Behind the Legend.* Nashville, TN: Cumberland House, 2000.

INDEX

ABOUT THE AUTHORS

Jerry Clark retired as a special agent with the Federal Bureau of Investigation in 2011 after twenty-seven years in law enforcement, including careers as a special agent with the Drug Enforcement Administration and the Naval Criminal Investigative Service. He received a PhD in public service leadership from Capella University, an MA in forensic psychology from the City University of New York John Jay College of Criminal Justice, and a BA in psychology from Edinboro University of Pennsylvania. Clark is an assistant professor of criminal justice at Gannon University in Erie, Pennsylvania, where he is also director of risk analysis and mitigation at McManis & Monsalve Associates.

Ed Palattella joined the *Erie Times-News*, in Erie, Pennsylvania, in 1990. He has won a number of awards, including for his investigative work and his coverage of crime. He arrived in Erie after reporting for the *Point Reyes Light*, in Marin County, California. Palattella received an MA in journalism from Stanford University and a BA in English literature from Washington University in St. Louis.

Clark and Palattella are the coauthors of *Pizza Bomber: The Untold Story of America's Most Shocking Bank Robbery*. As a special agent with the FBI, Clark led the investigation of the Pizza Bomber case, which was FBI Major Case 203. Palattella covered the case as a reporter for the *Erie Times-News*.